Emmett Dulaney

MCSE

FAST TRACK

TCP/IP

New Riders

201 West 103rd Street, Indianapolis, Indiana 46290

MCSE FAST TRACK: TCP/IP

Copyright © 1998 by New Riders Publishing

International Standard Book Number: 1-56205-937-8

Library of Congress Catalog Card Number: 98-86320

Printed in the United States of America

First Printing: September, 1998

00 99 98   4 3 2 1

TRADEMARKS

WARNING AND DISCLAIMER

Executive Editor
Mary Foote

Acquisitions Editor
Steve Weiss

Development Editor
Nancy Warner

Managing Editor
Sarah Kearns

Project Editors
Clint McCarty
Jade Williams

Copy Editor
Keith Cline

Indexer
Chris Wilcox

Technical Editors
Andrew Brice
Grant Jones

Production
John Etchison
JoAnna LaBarge
Heather Stephenson

Contents at a Glance

INTRODUCTION

Part I   What's Important to Know About
          Exam 70-059   11

    1   Planning   13
    2   Installation and Configuration   45
    3   Connectivity   149
    4   Monitoring and Optimization   193
    5   Troubleshooting   207

Objective Review Notes   233

Part II Inside Exam 70-059   251

    6   Fast Facts Review   253
    7   Insider's Spin on Exam 70-059   263
    8   Sample Test Questions   281
    9   Hotlist of Exam-Critical Concepts   301
   10   Did You Know?   331

Index   335

TABLE OF CONTENTS

Part I   What's Important to Know About Exam 70-059

1 Planning   13

Terminology   14

The OSI Model   20

Protocols and Standards   21

Fault Tolerance   22

The Physical Address   23

Network Connection Types   23

The Physical Address   23

Introduction to TCP/IP   25

Understanding the Four Layers of TCP/IP   27
Transmission Control Protocol (TCP)   30
User Datagram Protocol (UDP)   34
Internet Protocol (IP)   36
Internet Control Message Protocol (ICMP)   38
Internet Group Management Protocol (IGMP)   40
Address Resolution Protocol (ARP)   40
Network APIs   42
Windows Sockets   42
NetBIOS   43

What Is Important to Know   44

2 Installation and Configuration   45

Installing Services When Using Microsoft TCP/IP on Windows NT   47

Understanding DHCP   48
What DHCP Servers Can Do   50
Limitations of DHCP   51
Planning a DHCP Implementation   52
Using Multiple DHCP Servers   54
How DHCP Works   55
Installing the DHCP Server Service   57
Configuring the DHCP Server   58

Understanding WINS   58
Configuring a Client for WINS   60
Files Used for WINS   60
Backing Up the WINS Database   61
Restoring the WINS Database   61
Compacting the WINS Database   61

Understanding DNS   62
History of Microsoft DNS   63
Structure of DNS   63
Reverse Lookup   65

Installing TCP/IP   66

Configuring Scopes   67
Scope Options   69
Address Reservations   70
DHCP Clients   71
Windows NT and Windows 95 as DHCP Clients   71
Windows for Workgroups as a DHCP Client   72

Using Scope Options   72
Compacting the DHCP Database   73
Backing Up the DHCP Database   74
Restoring a Corrupt DHCP Database   75
Automatic Restoration   75
Registry RestoreFlag   75
Copying from the Backup Directory   76

Installing and Configuring a WINS Server   76

WINS Clients   77

Configuring WINS to be Used by Non-WINS Clients   77

Importing LMHOSTS Files to WINS   78

Running WINS on a Multihomed Computer   78

Configuring WINS Replication   79
Understanding the Replication Process   81
Using the WINS Manager   81
Initial Replication Configuration   82
Advanced Configuration Options   82

Configuring Static Mappings in the WINS Database   84

Configuring Subnet Masks   85
Subnet Masks, Host IDs, and Network IDs   86
Purpose of Subnet Masks   89
Default Subnet Masks   92

Subdividing a Network   94
Step 1: Determine the Number of Network IDs Required   95
Step 2: Determine the Number of Host IDs per Subnet Required   95
Step 3: Define the Subnet Mask   96
Step 4: Determine the Network IDs to Use   98
Step 5: Determine the Host IDs to Use   99

Configuring Windows NT to Function as an IP Router   99
Static Routing Environment   100
Default Gateways   103
Route Tables   103
Viewing the Route Table   104
Building a Static Routing Table   106
The TRACERT Utility   107
Dynamic Routing   108
Building a Multihomed Router   111

Installing and Configuring the DHCP Relay Agent   113

Installing and Configuring DNS   114
Enabling DNS on the Client   114
Using Existing BIND Files   116
Reinstalling Microsoft DNS Server   116
DNS Administration Tool   117
Creating a Subdomain   117
Updating DNS Startup Files   118
DNS Manager Preferences   118
NSLOOKUP   118

Integrating DNS with Other Name Servers   119
Adding HOSTS   120
Adding Other Records   121

Connecting a DNS Server to a DNS Root Server   123

Configuring DNS Server Roles   123
Configuring for Caching-Only   123
Configuring as an IP Forwarder   123
Creating a Primary DNS Server   124
Setting Up and Reviewing the SOA Record   125
Setting Up the Secondary DNS Server   126

Configuring HOSTS and LMHOSTS Files   127
Configure HOSTS Files   127
Configure LMHOSTS Files   129

Configuring a Windows NT Server to Support TCP/IP
Printing   131

Windows NT Client Printing to a Remote Host System   131
Using the LPR Command-Line Utility   132
Creating an LPR Printer on a Windows NT Computer   132

Remote Host Client Printing to a Windows NT Server   133

Configuring SNMP   133

SNMP Agents and Management   135
The SNMP Management System   135
The SNMP Agent   136

Management Information Base   137
Internet MIB II   138
LAN Manager MIB II   138
DHCP MIB   138
WINS MIB   139
MIB Structure   139

Microsoft SNMP Service   140
SNMP Architecture   140
SNMP Communities   141
Security   141

Installing and Configuring SNMP   141
SNMP Security Parameters   143
SNMP Agent   143
Using the SNMP Utility   144
What SNMP Is Really Doing   145

What Is Important to Know   147

3 Connectivity   149

Connectivity   150
Remote Execution Utilities   150
The REXEC Utility   151
The RSH Utility   151
The Telnet Utility   152

Data Transfer Utilities   153
RCP   153
FTP   154
TFTP   156
HTTP and Web Browsers   157

RAS Servers and Dial-Up Networking   158
PPP Versus SLIP   158
Modems   159
Ports   159
Configuring Modems   162

Other Communications Technologies   166
ISDN   166
X.25   167

Dial-In Permissions   167
PPP Problems   168
Dial-Up Networking   169
The RAS Server   172
Installing the RAS Server   172
Configuring the RAS Server   173
Configuring TCP/IP on the RAS Server   174

Monitoring the RAS Connection   174
Monitoring from the RAS Server   175
Dial-Up Networking Monitor   175

Common RAS Problems   176
Authentication   176
Call Back with Multilink   176

Browsing in a Multiple-Domain Routed Network   176
Browsing Tools   177
System Roles   178
Using the Direct Approach   179
Browsing Roles   180
Filling Roles   180
Controlling Your Browser Role   181
Understanding the Cost of Browsing   182

Windows NT Browsing Services   183
Collecting the Browse List   183
Distributing the Browse List   184
Browsing over Subnets   185
Announcement Periods   185
Domain Master Browser Failure   186

Servicing Client Requests   186
Browsing in an IP Internetwork   187
Internetwork Browsing Solutions   187
Using the WINS Solution   190

What Is Important to Know   192

4 Monitoring and Optimization   193
Utilities Used to Monitor TCP/IP Traffic   194
Performance Monitor   194
Network Monitor   195
Other Utilities   196
ARP   197
Event Log   198

IPCONFIG   198
NBTSTAT   199
NETSTAT   200
NSLOOKUP   201
Ping   202
ROUTE   202
SNMP   203
TRACERT   204

What Is Important to Know   206

5 Troubleshooting   207

Diagnosing and Resolving IP Addressing Problems   208
IP Address Configuration Problems   208
IP Address   209
Subnet Mask   211
Default Gateway   214
DHCP Client Configuration Problems   214

Microsoft Configuration Utilities   216

Microsoft IP Configuration Troubleshooting Utilities   218
Troubleshooting IP Protocol Installation by Pinging the Loopback Address   219
Troubleshooting Client Address Configuration by Pinging Local Address   220
Troubleshooting Router Problems by Pinging the Default Gateway   220
Pinging a Remote Host   221

Diagnosing and Resolving Name Resolution Problems   222
NBTSTAT   223
Hostname   224
Testing Name Resolution with Ping   226
Testing NetBIOS Name Resolution by Establishing a Session   226
Testing TCP Name Resolution by Establishing a Session   229

What Is Important to Know   230

Objective Review Notes   233

Planning   235
Installation and Configuration   236
Connectivity   244
Monitoring and Optimization   246
Troubleshooting   246

Part II Inside Exam 70-059   251

6 Fast Facts Review   253

What to Study   254
   Planning   254
   Installation and Configuration   254
   Connectivity   257
   Monitoring and Optimization   258
   Troubleshooting   258

7 Insider's Spin on Exam 70-059   263

Get into Microsoft's Mindset   265

Understand the Timeframe of the Exam   266

Get Used to Answering Questions Quickly   268

Become Acquainted with All the Things Available to You   269

Where the Questions Come From   275

Different Flavors of Questions   276

In the Future   277

8 Sample Test Questions   281

Questions   282

Answers and Explanations   295

9 Hotlist of Exam-Critical Concepts   301

10 Did You Know?   331

Circuit Switching   332

Message Switching   332

Packet Switching   333

Index   335

ABOUT THE AUTHOR

Emmett Dulaney, MCP+I, MCSE is a consultant for D S Technical Solutions, and instructor for a national training company. He has been teaching certification courses for the continuing education department of Indiana University/Purdue University at Fort Wayne for over four years, and is the Certification Corner columnist for *NT Systems Magazine*. In addition, Emmett is the author or co-author of over a dozen computer books, including *CNE Short Course, Teach Yourself MCSE Windows NT Workstation in 14 Days*, and *MCSE TestPrep: TCP/IP*. He has also written over 100 magazine articles on computing for several publications.

ABOUT THE TECHNICAL REVIEWERS

R. Andrew Brice currently works as a senior instructor for ProSoft I-Net Solutions in Austin, Texas. His certifications include Novell CNA and CNE, as well as the Microsoft Certified Trainer and Microsoft Certified Systems Engineer in both Windows NT 3.51 and 4.0. Since 1991, he has been providing consulting in network design and support to small and large organizations, including Fortune 1000 companies. This consulting has included training for Novell, Microsoft, and Netscape technical curricula, coupled with web-site development, security, and e-commerce. He specializes in the design and implementation of wide area networks (WANs). He credits his accomplishments to the love and support provided by both his wife, Susan, and his daughter, Katie. He can be reached at andrewb@flash.net.

Grant Jones has worked as a network engineer for the past five years, and is certified as an MCSE, MCP + Inet, MCT, CNE3/4 (Certified NetWare Engineer versions 3 and 4), and CNI (Certified NetWare Instructor). For the past three years, Grant has been teaching the official Microsoft core classes along with IIS and TCP/IP; he is currently working for ProSoft I-Net Solutions, where he is creating courseware for ePC certifications. Grant has written courses on Netscape Mail and IIS 4.0; the course he developed on IIS 4.0 was taught to Microsoft Visual Basic programmers in Redmond, WA. In addition, Grant has spoken at trade shows such as Internet World and Internet Commerce Expo on Internet fundamentals and electronic commerce.

DEDICATION

For Edna.

ACKNOWLEDGMENTS

First and foremost, I would like to thank Steve Weiss for his conviction and belief in the product and for his patience with it, as well. I would also like to thank Nancy Warner, Andrew Brice, Grant Jones, Clint McCarty and Jade Williams.

TELL US WHAT YOU THINK!

As the reader of this book, *you* are our most important critic and commentator. We value your opinion and want to know what we're doing right, what we could do better, what areas you'd like to see us publish in, and any other words of wisdom you're willing to pass our way.

As the Executive Editor for the Certification team at Macmillan Computer Publishing, I welcome your comments. You can fax, email, or write me directly to let me know what you did or didn't like about this book—as well as what we can do to make our books stronger.

Please note that I cannot help you with technical problems related to the topic of this book, and that due to the high volume of mail I receive, I might not be able to reply to every message.

When you write, please be sure to include this book's title and author, as well as your name and phone or fax number. I will carefully review your comments and share them with the author and editors who worked on the book.

Fax: 317-581-4663

Email: certification@mcp.com

Mail: Mary Foote
         Executive Editor
         Certification/Networking Group
         Macmillan Computer Publishing
         201 West 103rd Street

Introduction

The *MCSE Fast Track* series is written as a study aid for people preparing for Microsoft Certification Exams. The series is intended to help reinforce and clarify information with which the student is already familiar. This series is not intended to be a single source for student preparation, but rather a review of information and set of practice materials to help increase the likelihood of success when taking the actual exam.

WHY WE DID THIS SERIES: WORDS FROM THE AUTHOR AND PUBLISHER

First, let's state this once more: New Riders *MCSE Fast Tracks* are not intended to be single sources for exam preparation. These books have been uniquely written and developed to work as supplements to your existing knowledge base.

But exactly what makes them different?

1. **Brevity.** Many other exam training materials seek Microsoft approval (you've probably seen the official 'Microsoft Approved Study Guide' logo on other books, for example), meaning they must include 50% tutorial material and cover every objective for every exam in exactly the same manner, to the same degree. *MCSE Fast Tracks break away from that mold by focusing on what you really need to know to pass the exams.*

2. **Focus.** *Fast Tracks* are targeted primarily to those who know the technology but who don't yet have the certification. No superfluous information is included. *MCSE Fast Tracks* feature only what the more-experienced candidate needs to know to pass the exams. *Fast Tracks are affordable study material for the experienced professional.*

3. **Concentrated value and learning power.** Frankly, we wouldn't be surprised if Fast Tracks prove to appeal to a wider audience than just advanced-level candidates. We've tried to pack as much distilled

exam knowledge as possible into *Fast Tracks*, creating a 'digest' of exam-critical information. No matter what level you're at, you may well see this digest on certification training as a logical starting point for exam study.

4. **Classroom-tested, instructor-proven.** With tens of thousands of new certification candidates entering the training routine each year, trainers like Emmett Dulaney—on the forefront of the certification education lines—are finding themselves in front of classes comprised of increased numbers of candidates with the following:

   ◆ already a measurable base of understanding of the technology

   ◆ a desire for efficient 'just-the-facts' training

Emmett and New Riders pooled their thoughts and found that no books *truly* existed that adequately fill this need:

To provide an easy way to review the key elements of each certification technology without being bogged down with elementary-level information and to present this information in the light of an insider's perspective.

Emmett developed his instructional style and content to help this ever-increasing group of non-beginners, and they in turn helped him focus the material even more. He then worked with New Riders to develop this classroom-tested material into a refined, efficient self-instruction tool. What you see in this book is the result of that interaction.

Think of *Fast Tracks* as the set of instructor's notes you always wished you could get your hands on. These notes only truly help you if you already know the material and are ready to take on the exam itself. It's then that this book is truly designed to help you shine. Good luck and may your hard work pay off.

WHO SHOULD READ THIS BOOK

The TCP/IP book in the *MCSE Fast Track* series is specifically intended to help students prepare for Microsoft's Internetworking with Microsoft TCP/IP on Microsoft Windows NT 4.0 (70-059) exam; one of the electives available in the MCSE program.

What the TCP/IP Exam (70-059) Covers

The Internetworking with Microsoft TCP/IP on Microsoft Windows NT 4.0 certification exam measures your ability to implement, administer, and troubleshoot computer systems that are running TCP/IP. It focuses on determining your skill in five major categories. These categories follow:

- Planning
- Installation and Configuration
- Connectivity
- Monitoring and Optimization
- Troubleshooting

The Internetworking with Microsoft TCP/IP on Microsoft Windows NT 4.0 certification exam uses these categories to measure your ability. Before taking this exam, you should be proficient in the job skills discussed in the following pages.

Planning

The Planning section is designed to make sure that you understand the hardware requirements of TCP/IP, abilities of the protocol, and limitations, as well. The knowledge needed here also requires understanding of general networking concepts.

Objective for Planning

- Given a scenario, identify valid network configurations.

Installation and Configuration

The Installation and Configuration part of the TCP/IP exam is the meat of the exam. You are tested on virtually every possible component of the protocol.

Objectives for Installation and Configuration

 ◆ Given a scenario, select the appropriate services to install when using Microsoft TCP/IP on a Microsoft Windows NT Server computer.

 ◆ On a Windows NT Server Computer, configure Microsoft TCP/IP to support multiple network adapters.

 ◆ Configure scopes by using DHCP Manager.

 ◆ Install and configure a WINS server.

 ◆ Import LMHOSTS files to WINS.

 ◆ Run WINS on a multihomed computer.

 ◆ Configure WINS replication.

 ◆ Configure static mappings in the WINS database.

 ◆ Configure subnet masks.

 ◆ Configure a Windows NT Server computer to function as an IP router.

 ◆ Install and configure the DHCP Relay Agent.

 ◆ Install and configure the Microsoft DNS Server service on a Windows NT Server computer.

 ◆ Integrate DNS with other name servers.

 ◆ Connect a DNS server to a DNS root server.

 ◆ Configure DNS server roles.

 ◆ Configure HOSTS and LMHOSTS files.

 ◆ Configure a Windows NT Server computer to support TCP/IP printing.

 ◆ Configure SNMP.

Connectivity

The Connectivity component of the Internetworking with Microsoft TCP/IP on Microsoft Windows NT 4.0 certification exam concentrates on how to use the various interconnecting components of TCP/IP.

Objectives for Connectivity

◆ Given a scenario, identify which utility to use to connect to a TCP/IP-based UNIX host.

◆ Configure a RAS server and dial-up networking for use on a TCP/IP network.

◆ Configure and support browsing in a multiple-domain routed network.

Monitoring and Optimization

The Monitoring and Optimization component of the Internetworking with Microsoft TCP/IP on Microsoft Windows NT 4.0 certification exam has only one objective.

Objective for Monitoring and Optimization

◆ Given a scenario, identify which tool to use to monitor TCP/IP traffic.

Troubleshooting

The Troubleshooting component of the Internetworking with Microsoft TCP/IP on Microsoft Windows NT 4.0 certification exam has four components running the entire gamut of troubleshooting.

Objectives for Troubleshooting

◆ Diagnose and resolve IP addressing problems.

◆ Use Microsoft TCP/IP utilities to diagnose configuration problems.

◆ Identify which Microsoft TCP/IP utility to used to diagnose IP configuration problems.

◆ Diagnose and resolve name resolution problems.

HARDWARE AND SOFTWARE RECOMMENDED FOR PREPARATION

The *Fast Track* series is meant to help you review concepts with which you already have training and hands-on experience. To make the most of the review, you need to have as much background and experience as possible. The best way to do this is to combine studying with working on real networks using the products on which you will be tested. This section gives you a description of the minimum computer requirements you will need to build a solid practice environment.

Computers

The minimum computer requirements to ensure you can study on everything on which you'll be tested is one or more workstations running Windows 95 or NT Workstation, and two or more servers running Windows NT Server, all connected by a network.

Workstations: Windows 95 and Windows NT

- Computer on the Microsoft Hardware Compatibility list
- 486DX 33MHz
- 16MB or RAM
- 200MB hard disk
- 3.5-inch 1.44MB floppy drive
- VGA video adapter
- VGA monitor
- Mouse or equivalent pointing device
- Two-speed CD-ROM drive
- Network Interface Card (NIC)
- Presence on an existing network, or use of a hub to create a test network
- Microsoft Windows 95 or NT Workstation 4.0

Servers: Windows NT Server

- Two computers on the Microsoft Hardware Compatibility List

- 486DX2 66MHz

- 32MB of RAM

- 340MB hard disk

- 3.5-inch 1.44MB floppy drive

- VGA video adapter

- VGA monitor

- Mouse or equivalent pointing device

- Two-speed CD-ROM drive

- Network Interface Card (NIC)

- Presence on an existing network, or use of a hub to create a test network

- Microsoft Windows NT Server 4.0

OBJECTIVE REVIEW NOTES

The Objective Review Notes feature of the *Fast Track* series contains a separate section—two to a page—for each subobjective covered in the book. Each subobjective section falls under the main exam objective category, just as you'd expect to find it. It is strongly suggested that you review each subobjective and immediately make note of your knowledge level; then return to the Objective Review Notes section repeatedly and document your progress. Your ultimate goal should be to be able to review only this section and know if you are ready for the exam.

Suggested use:

1. Read the objective. Refer to the part of the book where it's covered. Then ask yourself the following questions:

    - Do you already know this material? Then check "Got it" and make a note of the date.

    - Do you need some brushing up on the objective area? Check "Review it" and make a note of the date. While you're at it, write down the page numbers you just checked, because you'll need to return to that section.

- Is this material something you're largely unfamiliar with? Check the "Help!" box and write down the date. Now you can get to work.

2. You get the idea. Keep working through the material in this book and in the other study material you probably have. The more you get the material, the quicker you can update and upgrade each objective notes section from "Help!" to "Review it" to "Got it."

3. Cross reference to the materials YOU are using. Most people who take certification exams use more than one resource at a time. Write down the page numbers of where this material is covered in other books you're using, or which software program and file this material is covered on, or which video tape (and counter number) it's on, or whatever you need that works for you.

Think of this as your personal study diary—your documentation of how you beat this exam.

PART II: ROUNDING OUT YOUR EXAM PREPARATION

Part II of this book is designed to round out your exam preparation by providing you with chapters that do the following:

- "Fast Facts Review"is a digest of all "What Is Important to Know" sections from all Part I chapters. Use this chapter to review just before you take the exam: It's all here, in an easily-reviewable format.

- "Insider's Spin on Exam 70-059" grounds you in the particulars for preparing mentally for this examination and for Microsoft testing in general.

- "Sample Test Questions" provides a full-length practice exam that tests you on the actual material covered in Part I. If you mastered the material there, you should be able to pass with flying colors here.

- "Hotlist of Exam-Critical Concepts" is your resource for cross-checking your tech terms. Although you're probably up to speed on most of this material already, double-check yourself anytime you run across an item you're not 100 percent certain about; it could make a difference at exam time.

- "Did You Know?" is the last-day-of-class bonus chapter: A brief touching-upon of peripheral information designed to be helpful and of interest to people using this technology to the point that they wish to be certified in its mastery.

I

WHAT'S IMPORTANT TO KNOW ABOUT EXAM 70-059

MCSE Fast Track: TCP/IP is written as a study aid for people preparing for Microsoft Certification Exam 70-059. The book is intended to help reinforce and clarify information with which the student is already familiar. This series is not intended to be a single source for exam preparation, but rather a review of information and set of practice materials to help increase the likelihood of success when taking the actual exam.

Part I of this book is designed to help you make the most of your study time by presenting concise summaries of information that you need to understand to succeed on the exam. Each chapter covers a specific exam objective area as outlined by Microsoft:

1 **Planning**

2 **Installation and Configuration**

3 **Connectivity**

4 **Monitoring and Optimization**

5 **Troubleshooting**

ABOUT THE EXAM

Exam Number	70-059
Minutes	90*
Questions	58*
Passing Score	750*
Single Answer Questions	Yes
Multiple Answer With Correct Number Given	Yes
Multiple Answer Without Correct Number Given	Yes
Ranking Order	Yes
Choices of A–D	Yes
Choices of A–E	Yes
Objective Categories	5

*Note: These exam criteria will no longer apply when this exam goes to an adaptive format.

▶ Given a scenario, identify valid network configurations

CHAPTER 1

Planning

To implement a successful network, you must understand the basics of networking. This chapter provides the foundation of standard networking information and can be easily skimmed if you have already passed the Networking Essentials exam (70-058).

TERMINOLOGY

Brush up on key concepts and definitions. Table 1.1 is a list of the most important terms to focus on.

TABLE 1.1

KEY CONCEPTS AND DEFINITIONS.

Term	Definition
ACK	Acknowledgment—A response from a receiving computer to a sending computer to indicate successful reception of information. TCP requires that packets be acknowledged before it considers the transmission safe.
Active open	An action taken by a client to initiate a TCP connection with a server.
Address classes	Grouping of IP addresses with each class, defining the maximum number of networks and hosts available. The first octet of the address determines the class.
Address mask	A 32-bit binary number used to select bits from an IP address for subnet masking.
Address resolution	A translation of an IP address to a corresponding physical address.
Analog	A form of electronic communication using a continuous electromagnetic wave, such as television or radio. Any continuous wave form as opposed to digital on/off transmissions.
ANSI	American National Standards Institute—the membership organization responsible for defining U.S. standards in the information technology industry.
API	Application Programming Interface—A language and message format that enables a programmer to use functions in another program or in the hardware.
ARP	Address Resolution Protocol—A protocol in the TCP/IP suite used to bind an IP address to a physical hardware (MAC) address.

Term	*Definition*
ARPA	Advanced Research Projects Agency—A government agency that originally funded the research on the ARPAnet (became DARPA in the mid-1970s).
ARPAnet	The first network of computers funded by the U.S. Department of Defense Advanced Projects Agency. An experimental communications network funded by the government that eventually developed into the Internet.
ASCII	American Standard Code for Information Interchange—Data that is limited to letters, numbers, and punctuation.
ATM	Asynchronous Transfer Mode—Broadband technology that speeds transfer speeds.
Backbone	Generally very high-speed, T3 telephone lines that connect remote ends of networks and networks to one another; only service providers are connected to the Internet in this way.
Baseband	A network technology that requires all nodes attached to the network to participate in every transmission. Ethernet, for example, is a baseband technology.
BOOTP	Bootstrap Protocol—A protocol used to configure systems across internetworks with an IP address, subnet mask, and a default gateway.
Bps	Bits per second—A measurement that expresses the speed at which data is transferred between computers.
Bridge	A device that connects one physical section of a network to another, often providing isolation.
Broadband	A network technology that multiplexes multiple network carriers into a single cable.
Broadcast	A packet destined for all hosts on the network.
Brouter	A computer device that works as both a bridge and a router. Some network traffic may be bridged, while other is routed.
Buffer	A storage area used to hold input or output data.
Checksumming	A service performed by UDP that checks to see whether packets were changed during transmission.
Connectionless service	A delivery service that treats each packet as a separate entity. Often results in lost packets or packets delivered out of sequence.
CRC	Cyclic Redundancy Check—A computation about a frame of which the result is a small integer. The value is appended to the end of the frame and recalculated when the frame is received. If the results differ from the appended value, the frame has presumably been corrupted and is therefore discarded. It is used to detect errors in transmission.

continues

TABLE 1.1 continued

Term	*Definition*
CSMA	Carrier Sense Multiple Access—A simple media access control protocol that enables multiple stations to contend for access to the medium. If no traffic is detected on the medium, the station may send a transmission.
CSMA/CD	Carrier Sense Multiple Access with Collision Detection—A characteristic of network hardware that uses CSMA in conjunction with a process that detects when two stations transmit simultaneously. If that happens, both back off and retry the transmission after a random time period has elapsed.
DARPA	Defense Advanced Research Projects Agency, originally ARPA—The government agency that funded the research that developed the ARPAnet.
Datagram	A packet of data and delivery information.
DHCP	Dynamic Host Configuration Protocol—A protocol that provides dynamic address allocation and automatic TCP/IP configuration.
Digital	Type of communications used by computers, consisting of individual on and off pulses. Compare to analog.
Directed Broadcast Address	An IP address that specifies all hosts on the network.
Domain	Highest subdivision of the Internet, for the most part by country (except in the United States, where it is by type of organization, such as educational, commercial, and government). Usually the last part of a hostname; for example, the domain part of ibm.com is .com, which represents the domain of commercial sites in the United States.
Domain Name System (DNS)	The system that translates between Internet IP address and Internet hostnames.
Ethernet	A type of local area network hardware. Many TCP/IP networks are Ethernet based.
FDDI	Fiber Distributed Data Interface—The formal name for fiber wiring.
FDM	Frequency Division Multiplexing—A technique of passing signals across a single medium by assigning each signal a unique carrier frequency.
Firewall	A device placed on a network to prevent unauthorized traffic from entering the network.
FQDN	Fully qualified domain name—A combination of the hostname and the domain name.

Term	*Definition*
Frame	Packets as transmitted across a medium. Differing frame types have unique characteristics.
frame relay	A type of digital data communications protocol.
FTP	File Transfer Protocol—A popular Internet communications protocol that enables you to transfer files between hosts on the Internet.
Gateway	A device that interfaces two networks using different protocols.
Hardware address	The physical address of a host used by networks.
Host	A server using TCP/IP, and/or connected to the Internet.
Host address	A unique number assigned to identify a host on the Internet (also called IP address or dot address). This address is usually represented as four numbers between 1 and 254 and separated by periods (for example, 192.58.107.230).
Host ID	The portion of an IP address that identifies the host in a particular network. It is used in conjunction with network IDs to form a complete IP address.
Hostname	A unique name for a host that corresponds to the host address.
HTML	Hypertext Markup Language—The formatting language/protocol used to define various text styles in a hypertext document, including emphasis and bulleted lists.
HTTP	Hypertext Transfer Protocol—The communications protocol used by WWW services to retrieve documents quickly.
ICMP	Internet Control Message Protocol—A maintenance protocol that handles error messages to be sent when datagrams are discarded or when systems experience congestion.
IGMP	Internet Group Management Protocol—A protocol used to carry group membership information in a multicast system.
ISDN	Integrated Services Digital Network—A dedicated telephone line connection that transmits digital data at rates of 64Kbps and 128Kbps. In reality with the overhead, the data transfers are approximately 56/112.
LAN	Local area network—A network of computers that is usually limited to a small physical area, like a building.
LLC	Logical Link Control—A protocol that provides a common interface point to the MAC layers.
MAC	Media Access Control—A protocol that governs the access method a station has to the network.

continues

TABLE 1.1 **continued**

Term	Definition
MAN	Metropolitan area network—A physical communications network that operates across a metropolitan area.
MIME	Multipurpose Internet Mail Extension—A protocol that describes the format of Internet messages.
Name resolution	The process of mapping a computer name to an IP address. DNS and DHCP are to ways of resolving names.
NFS	Network File System—A file system developed by Sun Microsystems that is now widely used on many different networks.
NIC	Network interface card—An add-on card to allow a machine to access a LAN (most commonly an Ethernet card).
Nodes	Individual computers connected to a network.
OSI	Open Systems Interconnection—A set of ISO standards that define the framework for implementing protocols in seven layers.
Packet	The unit of data transmission on the Internet. A packet consists of the data being transferred with additional overhead information, such as the transmitting and receiving addresses.
Packet switching	The communications technology that the Internet is based on, where data being sent between computers is transmitted in packets.
Ping	A utility that sends out a packet to an Internet host and waits for a response (used to check whether a host is up).
POP	Point of Presence—indicates availability of a local access number to a public data network.
PPP	Point-to-Point Protocol—A driver that enables you to use a network communications protocol over a phone line, used with TCP/IP to enable you to have a dial-in Internet host.
PPTP	Point-to-Point Tunneling Protocol—A revision to PPP used mostly for virtual private networks.
Protocol	The standard that defines how computers on a network communicate with one another.
RARP	Reverse Address Resolution Protocol—A protocol that enables a computer to find its IP address by broadcasting a request. It is usually used by diskless workstations at startup to find their logical IP address.
Repeater	Device that enables you to extend the length of your network by amplifying and repeating the information it receives.
RIP	Routing Information Protocol—A router-to-router protocol used to exchange information between routers. RIP supports dynamic routing.

Term	*Definition*
Router	Equipment that receives an Internet packet and sends it to the next machine in the destination path.
Segment	Protocol data unit consisting of part of a stream of bytes being sent between two machines. It also includes information about the current position in the stream and a checksum value.
Server	Provider of a service; a computer that runs services. It also often refers to a piece of hardware or software that provides access to information requested from it.
Service	Application that processes requests by client applications (for example, storing data or executing an algorithm).
SLIP	Serial Line Internet Protocol—A way of running TCP/IP via the phone lines to enable you to have a dial-up Internet host.
SMTP	Simple Mail Transport Protocol—The accepted communications protocol standard for exchange of e-mail between Internet hosts.
SNA	System Network Architecture—A protocol suite developed and used by IBM.
SNMP	Simple Network Management Protocol—A communications protocol used to control and monitor devices on a network.
Socket	A means of network communications via special entities.
Subnet	Any lower network that is part of the logical network—identified by the network ID.
Subnet mask	A 32-bit value that distinguishes the network ID from the host ID in an IP address.
TCP/IP	Transmission Control Protocol/Internet Protocol—A communications protocol suite that allows computers of any make to communicate when running TCP/IP software.
TFTP	Trivial File Transfer Protocol—A basic, standard protocol used to upload or download files with minimal overhead. TFTP depends on UDP and is often used to initialize diskless workstations, as it has no directory and password capabilities.
Transceiver	A device that connects a host interface to a network. It is used to apply signals to the cable and sense collisions.
UDP	User Datagram Protocol—A simple protocol that enables an application program on one machine to send a datagram to an application program on another machine. Delivery is not guaranteed, nor is it guaranteed the datagrams will be delivered in proper order.
URL	Universal resource locator—A means of specifying the location of information on the Internet for WWW clients.

continues

TABLE 1.1   continued

Term	Definition
WAN	Wide area network—A network of computers that are geographically dispersed.
X.25	An CCITT standard for connecting computers to a network that provides a reliable stream transmission service, which can support remote logons.
X.400	An CCITT standard for message transfer and interpersonal messaging, like electronic mail.

THE OSI MODEL

Commit to memory the OSI model, the type of data each layer works with, hardware devices, and everything else presented in Table 1.2. (Hint: Most people use the mnemonic All People Seem To Need Data Processing to memorize the order of the layers).

TABLE 1.2

OSI MODEL.

Layer	Purpose	Data Type	Hardware
Application	Interface to network services	Message	Gateway
Presentation	Translates between Application and all others; redirector; encryption; compression	Packet	Gateway
Session	Establishes rules for communication; synchronization	Packet	Gateway
Transport	Handles network transmission and is responsible for data segmentation	Datagram segment (and packet)	Gateway

Layer	Purpose	Data Type	Hardware
Network	Addressing; traffic; switching	Datagram (and packet)	Router—uses routing table, can determine best path, can be static or dynamic, can support multiple paths
Data Link	Error checking; manages link control; communicates with card	Frame	Bridge—uses MAC addresses, can connect different media and unlike segments
Physical	The connection, wire, cards, and so on (what you can see and touch)	Bits and signals	Repeater—no filtering or processing, just regeneration; can connect different media

> **NOTE**
>
> Mnemonics for memorizing the ordering of the layers include: All People Seem To Need Data Processing and Please Do Not Throw Sausage Pizza Away.

Headers are added to the message as it travels down the layers, and stripped from the message as it travels up the layers. Brouters operate at both the Data Link and Network layer and perform the function of a bridge and a router.

PROTOCOLS AND STANDARDS

Most protocols are routable, and it is easier to remember those that are not: NetBEUI, DLC, and LAT (a DEC protocol). The IEEE 802 standards are as follows:

- 802.1   Internetworking
- 802.2   Logical Link Control

- 802.3 Carrier Sense W/ Multiple Access & Collision Detection (CSMA/CD)

- 802.4 Token Bus LAN

- 802.5 Token Ring LAN

- 802.6 Metropolitan Area Network (MAN)

- 802.7 Broadband Technical Advisory Group

- 802.8 Fiber Optic Tech Advisory Group

- 802.9 Integrated Voice/Data Networks

- 802.10 Network Security

- 802.11 Wireless Networks

- 802.12 Demand Priority Access LAN, 100BaseVG AnyLAN

FAULT TOLERANCE

Software implemented fault tolerance can be provided by stripe sets with parity (RAID level 5), or mirror sets (RAID level 1). Both allow data to be recovered in the event of a system or hardware failure. Stripe sets with parity require a minimum of three physical disks, and the system and boot partitions cannot be a part of the stripe set.

Disk striping without parity (RAID level 0) requires only two disks and is not a fault-tolerant solution because data cannot be recovered in the event of a disk failure (no data redundancy). Its major benefit is that it offers the highest level of read and write performance of any of the available disk management systems—allowing concurrent requests to be processed on all drives simultaneously.

Disk striping with parity always uses the smallest amount of free space on any drive because the amount is then used on all other drives. Therefore if you have drives with 100, 200, 300, and 400MB free on each of four drives, respectively, only 100MB would be used on each drive. Four times 100MB means the stripe set would be 400MB in size. Of that, $\frac{1}{4}$th is used for storing parity information, and there is only 300MB of data that can be stored on the stripe set.

Disk mirroring can only support two hard drives, and amounts to two drives running off of the same controller. Disk duplexing is the same as mirroring, only using two disk controllers rather than one (a hardware enhancement versus a software enhancement). Mirror sets are the only form of fault tolerance that can include system and boot partitions.

NETWORK CONNECTION TYPES

At A Glance: Cabling

Connection Type	Installation	Maintenance	Expense	Notes
10BASE-2 coaxial cable	Easy	Easy	Cheap	Traffic seen by all machines on a coax segment.
10BASE-T unshielded twisted pair	Moderately easy	Easy	Moderately inexpensive	Traffic can be easily isolated.
Token ring	Moderately difficult	Difficult	Expensive	Traffic isolated, large data throughput.
FDDI (fiber)	Difficult	Difficult	Very expensive	Immune to electrical disturbances, very large data throughput.

THE PHYSICAL ADDRESS

A *physical address* is a 48-bit address represented by six sections of two hexadecimal values (for example, 00-C0-DF-48-6F-13). It is assigned by the manufacturer of the network card before it is shipped to be sold. This identifier is designed to be unique and is often used to help identify a single machine on a network. At this level of the networking model, the Physical layer, data being passed over the network appears to be nothing more than the transmission and error-checking of voltage (1s and 0s) on the wire. These 1s and 0s are transmitted in a certain sequence based on the type of network used. This sequence is referred to as a frame. Within the frame, various pieces of information can be deciphered. The first active component to receive and process the voltage being transmitted on to the network is the network card.

The network card is responsible for determining whether the voltage is intended for it or some other machine. Each network card is given a set of rules that it must obey. First it listens to the preamble to synchronize itself so that it can determine where the data within the frame begins. After it determines where the data begins, it discards both the preamble and the frame check sequence before continuing to the next process. In the second process, the network card deciphers the data to determine for what physical address the frame is destined. If the destination address matches the physical address of the network card, it continues to process the information and pass the remaining data on for further action. If the destination address specifies some other machine's physical address, it silently discards the data within the frame and starts listening for other messages.

On a machine running Windows NT 4.0, it is relatively easy to determine its IP address. To do so, follow these steps:

1. From the Start menu, choose Programs, Command Prompt.

2. After the Command Prompt window appears, type **IPCONFIG /all**.

3. Read the information provided by the IPCONFIG utility until you see a section called "Ethernet Address." The value represented is the physical address of the machine.

If a network card discards the preamble and determines that the destination physical address is an Ethernet broadcast, for example FF-FF-FF-FF-FF-FF, this means the message is intended for all machines connected on that network segment. Whenever a network card receives a broadcast, it assumes the data is relevant and passes the data to the rest of the system for further processing. Network protocols such as NetBEUI use broadcasts to begin communication with a single machine on the network, requiring all machines on the network segment to listen, process the frame, and allow higher layers in the networking model to discard the information. Network protocols such as TCP/IP, although capable of broadcasting, typically determine the specific physical address of the destination machine, eliminating a great deal of broadcast traffic.

It would be unfair to say that TCP/IP does not utilize any broadcasts to communicate, but in general, machines on a network using NetBEUI spend more time deciphering broadcast traffic than machines on a TCP/IP network. This is primarily because NetBEUI is optimized for use on a local area network (LAN), where bandwidth and resources are plenty. NetBEUI is also enormously easy to install and configure and requires almost no ongoing intervention on behalf of the user. Its only significant weakness is that it is not a routeable protocol, meaning that it has no addressing characteristics that allow packets to be moved from one logical network to another.

TCP/IP, on the other hand, is designed for wide area network (WAN) environments where routers are the common connection method between two locations. Because of its routability and almost surgical (precise and efficient) use of bandwidth resources, it is clearly the favorite for this type of environment. It does require significantly more knowledge and experience on the user's part, however, to install and configure it correctly before it can be utilized. This is probably why Microsoft deems it necessary to test users' and administrators' knowledge of this protocol (that is, they don't have a test dedicated to NetBEUI or NWLink).

INTRODUCTION TO **TCP/IP**

The Transmission Control Protocol/Internet Protocol (TCP/IP) is an industry-standard suite of protocols designed to be routeable, robust, and functionally efficient. TCP/IP was originally designed as a set of wide area network (WAN) protocols for the express purpose of maintaining communication links and data transfer between sites in the event of a atomic/nuclear war. Since those early days, development of the protocols has passed from the hands of the government and has been the responsibility of the Internet community for some time.

The evolution of these protocols from a small five-site project into the foundation of the worldwide Internet has been extraordinary. But, despite more than 25 years of work and numerous modifications to the protocol suite, the inherent spirit of the original specifications is still intact.

Installing Microsoft's TCP/IP as a protocol on your machine or network provides the following advantages:

- **An industry-standard protocol**. Because TCP/IP is not maintained or written by one company, it is not proprietary or subject to as many compatibility issues. The Internet community as a whole decides whether a particular change or implementation is worthwhile. Naturally, this slows down the implementation of new features and characteristics compared to how quickly one directed company might make changes, but it does guarantee that changes are well thought out, that they provide functionality with most (if not all) other implementations of TCP/IP, and that a set of specifications is publicly available that can be referenced at any time over the Internet, detailing how the protocol suite should be used and implemented.

- **A set of utilities for connecting dissimilar operating systems**. Many connectivity utilities have been written for the TCP/IP suite, including the File Transfer Protocol (FTP) and Terminal Emulation Protocol (Telnet). Because these utilities use the Windows Sockets API, connectivity from one machine to another is not dependent on the network operating system used on either machine. A UNIX FTP server could be accessed by a Microsoft FTP client to transfer files without either party having to worry about compatibility issues. This functionality also allows a Windows NT machine running a Telnet client to access and run commands on an IBM mainframe running a Telnet server, for example.

- **A scalable, cross-platform client-server architecture.** Consider what happened during the initial development of applications for the TCP/IP protocol suite. Vendors wanted to be able to write their own client/server applications (for instance, SQL server and SNMP). The specification for how to write applications was also up for public perusal. Which operating systems would be included? Users everywhere wanted to be able to take advantage of the connectivity options promised through utilizing TCP/IP, regardless of the operating system they were currently running. Therefore, the Windows Sockets API was established so that applications utilizing the TCP/IP protocol could write to a standard, agreed-upon interface. Because the contributors included everyone, and therefore every kind of operating system, the specifications for Windows

Sockets on TCP/IP were written to make the operating system transparent to the application. Microsoft TCP/IP includes support for Windows Sockets and for connectivity to other Windows Sockets–compliant TCP/IP stacks.

♦ **Access to the Internet.** TCP/IP is the de facto protocol of the Internet and allows access to a wealth of information that can be found at thousands of locations around the world. To connect to the Internet, however, a valid IP address is required. Because IP addresses have become more and more scarce, and as security issues surrounding access to the Internet have been raised, many creative alternatives have been established to allow connections to the Internet. However, all these implementations utilize gateways or firewalls that act on behalf of the requesting machines.

Now that you understand the benefits of installing TCP/IP, you are ready to learn about how the TCP/IP protocol suite maps to a four-layer model.

Understanding the Four Layers of TCP/IP

At A Glance: TCP/IP and OSI

OSI	TCP/IP
Application	
Presentation	
Session	Application
Transport	Transport
Networking	Internet
Data Link	Network Interface
Physical	

TCP/IP maps to a four-layer architectural model. This model is called the *Internet Protocol Suite* and is broken into the Network Interface, Internet, Transport, and Application layers. Each of these layers corresponds to one or more layers of the OSI model. The Network Interface layer corresponds to the Physical and Data Link layers. The Internet layer corresponds to the Network layer. The Transport layer corresponds to the Transport layer, and the Application layer corresponds to the Session, Presentation, and Application layers of the OSI model.

Each of the four layers of the model is responsible for all the activities of the layers to which it maps. Each layer is described as follows:

- The *Network Interface layer* is responsible for communicating directly with the network. It must understand the network architecture being used, such as token ring or Ethernet, and provide an interface allowing the Internet layer to communicate with it. The Internet layer is responsible for communicating directly with the network Interface layer.

- The *Internet layer* is primarily concerned with the routing and delivery of packets through the Internet Protocol (IP). All the protocols in the Transport layer must use IP to send data. The Internet Protocol includes rules for how to address and direct packets, fragment and reassemble packets, provide security information, and identify the type of service being used. Because IP is not a connection-based protocol, however, it does not guarantee that packets transmitted on to the wire will not be lost, damaged, duplicated, or out of order. This is the responsibility of higher layers of the networking model, such as the Transport layer or the Application layer. Other protocols that exist in the Internet layer are the Internet Control Messaging Protocol (ICMP), Internet Group Management Protocol (IGMP), and the Address Resolution Protocol (ARP).

- The *Transport layer* maps to the Transport layer of the OSI model and is responsible for providing communication between machines for applications. This communication can be connection based or non-connection based. The primary difference between these two types of connections is whether there is a mechanism for tracking data and guaranteeing the delivery of the data to its destination. Transmission Control Protocol (TCP) is the protocol used for connection-based communication between two machines providing reliable data transfer. User Datagram Protocol (UDP) is used for non-connection–based communication with no guarantee of delivery.

- The *Application layer* of the Internet protocol suite is responsible for all the activities that occur in the Session, Presentation, and Application layers of the OSI model. Numerous protocols have been written for use in this layer, including HTTP, Simple Network Management Protocol (SNMP), File Transfer Protocol (FTP), Simple Mail Transfer Protocol (SMTP), as well as many others.

The interface between each of these layers is written to have the capability to pass information from one layer to the other.

The interface between the Network Interface layer and the Internet layer does not pass a great deal of information, although it must follow certain rules. Namely, it must listen to all broadcasts and send the rest of the data in the frame up to the Internet layer for processing, and if it receives any frames that do not have an IP frame type, they must be silently discarded.

The interface between the Internet layer and the Transport layer must be able to provide each layer full access to such information as the source and destination addresses, whether TCP or UDP should be utilized in the transport of data, and all other available mechanisms for IP. Rules and specifications for the Transport layer include giving the Transport layer the capability to change these parameters or to pass parameters it receives from the Application layer down to the Internet layer. The most important thing to remember about all these boundary layers is that they must use the agreed-upon rules for passing information from one layer to the other.

The interface between the Transport layer and the Application layer is written to provide an interface to applications, whether they are using the TCP or UDP protocol for transferring data. The interface utilizes the Windows Sockets and NetBIOS APIs to transfer parameters and data between the two layers. The Application layer must have full access to the Transport layer to change and alter parameters as necessary.

The layers provide only guidelines, however; the real work is done by the protocols contained within the layers. This section describes the TCP/IP protocol as being a suite of protocols, not just two (TCP and IP). In fact, six primary protocols are associated with TCP/IP:

- Transmission Control Protocol (TCP)
- User Datagram Protocol (UDP)

- Internet Protocol (IP)
- Internet Control Message Protocol (ICMP)
- Internet Group Management Protocol (IGMP)
- Address Resolution Protocol (ARP)

Transmission Control Protocol (TCP)

The first protocol that lives in the Transport layer is the Transmission Control Protocol (TCP). This protocol is a connection-based protocol and requires the establishment of a session before data is transmitted between two machines. TCP packets are delivered to sockets or ports. Because TCP sets up a connection between two machines, it is designed to verify that all packets sent by a machine are received on the other end. If, for some reason, packets are lost, the sending machine resends the data. Because a session is established and delivery of packets is guaranteed, there is additional overhead involved with using TCP to transmit packets.

To understand TCP further, you must understand ports and sockets, connection-oriented communications, sliding windows, and acknowledgments. The following sections cover each of these areas.

Ports and Sockets

The communication process between the Transport layer and the Application layer involves identifying the application that has requested either a reliable or unreliable transport mechanism. Port assignments are the means used to identify application processes to the Transport layer. Ports identify to which process on the machine data should be sent for further processing. Specific port numbers have been assigned by the Internet Assigned Numbers Authority (IANA), specifically those from 1 to 1023. These port assignments are called the well-known ports and represent the ports to which standard applications listen. Defining these standard port numbers helps eliminate having to guess to which port an application is listening so that applications can direct their queries or messages directly. Port numbers above the well-known port range are available for running applications, and work in exactly the same way. In this case, however, the client or user has to be able to identify to which port the application is connecting. Ports can be used by both TCP and

UDP for delivering data between two machines. Ports themselves do not care whether the data they receive is in order, but the applications running on those ports might.

To identify both the location and application to which a stream of data needs to be sent, the IP address (location) and the port number (application) are often combined into one functional address called a socket.

Connection-Orientation Communication

The Transmission Control Protocol (TCP) is a connection-based protocol that establishes a connection, or session, between two machines before any data is transferred. TCP exists within the Transport layer, between the Application layer and the IP layer, providing a reliable and guaranteed delivery mechanism to a destination machine. Connection-based protocols guarantee the delivery of packets by tracking the transmission and receipt of individual packets during communication. A session can track the progress of individual packets by monitoring when a packet is sent, in what order it was sent, and by notifying the sender when it is received so that it can send more.

The first step in the communication process is to send a message indicating a desire to synchronize the systems. This is equivalent to dialing a phone number and waiting for someone to answer. The second step is for the machine to send an acknowledgment that it is listening and willing to accept data. This step is equivalent to a person answering the phone, and then waiting for the caller to say something. The third step is for the calling machine to send a message indicating that it understands the receiving machine's willingness to listen and that data transmission will now begin.

After the TCP session has been created, the machines begin to communicate just as people do during a phone call. In the example of the telephone, if the caller uses a cellular phone and some of the transmission is lost, the user indicates that she did not receive the message by saying, "What did you say? I didn't hear that." This indicates to the sender that he needs to resend the data.

Included in the header are sections defining the sequence numbers and acknowledgment numbers that help verify the delivery of a datagram. A datagram or packet is just the data being transferred to the destination machine. This data often has to be broken up into smaller pieces (datagrams) because the underlying network can only transmit so much data at one time. Other parameters include the SYN and FIN options for starting and ending communication sessions between two machines, the size of the window to be used in transferring data, a checksum for verifying the headers information, and other options that can be specific implementations of TCP/IP. The last part of the frame is the actual data being transmitted. A full discussion of each of these parameters is beyond the scope of this book or the TCP/IP test. More academic texts and RFCs on the Internet describe in fuller detail the specifications for each parameter.

During the initialization of a TCP session, often called the *three-way handshake*, both machines agree on the best method to track how much data is to be sent at any one time, acknowledgment numbers to be sent upon receipt of data, and when the connection is no longer necessary because all data has been transmitted and received. It is only after this session is created that data transmission begins. To provide reliable delivery, TCP places packets in sequenced order and requires acknowledgments that these packets reached their destination before it sends new data. TCP is typically used for transferring large amounts of data, or when the application requires acknowledgment that data has been received. Given all the additional overhead information that TCP needs to keep track of, the format of a TCP packet can be somewhat complex.

Sliding Windows

TCP uses the concept of sliding windows for transferring data between machines. Sliding windows are often referred to in the UNIX environment as *streams*. Each machine has both a send window and a receive window that it utilizes to buffer data and make the communication process more efficient. A window represents the subset of data currently being sent to a destination machine, and is also the amount of data being received by the destination machine. At first this seems redundant, but it really isn't. Not all data that is sent is guaranteed to be received, so they must be kept track of on both machines. A sliding window allows a sending machine to send the window data in a stream without having to wait for an acknowledgment for every single packet.

A receiving window allows a machine to receive packets out of order and reorganize them while it waits for more packets. This reorganization may be necessary because TCP utilizes IP to transmit data, and IP does not guarantee the orderly delivery of packets. By default, window sizes in

Windows NT are a little more than 8KB in size, representing eight standard Ethernet frames. Standard Ethernet frames are a little more than 1KB apiece.

Packets do not always make it to their destination, however. TCP has been designed to recover in the event that packets are lost along the way, perhaps by busy routers. TCP keeps track of the data that has been sent out, and if it doesn't receive an acknowledgment for that data from the destination machine in a certain amount of time, the data is re-sent. In fact, until acknowledgment for a packet of data is received, further data transmission is halted completely.

Acknowledgments

Acknowledgments are a very important component necessary to ensure the reliable delivery of packets. As the receiving window receives packets, it sends acknowledgments to the sending window that the packets arrived intact. When the send window receives acknowledgments for data it has sent, it slides the window to the right so that it can send any additional data stored in memory. But it can only slide over by the number of acknowledgments it has received. By default, a receive window sends an acknowledgment for every two sequenced packets it receives.

As long as the acknowledgments begin flowing back regularly from the receiving machine, data flows smoothly and efficiently. On busy networks, however, packets can get lost and acknowledgments may be delayed. Because TCP guarantees delivery and reliability of traffic flow, the window cannot slide past any data that has not been acknowledged. If the window cannot slide beyond a packet of data, no more data beyond the window is transmitted, TCP eventually has to shut down the session, and the communication fails.

Each machine is therefore instructed to wait a certain amount of time before either retransmitting data or sending acknowledgments for packets that arrive out of sequence. Each window is given a timer: The send window has the Retransmit Timer; the receive window has the Delayed Acknowledgment Timer. These timers help define what to do when communication is not flowing very smoothly.

In the send window, a Retransmit Timer is set for each packet, specifying how long to wait for an acknowledgment before making the assumption that the packet did not get to its destination. After this timer has expired, the send window is instructed to resend the packet and wait twice as long as the time set on the preceding timer. The default starting point for this timer is approximately three seconds, but is usually reduced to less than a second almost immediately. Each time an acknowledgment is not received, the Retransmit Timer doubles. If the Retransmit Timer started at approximately one second, for example, the second Retransmit Timer is set for two seconds, the third for four seconds, the fourth for eight seconds, up to a fifth attempt that waits 16 seconds. The number of attempts can be altered in the Registry; if after these attempts an acknowledgment still cannot be received, however, the TCP session is closed and errors are reported to the application.

In the receiving window, a Delayed Acknowledgment Timer is set for those packets that arrive out of order. Remember, by default an acknowledgment is sent for every two sequenced packets, starting from the left-hand side of the window. If packets arrive out of order (if, for instance, 1 and 3 arrive but 2 is missing), an acknowledgment for two sequenced packets is not possible. When packets arrive out of order, a Delayed Acknowledgment Timer is set on the first packet in the pair. In the parenthetical example, a timer is set on packet number 1. The Delayed Acknowledgment Timer is hard-coded for 200 milliseconds, or $\frac{1}{5}$ the Retransmit Timer. If packet 2 does not show up before the Delayed Acknowledgment Timer expires, an acknowledgment for packet 1, and only packet 1, is sent. No other acknowledgments are sent, including those for packets 3 through 8 that might have appeared. Until packet 2 arrives, the other packets are considered interesting, but useless. As data is acknowledged and passed to the Application layer, the receive window slides to the right, enabling more data to be received. Again however, if a packet doesn't show up, the window is not enabled to slide past it.

User Datagram Protocol (UDP)

The second protocol that lives in the Transport layer is the User Datagram Protocol, or UDP. This protocol is a non-connection–based protocol and does not require a session to be established between two machines before data is transmitted. UDP packets are still delivered to sockets or ports, just as they are in TCP. But because UDP does not create a session between machines, it cannot guarantee that packets are delivered or that they are delivered in order or retransmitted if the packets are lost. Given the apparent unreliability of this protocol, some may wonder why a protocol such as UDP was developed.

Sending a UDP datagram has very little overhead involved. A UDP datagram has no synchronization parameters or priority options. All that exists is the source port, destination port, the length of the data, a checksum for verifying the header, and then the data.

There are actually a number of good reasons to have a transport protocol that does not require a session to be established. For one, very little overhead is associated with UDP, such as having to keep track of sequence numbers, Retransmit Timers, Delayed Acknowledgment Timers, and retransmission of packets. UDP is quick and extremely streamlined functionally; it is just not guaranteed. This makes UDP perfect for communications that involve broadcasts, general announcements to the network, or real-time data.

Another really good use for UDP is in streaming video and streaming audio. Not only does the unguaranteed delivery of packets enable more data to be transmitted (because a broadcast has little to no overhead), but the retransmission of a packet is pointless, anyway. In the case of a streaming broadcast, users are more concerned with what's coming next than with trying to recover a packet or two that may not have made it. Compare it to listening to a music CD and a piece of dust gets stuck in one of the little grooves. In most cases, the omission of that piece is imperceptible; your ear barely notices and your brain probably filled in the gap for you anyway. Imagine instead that your CD player decides to guarantee the delivery of that one piece of data that it can't quite get, and ends up skipping and skipping indefinitely. It can definitely ruin the listening experience. It is easier to deal with an occasional packet dropping out to have as fulfilling a listening experience as possible. Thankfully, UDP was developed for applications to utilize in this very same fashion.

> **NOTE**
> An application that uses UDP can guarantee delivery, but it is the responsibility of the application, not UDP.

Internet Protocol (IP)

A number of protocols are found in the Internet layer, including the most important protocol in the entire suite, the Internet Protocol (IP). The reason that this is probably the most important protocol is that the Transport layer cannot communicate at all without communicating through IP in the Internet layer.

Addressing

The most fundamental element of the Internet Protocol is the address space that IP uses. Each machine on a network is given a unique 32-bit address called an Internet address or IP address. Addresses are divided into five categories, called classes. There are currently A, B, C, D, and E classes of addresses. The unique address given to a machine is derived from the class A, B, or C addresses. Class D addresses are used for combining machines into one functional group, and Class E addresses are considered experimental and are not currently available. For now, the most important concept to understand is that each machine requires a unique address and IP is responsible for maintaining, utilizing, and manipulating it to provide communication between two machines. The whole concept behind uniquely identifying machines is to be able to send data to one machine and one machine only, even in the event that the IP stack has to broadcast at the Physical layer.

If IP receives data from the Network Interface layer that is addressed to another machine or is not a broadcast, its directions are to silently discard the packet and not continue processing it.

IP receives information in the form of packets from the Transport layer, from either TCP or UDP, and sends out data in what are commonly referred to as datagrams. The size of a datagram depends on the type of network being used, such as token ring or Ethernet. If a packet has too much data to be transmitted in one datagram, it is broken into pieces and transmitted through several datagrams. Each of these datagrams has to then be reassembled by TCP or UDP.

Broadcasts

Despite the fact that IP was designed to be able to send packets directly to a particular machine, at times it is preferable to send a message to all machines connected to a physical segment. IP supports broadcasts at the Internet layer and if it receives a broadcast datagram from the Network Interface layer, it must process the packet as if it had been addressed to it.

Fragmentation and Reassembly

Fragmentation and reassembly occurs when data is too large to be transmitted on the underlying network. Combining a token-ring and Ethernet network is the most common example. Token-ring networks support much larger frame sizes and therefore support larger datagram sizes. It may also be the case that the Transport layer sends the Internet layer more data than one datagram can handle. In either of these cases, IP must break down the data into manageable chunks through a process called fragmentation. After data is fragmented, each datagram gets a fragment ID, identifying it in the sequence so that each fragment can be reassembled at the destination machine. This whole process is transparent to the user.

After the fragments have been received and reassembled at the destination machine, the data can be sent up to the higher layers for processing.

Routeability

IP is responsible for routing IP datagrams from one network to another. Machines on a network can be configured to support routing. With routing, when a machine receives a datagram that is neither addressed to it nor is a broadcast, it is given the additional responsibility of trying to find where the datagram should be sent so that it can reach its destination. Not all machines on a TCP/IP network are routers. But all routers have the capability to forward datagrams from one network to another. Connections to the Internet are often through one form of router or another.

Time to Live

The Time to Live (TTL) specification is set in Windows NT to a default of 128. This represents either 128 hops or 128 seconds, or a combination of the two. Each time a router handles a datagram, it decrements the TTL by one. If a datagram is held up at a router for longer than one second before it is transmitted, the router can decrement the TTL by more than one.

One way to visualize how the TTL works is to think of a deadly poison. Each time a datagram is sent out onto the network, it is injected with this deadly poison. The datagram has only the length of time specified in the TTL to get to its destination and receive the antidote for the poison. If the datagram gets routed through congested routers, traffic jams, narrow bandwidth communication avenues, and so on, it just might not make it. If the TTL expires before the datagram reaches its destination, it is discarded from the network.

Although this concept may seem strange at first, in reality it prevents datagrams from running around a network indefinitely wreaking havoc with bandwidth and the synchronization of data. Imagine a scenario in which 100 datagrams are sent to a machine. Twenty-five of them have to be resent because the Retransmit Timer on the sending machine expired. After the communication is complete and the session broken down, suddenly 25 packets appear out of nowhere hitting the destination machine. It may be that these 25 packets got rerouted through some extremely slow network path and were never discarded. At least in this case the destination machine can just ignore the datagrams. However, in routed environments it would be pretty easy to set up infinite loops where packets would bounce in between two routers indefinitely.

So here we have TCP, UDP, and IP working together to provide both connection-oriented and non-connection–oriented communication. These three protocols work together to provide communication between two machines.

Internet Control Message Protocol (ICMP)

Internet Control Message Protocol (ICMP) is part of the Internet layer and is responsible for reporting errors and messages regarding the delivery of IP datagrams. It can also send *source quench* and other self-tuning signals during the transfer of data between two machines without the intervention of the user. These signals are designed to fine-tune and optimize the transfer of data automatically. ICMP is the protocol that warns you when a destination host is unreachable, or how long it took to get to a destination host.

ICMP messages can be broken down into two basic categories: the reporting of errors and the sending of queries. Error messages include the following:

- Destination unreachable
- Redirect
- Source quench
- Time exceeded

The destination unreachable error message is generated by ICMP when an IP datagram is sent out and the destination machine either cannot be located or does not support the designated protocol. A sending machine may receive a destination host unreachable message when trying to communicate through a router that does not know to which network to send a datagram, for example.

The first important thing to realize about redirect messages is that these are only sent by routers in a TCP/IP environment, not individual machines. A machine may have more than one default gateway defined for redundancy. If a router detects a better route to a particular destination, it forwards the first packet it receives, but sends a redirect message to the machine to update its route tables. In this way, the machine can use the better route to reach the remote network.

Sometimes a machine has to drop incoming datagrams because it has received so many that it cannot process them all. In this case, a machine can send a source quench message to the source, indicating that it needs to slow up transmission. The source quench message can also be sent by a router if it is in between the source and destination machines and is encountering trouble routing all the packets in time. Upon receiving a source quench message, the source machine immediately reduces its transmissions. It continues to try to increase the amount of data as time progresses, however, to the original amount of data it was sending before.

The time exceeded error message is sent by a router whenever it drops a packet because of the expiration of the TTL. This error message is sent to the source address to notify the machine of a possible infinite routing loop or that the TTL is set too low to get to the destination.

N O T E	The router should be capable of processing ICMP to send the specific error message mentioned.

ICMP also includes general message queries. The two most commonly used are the following:

- ◆ Echo request
- ◆ Echo reply

The most familiar tool for verifying that an IP address on a network actually exists is the Personal Internet Groper (Ping) utility. This utility uses the ICMP echo request and reply mechanisms. The echo request is a simple directed datagram that asks for acknowledgment that a particular IP address exists on the network. If a machine with this IP address exists and receives the request, it is designed to send an ICMP echo reply. This reply is sent back to the destination address to notify the source machine of its existence. The Ping utility reports the existence of the IP address and how long it took to get there.

Internet Group Management Protocol (IGMP)

Internet Group Management Protocol (IGMP) is a protocol and set of specifications that allow machines to be added and removed from IP address groups, utilizing the Class D range of addresses mentioned earlier. IP allows the assignment of Class D addresses to groups of machines so that they may receive broadcast data as one functional unit. Machines can be added and removed from these units or groups, or be members of multiple groups.

Most implementations of the TCP/IP protocol stack support this on the local machine; however, routers designed to broadcast IGMP messages from one network to another are still in the experimental stage. Routers are designed to initiate queries for multicast groups on local network segments to determine whether they should be broadcasting on that segment. If at least one member of an IGMP group exists or responds with an IGMP response, the router processes IGMP datagrams and broadcasts them on the segment.

Address Resolution Protocol (ARP)

Unless IP is planning to initiate a full broadcast on the network, it has to have the physical address of the machine to which it is going to send datagrams. For this information, it relies on Address Resolution Protocol (ARP). ARP is responsible for mapping IP addresses on the network to physical addresses in memory. This way, whenever IP needs a physical address for a particular IP address, ARP can deliver. But ARP's memory does not last indefinitely, and occasionally IP will ask for an IP address that is not in ARP's memory. When this happens, ARP has to go out and find one.

ARP is responsible for finding a map to a local physical address for any local IP address that IP may request. If ARP does not have a map in memory, it has to go find one on the network. ARP uses local broadcasts to find physical addresses of machines and maintains a cache in memory of recently mapped IP addresses to physical addresses. Although this cache does not last indefinitely, it enables ARP to not have to broadcast every time IP needs a physical address.

As long as the destination IP address is local, all ARP does is a local broadcast for that machine and returns the physical address to IP. IP, realizing that the destination IP address is local, just formulates the datagram with the IP address above the physical address of the destination machine.

But IP does not always need to send datagrams to local IP addresses. In fact, often the destination address is on a remote network where the path may include several routers along the way. The hardest thing to realize conceptually is that ARP operates so close to the Network Interface layer that it is really only good for finding local physical addresses. This is true even in environments where routers exist. ARP never reports a physical address that exists on a remote network to IP.

To get the packet to the other network, the router is supposed to listen to the packet and forward it on. The only way to get it to listen to the packet, however, is to either do a broadcast or send the packet to the router's physical address. IP is smart enough to realize that the destination IP address is on a remote network and that the datagram must be sent to the router. It has no idea what the physical address of the router is, however, and therefore relies on ARP to discover that for it.

To route a packet, IP asks ARP whether it has the physical address of the router, not of the destination machine. This is one of the more subtle and elegant features of the TCP/IP suite, in that it cleverly redirects packets based on what layer is being communicated with. After IP receives the physical address of the router from ARP, it formulates the datagram, placing the destination IP address directly above the router's physical address.

Network APIs

The Application layer provides the interface between applications and the transport protocols. Microsoft supports two APIs for applications to use: Windows Sockets and NetBIOS. This functionality is included because Microsoft networks still use NetBIOS for a number of internal mechanisms within the Windows NT operating system. It is also used because it provides a standard interface to a number of other protocols as well. TCP/IP, NetBEUI, and NWLink all have a NetBIOS interface to which applications can be written to use networking protocols. Strict UNIX flavors of TCP/IP may not support the NetBIOS interface and may only support Windows Sockets as their API; Microsoft's implementation of TCP/IP therefore includes support for both.

Windows Sockets

The Windows Sockets interface defines an industry-standard specification for how Windows applications communicate with the TCP/IP protocol. This specification includes definitions for how to use the transport protocols and how to transfer data between two machines, including the establishment of connection-oriented sessions (TCP three-way handshake) and non-connection–oriented datagrams (broadcasts). The Windows Sockets API also defines how to uniquely address packets destined for a particular application on another machine. The concept of a socket (the combination of the TCP/IP address and the port number) is a common example of the relative ease of uniquely identifying a communications path. Because of the ease and standardization of the Windows Sockets specifications, this API is enjoying a tremendous amount of exposure and success, particularly in terms of its use in Internet applications.

Windows Sockets uniquely identifies machines through their IP address, so machine names in the TCP/IP environment are entirely optional. Given that it is tremendously more difficult for users to remember 100 IP addresses over some form of an alias for these machines, a name space was created to help identify machines on a TCP/IP network. A name space is a hierarchical naming scheme that uniquely identifies machine aliases to IP addresses. This scheme allows two machines to have the same alias as long as they are not in the same domain. This is very useful for people, but entirely unnecessary for applications because applications can use the IP address. This is why you can use any alias you wish to establish a connection to a particular machine. As long as the name resolution method (DNS, HOSTS file) returns a valid IP address, a communication path can be created. The IP address is what's most important. With the NetBIOS API, the IP address is only part of the information necessary to establish communication between two machines, and the name of the machine (hostname) is required.

NetBIOS

The NetBIOS API was developed on local area networks and has evolved into a standard interface for applications to use to access networking protocols in the Transport layer for both connection-oriented and non-connection–oriented communications. NetBIOS interfaces have been written for the NetBEUI, NWLink, and TCP/IP protocols so that applications need not worry about which of these protocols is providing the transport services. Because each of these protocols supports the NetBIOS API, all the functionality for establishing sessions and initiating broadcasts is provided. Unlike Windows Sockets, NetBIOS requires not only an IP address to uniquely identify a machine, but a NetBIOS name as well.

Every machine on a network must be uniquely identified with a NetBIOS name. This name is required for establishing a NetBIOS session or sending out a broadcast. When utilizing names through a NetBIOS session, the sending machine must be able to resolve the NetBIOS name to an IP address. Because both an IP address and name are needed, all name resolution methods have to supply the correct IP address before successful communication can occur.

The Microsoft TCP/IP stack supports connection-oriented and non-connection–oriented communications established through either of these popular APIs. Microsoft includes NetBT (NetBIOS over TCP/IP) for applications that would like to utilize the NetBIOS API over a TCP/IP network. This small, seemingly insignificant piece of software is what prevents your machine from having to run two protocols (one for Windows Sockets, and one for NetBIOS). By providing NetBT with Microsoft's TCP/IP protocol stack, all NetBIOS calls an application may initiate are supported.

WHAT IS IMPORTANT TO KNOW

The following bullets summarize the chapter and accentuate the key concepts to memorize for the exam:

- Support and implementation of the TCP/IP protocol is built in to Windows NT 4.0 (Server and Workstation). To use TCP/IP, every host (computer) must have a unique IP address.

- Windows NT enhances TCP/IP by including services for DNS and DHCP.

OBJECTIVES

Installation and Configuration Objectives:

▶ Given a scenario, select the appropriate services to install when using Microsoft TCP/IP on a Microsoft Windows NT Server computer

▶ On a Windows NT Server computer, configure Microsoft TCP/IP to support multiple network adapters

▶ Configure scopes by using DHCP Manager

▶ Install and configure a WINS server

▶ Import LMHOSTS files to WINS

▶ Run WINS on a multihomed computer

▶ Configure WINS replication

▶ Configure static mappings in the WINS database

▶ Configure subnet masks

▶ Configure a Windows NT Server computer to function as an IP router

▶ Install and configure the DHCP Relay Agent

▶ continues . . .

C H A P T E R *2*

Installation and Configuration

Oʙᴊᴇᴄᴛɪᴠᴇs continued

▶ Install and configure the Microsoft DNS Server service on a Windows NT Server computer

▶ Integrate DNS with other name servers

▶ Connect a DNS server to a DNS root server

▶ Configure DNS server roles

▶ Configure HOSTS and LMHOSTS files

▶ Configure a Windows NT Server computer to support TCP/IP printing

▶ Configure SNMP

INSTALLING SERVICES WHEN USING MICROSOFT TCP/IP ON WINDOWS NT

When installing the TCP/IP protocol, you have the choice of installing and using several different services that work in conjunction with it.

At A Glance: Services

Service	*Purpose*
IIS	Create a Windows NT Internet site
LPD	Provide TCP/IP printing services
DHCP	Dynamically assign TCP/IP configuration information to clients
WINS	Resolve Windows (NetBIOS) names to IP addresses
SNMP	Gather TCP/IP statistics
DNS	Resolve hostnames to IP addresses

You may want or need to install the following services:

- **Internet Information Server.** The Internet Information Server provides you the ability to share information to any type of computer that can use the TCP/IP protocol. IIS 3 includes FTP, Gopher, and WWW servers. IIS 4 does not include Gopher.

- **Line Printer Daemon.** This server enables you to share your printers with many different types of hosts, including mainframes and UNIX-based hosts.

- **Dynamic Host Configuration Protocol (DHCP).** Provides automatic configuration of remote hosts, making management of a TCP/IP environment easy.

- **DHCP Relay Agent.** Extends the capabilities of the DHCP service by allowing it to work across various different subnets.

- **Windows Internet Name Service.** Without the ability to find another computer on the network, you would never be able to communicate. The WINS server provides a centralized method of name management that is both flexible and dynamic in a Microsoft-only network.

♦ **Simple Network Management Protocol Agent.** In areas where you will use SNMP managers, or even if you want to track the performance of your TCP/IP protocols, you will want to install the SNMP agent.

♦ **Domain Name Server.** Where the WINS server provides the capability to find NetBIOS names, the DNS server will work with hostnames to enable you to integrate your systems into the Internet or to resolve hosts on the Internet.

IIS is covered in great detail in an exam of its own; the Line Printer Daemon is covered in detail in later sections of this chapter. DHCP, WINS, and DNS are all examined in the following sections.

Understanding DHCP

The configuration of Microsoft TCP/IP involves knowing the correct values for several fields for each TCP/IP host and entering them manually. At the minimum, the host IP address and the subnet mask need to be configured. In most cases, other parameters such as WINS and DNS server addresses also need to be configured on each host. DHCP relieves the need for manual configuration and provides a method of configuring and reconfiguring all the TCP/IP-related parameters.

It is critical that the correct TCP/IP address is configured on each host; otherwise, hosts on the internetwork might

♦ Fail to communicate

♦ Fail to initialize

♦ Cause other hosts on the internetwork to hang

The Dynamic Host Configuration Protocol is an open industry standard that enables the automatic TCP/IP configuration of DHCP client computers. The use of Microsoft's DHCP server greatly reduces the administrative overhead of managing TCP/IP client computers by eliminating the need to manually configure clients. The DHCP server also allows for greater flexibility and mobility of clients on a TCP/IP network without administrator intervention. If used correctly, DHCP can eliminate nearly all the problems associated with TCP/IP. The administrator enters the valid IP addresses or ranges of IP addresses (called a scope) in the DHCP server database, which then assigns (or leases) the IP addresses to the DHCP client hosts.

Having all the TCP/IP configuration parameters stored on the DHCP server provides the following benefits:

+ The administrator can quickly verify the IP address and other configuration parameters without having to go to each host. Also, reconfiguration of the DHCP database is accomplished at one central location, thereby eliminating the need to manually configure each host.

+ DHCP does not lease the same IP address from a scope to two hosts at the same time; this can prevent duplicate IP addresses if used properly.

NOTE

DHCP cannot detect which IP addresses are already being used by non-DHCP clients. If a host has a manually configured IP address and a DHCP scope is configured with that same address, the DHCP server may lease the address to a DHCP client, creating a duplicate IP address on the network. To prevent this situation, you must exclude all manually configured IP addresses from any scopes configured on the DHCP server.

+ The DHCP administrator controls which IP addresses are used by which hosts. DHCP uses local network broadcasts to lease IP addresses to client hosts. If a second DHCP server resides on the same local network segment, the DHCP client can communicate with either server and may receive an IP address lease from the unintended DHCP server.

+ The chance of clerical and typing errors is reduced because the TCP/IP configuration parameters are entered in one place—the DHCP server database.

+ Several options can be set for each DHCP scope (or globally for all scopes) configured on the client along with the IP address, for example, default gateway, WINS server addresses, and so on.

+ An IP address may be leased for a limited time, which requires the DHCP client periodically to renew its lease before the lease expires. If the host is no longer using the IP address (is no longer running

TCP/IP or is powered off), the lease expires and can then be assigned to another TCP/IP host. This feature is useful if the number of hosts requesting IP addresses is larger than the number of available valid IP addresses (such as when the network is part of the Internet).

◆ If a host is physically moved to a different subnet, the DHCP server on that subnet automatically reconfigures the host with the proper TCP/IP configuration information for that subnet.

What DHCP Servers Can Do

To enable automatic TCP/IP configuration by using DHCP, the DHCP administrator first enters the valid IP addresses as a scope in the DHCP server database and then activates the scope. The DHCP administrator now enters other TCP/IP configuration information that will be given to the clients. The administrator or user then selects the Enable Automatic DHCP Configuration option on the client (found in their network configuration).

When a DHCP client host starts up, TCP/IP initializes and the client requests an IP address from a DHCP server by issuing a DHCPDISCOVER packet. The DHCPDISCOVER packet represents the client's IP lease request.

After a DHCP server receives the DHCPDISCOVER packet, the DHCP server offers (DHCPOFFER) one of the unassigned IP addresses from the scope of addresses that are valid for that host. This ensures that no two DHCP clients on that subnet have the same IP address. This DHCPOFFER information is sent back to the host. If your network contains more than one DHCP server, the host may receive several DHCPOFFERS. In most cases, the host or client computer accepts the first DHCPOFFER that it receives. The client then sends a DHCPREQUEST packet containing the IP address offered by the DHCP server.

The DHCP server then sends the client an acknowledgment (DHCPACK) that contains the IP address originally sent and a lease for that address. The DHCP server leases the IP address to the DHCP client host for the specified period. The DHCP client must renew its lease before the lease expires. During the life of the lease, the client attempts to renew the lease.

The renewal request is sent automatically if the host still has TCP/IP initialized, can communicate with the DHCP server, and is still on the same subnet or network. After 50% of the lease time expires, the client attempts to renew its lease with the DHCP server that assigned its TCP/IP configuration. At 87.5% of the active lease period, the client, if unable to contact and renew the lease with the original DHCP server, attempts to communicate with any DHCP server to renew its configuration information. If the client cannot make contact with a DHCP server and consequently fails to maintain its lease, the client must discontinue use of the IP address and begin the entire process again by issuing a DHCPDISCOVER packet.

Limitations of DHCP

Although DHCP can substantially reduce the headaches and time required to administer IP addresses, you should note a few limiting characteristics of DHCP:

+ DHCP does not detect IP addresses already in use on a network by non-DHCP clients. These addresses should be excluded from any scopes configured on the DHCP server.

+ A DHCP server does not communicate with other DHCP servers and cannot detect IP addresses leased by other DHCP servers. Therefore, two DHCP servers should not use the same IP addresses in their respective scopes.

+ DHCP servers cannot communicate with clients across routers unless BOOTP forwarding is enabled on the router, or the DHCP Relay Agent is enabled on the subnet.

+ As with manually configured TCP/IP, incorrect values configured for a DHCP scope can cause unexpected and potentially disastrous results on the internetwork.

Other than the IP address and subnet mask, any values configured manually through the Network Control Panel applet or Registry Editor of a DHCP client override the DHCP server scope settings. If you intend to use the server-configured values, be sure to clear the values from the host TCP/IP configuration dialog boxes. Enabling DHCP on the client host does not automatically clear any pre-existing values, although DHCP clears the IP address and subnet mask.

Planning a DHCP Implementation

As with all network services that you will use, you should plan the implementation of DHCP. A few conditions must be met; the next few sections examine these conditions.

Network Requirements

The following requirements must be met to implement Microsoft TCP/IP using DHCP:

* The DHCP Server service must be running on a Windows NT Server.

* The DHCP server must have a manually configured IP address.

* A DHCP server must be located on the same subnet as the DHCP clients, the clients subnet must have a DHCP Relay Agent running, or the routers connecting the two subnets involved must be able to forward DHCP (BOOTP) datagrams.

* Pools of IP addresses known as *scopes* must be configured on the DHCP server, and the scopes must be activated, as well.

It is easiest to implement DHCP with only one DHCP server on a subnet (local network segment). If more than one DHCP server is configured to provide addresses for a subnet, either can provide the address—there is no way to specify which server to use as you can in WINS (Windows Internet Name Service). Because DHCP servers do not communicate with each other, a DHCP server has no way of knowing whether an IP address is leased to a client from another DHCP server.

To prevent two DHCP servers from assigning the same IP address to two clients, you must ensure that each IP address is made available in a scope on only one DHCP server on the internetwork. In other words, the IP address scopes cannot overlap or contain the same IP addresses.

If no DHCP server is available to lease an IP address to a DHCP client—because of hardware problems, for example—the client cannot initialize. For this reason, you may want to have a second DHCP server, with unique IP address scopes, on the network. This scenario works best when the second DHCP server is on a different subnet connected by a router that forwards DHCP datagrams.

A DHCP client accepts the first IP address offer it receives from a DHCP server. This address would normally be from the DHCP server on the local network, because the IP address request broadcast would reach the local DHCP server first. If the local DHCP server is not responding and if the DHCP broadcasts were forwarded by the router, for example, the DHCP client could accept a lease offer from a DHCP server on a remote network.

Finally, the DHCP server must have one or more scopes created by using the DHCP Server Manager application (Start, Programs, Administrative Tools, DHCP Manager). A *scope* is a range of IP addresses available for lease by DHCP clients; for example, 200.20.5.1 through 200.20.5.20 may be a scope for a given subnet, and 200.20.6.1 through 200.20.6.50 may be a scope for another subnet.

Client Requirements

A Microsoft TCP/IP DHCP client can be any of the following Microsoft TCP/IP clients:

- Windows NT Server 3.5 or later, which is not a DHCP server

- Windows NT Workstation 3.5 or later

- Windows 95

- Windows for Workgroups 3.11, running the Microsoft TCP/IP-32 software from the Windows NT Server CD-ROM

- Microsoft Network Client for MS-DOS 3.0 from the Windows NT Server CD-ROM

- LAN Manager server for MS-DOS 2.2c from the Windows NT Server CD-ROM

If some clients on the network do not use DHCP for IP address config- uration—because they do not support DHCP or otherwise need to have TCP/IP manually configured—the IP addresses of these non-DHCP clients must not be made available for lease to the DHCP clients. Non- DHCP clients can include clients that do not support Microsoft DHCP (see the preceding list), and clients that must always use the same IP address, such as Windows Internet Name Service (WINS) servers, Domain Name Service (DNS) servers, and other DHCP servers.

NOTE

You should not assign the addresses of servers (file and print, DNS, WINS, and so on) with DHCP because the address could change. If you do, you have to reconfigure the scope options every time one of these servers restarts.

Using Multiple DHCP Servers

It is not recommended to have more than one DHCP server on a subnet because there is no way to control from which DHCP server a client receives an IP address lease. Any DHCP server that receives a client's DHCP request broadcast can send a DHCP offer to that client. The client accepts the first lease offer it receives from a DHCP server.

If more than one subnet exists on a network, it is generally recommended to have a DHCP server on each subnet. If the DHCP Relay Agent or routers that support the forwarding of BOOTP broadcasts are used, requests for DHCP addresses can be handled by a single DHCP server.

A DHCP server has an IP address scope configured for each subnet to which it sends DHCP offers. If the DHCP server receives a relayed DHCP request from a remote subnet, it offers an IP address lease from the scope for that subnet. To ensure that a DHCP client can receive an IP address lease even if a DHCP server is not functioning, you should configure an IP address scope for a given subnet on more than one DHCP server. Thus, if a DHCP client cannot obtain a lease from the local DHCP server, the DHCP Relay Agent or router passes the request to a DHCP server on a remote network that can offer a DHCP lease to the client.

Consider a network with two subnets, for example, each with a DHCP server, joined by a RFC 1542-compliant router. For this scenario, Microsoft recommends that each DHCP server should contain approximately 75% of the available IP addresses for the subnet the DHCP server is on, and 25% of the available IP addresses for the remote subnet. Most of the IP addresses available for a subnet can be obtained from the local DHCP server. If the local DHCP server is unavailable, the remote DHCP server can offer a lease from the smaller range of IP addresses available from the scope on the remote DHCP server.

If the range of IP addresses available are 120.50.7.10 through 120.50.
7.110 for Subnet A and 120.50.8.10 through 120.50.8.110 for Subnet
B, you can configure the scopes on each DHCP server as follows:

Subnet	*DHCP Server A*	*DHCP Server B*
A	120.50.7.10 – 120.50.7.84	120.50.7.85 – 120.50.7.110
B	120.50.8.10 – 120.50.8.34	120.50.8.35 – 120.50.8.110

NOTE
You must ensure that no IP address is duplicated on another DHCP server.
If two DHCP servers contain the same IP address, that IP address could
potentially be leased to two DHCP clients at the same time. Therefore, IP
address ranges must be split among multiple DHCP servers, as shown in
the preceding example.

How DHCP Works

DHCP client configuration is a four-part process:

1. When the DHCP client initializes, it broadcasts a request for an IP
   lease called a DHCPDISCOVER from a DHCP server.

2. All DHCP servers that receive the IP lease request respond to the
   DHCP client with an IP lease offer known as a DHCPOFFER. This
   includes DHCP servers on the local network and on remote networks when the Relay Agent is used or a router that passes BOOTP
   requests.

3. The DHCP client selects the first offer it receives and broadcasts an
   IP lease-selection message specifying the IP address it has selected.
   This message is known as a DHCPREQUEST.

4. The DHCP server that offered the selected lease responds with a
   DHCP lease-acknowledgment message known as a DHCPACK. The
   DHCP server then updates its DHCP database to show that the
   lease can no longer be offered to other DHCP clients. The DHCP
   servers offering leases that were not selected can offer those IP
   addresses in future lease offers.

DHCPACK Phase

After the server that offered the lease receives the DHCPREQUEST message, it checks its DHCP database to ensure that the IP address is still available. If the requested lease remains available, the DHCP server marks that IP address as being leased in its DHCP database and broadcasts a DHCPACK to acknowledge that the IP address has been leased to the DHCP client. The DHCPACK contains the same information as the DHCPOFFER sent, and any optional DHCP information that has been configured for that scope as a scope option. If the requested lease is no longer available, the DHCP server broadcasts a DHCP negative acknowledgment (DHCPNACK) containing the DHCP client's hardware address. When the DHCP client receives a DHCPNACK, it must start the lease request process over with a DHCPDISCOVER message. After receiving a DHCPACK, the DHCP client can continue to initialize TCP/IP, and it updates its Registry with the IP addressing information included with the lease. The client continues to use the leased IP address information until the command ipconfig/ release is typed from a command prompt, or until it receives a DHCPNACK from the DHCP server after unsuccessfully renewing its lease.

DHCP Lease Renewal

The DHCP client attempts to renew its IP address lease after 50% of its lease time has expired (or when manually requested to renew the lease by the ipconfig/renew command from a command prompt). To renew the lease, a DHCP client sends a DHCPREQUEST directly to the DHCP server that gave it the original lease. Again, the DHCPREQUEST contains the hardware address of the client and the requested IP address, but this time uses the DHCP server IP address for the destination and the DHCP client IP address for the source IP address in the datagram. If the DHCP server is available and the requested IP address is still available (has not been removed from the scope), the DHCP server responds by sending a DHCPACK directly to the DHCP client. If the server is available but the requested IP address is no longer in the configured scopes, a DHCPNACK is sent to the DHCP client, which then must start the lease process over with a DHCPDISCOVER. A DHCPNACK can be sent because of the following reasons:

- The IP address requested is no longer available because the lease has been manually expired on the server and has been given to another client.

- The IP address requested has been removed from the available scopes on the DHCP server.

- The DHCP client has been physically moved to another subnet that will use a different scope on the DHCP server for that subnet. Hence, the IP address changes to a valid IP address for the new subnet. If the server does not respond to the DHCPREQUEST sent after the lease is 50% expired, the DHCP client continues to use the original lease until it is seven-eighths expired (87.5% of the lease time has expired). Because this DHCPREQUEST is broadcast rather than directed to a particular DHCP server, any DHCP server can respond with a DHCPACK or DHCPNACK to renew or deny the lease.

Installing the DHCP Server Service

The DHCP Server service can be installed on a computer running Microsoft TCP/IP and Windows NT Server version 3.5 or later. To install the DHCP Server service, follow these steps:

1. Open the Control Panel and double-click the Network icon.

2. From the Network Settings dialog box, choose the Services tab, and then click Add.

3. Choose the Microsoft DHCP Service from the list that appears and click OK. When prompted, enter the directory for the NT source files.

4. Click Close on the Network Settings dialog box, and when prompted restart your computer.

The DHCP server must have a manually configured IP address, subnet mask, and default gateway. It cannot be assigned an address from another DHCP server, even if an address is reserved for the DHCP server.

NOTE

This is an important thing to remember for the exam: A DHCP server *cannot* be a DHCP client.

Configuring the DHCP Server

After a DHCP server has been installed on an internetwork, you need to configure the following items:

◆ One or more IP address scopes (ranges of IP addresses to be leased) must be defined on the DHCP server.

◆ Non-DHCP client IP addresses must be excluded from the defined scopes.

◆ The options for the scope must be configured—for example, the default gateway for a subnet.

◆ IP address reservations for DHCP clients requiring a specific IP address to be assigned must be created.

◆ The DHCP clients must have automatic DHCP configuration enabled and should have unwanted manually configured TCP/IP parameters deleted.

Understanding WINS

WINS is used to map NetBIOS (computer) names to IP addresses dynamically. The same function can be performed in the absence of a WINS server with LMHOSTS files, but the files are static and do not incorporate changes. The only time a WINS server automatically collects entries is when a WINS client is configured with that WINS server's address. When the client starts up, it sends a registration request to the WINS server.

After a client registers its NetBIOS name with a WINS server, it is the client's responsibility to renew that registration. The WINS server does not initiate any registration renewals with clients. The registration is released if not renewed by the time the TTL expires. The entry is not scavenged, however, until the Extinction Interval and the Extinction Timeout have expired.

WINS writes its error messages to the Windows NT Event log. Because WINS uses a JET database to store its entries, however, messages are written in the Application log rather than the System log.

You can also enable non-WINS clients to use a WINS server to resolve NetBIOS names by installing a *WINS proxy agent*. By definition, a non-

WINS client cannot directly communicate with a WINS server to resolve a name. The non-WINS client resolves names by resorting to a b-node broadcast. If you install a WINS proxy agent, the proxy agent forwards any broadcasts for name resolution to the WINS server. The proxy agent must be located on the same subnet as non-WINS clients so that the proxy agent receives the broadcast for name resolution.

When a non-WINS client broadcasts a name resolution request, a proxy agent that hears the broadcast checks its own NetBIOS name cache to see whether an entry exists for the requested name. If the entry does not exist, the proxy agent adds to the cache an entry for that name with the status of pending. The proxy agent then sends a name resolution request for the same name to the WINS server. After the WINS server responds with the name resolution, the proxy agent adds the entry to its cache and then removes the pending status from the entry. The proxy agent does not forward the response to the non-WINS client making the request. When the non-WINS client broadcasts another request for the name resolution, the proxy agent now finds an entry for the name in its cache and the proxy agent can respond to the non-WINS client with a successful name resolution response.

The WINS proxy agent also forwards registration requests to the WINS server. However, registration requests for non-WINS clients are not added to the WINS server's database. The WINS server uses these forwarded registration requests to see whether there are any potential conflicts in its database with the requested name registration. You must still add static entries to the WINS database so that names of non-WINS clients can be resolved.

You must place a WINS proxy agent on each subnet where non-WINS clients are located so that those clients have access to the WINS server. Because those clients resolve names only by using broadcasts, which are not typically routed, those broadcasts never go beyond the subnet. With a proxy agent on each subnet, broadcasts on each subnet can then be forwarded to the WINS server. You can have two proxy agents on a subnet, but you shouldn't exceed this limit. Even having more than one proxy agent on a subnet can generate excessive work for the WINS server because each proxy agent forwards name resolution and name registration requests to the WINS server. The WINS server has to respond to duplicate messages from proxy agents if more than one proxy agent is on a subnet.

Any Windows-based WINS client can be a WINS proxy agent. To config-ure a Windows NT server or workstation to be a proxy agent, you must turn on a parameter in the Registry. This proxy agent cannot be a WINS server. Windows 95 and Windows for Workgroups computers are more easily configured by turning on a switch in the TCP/IP configuration.

After you configure a WINS client to be a proxy agent, you must reboot the machine for this change to take effect. No other configuration is needed for this proxy agent. This WINS client remains a proxy agent until you turn off the proxy agent parameter and reboot the computer.

Configuring a Client for WINS

To manually configure a WINS client, you specify the WINS server address as part of the TCP/IP configuration. Open the TCP/IP prop-erties in the Protocol tab of the Network Properties dialog box (opened with Control Panel, Network). Select the WINS tab in the TCP/IP Properties dialog box and then just specify the address of a primary WINS server. If you are using a secondary WINS server (recommended for every 10,000 clients), you should also type in the IP address of the secondary WINS server.

To configure a DHCP client to be a WINS client, you must add two properties to the DHCP scope created on the DHCP server. Under the DHCP scope options, add the following parameters:

- **044 WINS/NBNS Servers.**   Configure this with the address of the primary WINS server and a secondary WINS server, if desired.

- **046 WINS/NBT Node.**   By default, this is set to 2, a b-node broadcast. WINS clients use h-node broadcasts, so you must change the value of this parameter to 8.

Files Used for WINS

The WINS database is stored in the path \WINNT\SYSTEM32\WINS, and sev-eral files make up the WINS database:

- WINS.MDB   This is the WINS database itself.

- WINSTMP.MDB   This is a temporary working file used by WINS. This file is deleted when the WINS server is shut down normally, but a copy could remain in the directory after a crash.

- ◆ `J50.LOG`   This is the Transaction log of the WINS database.

- ◆ `J50.CHK`   This is a checkpoint file used by the WINS database. This is equivalent to a cache for a disk drive.

Backing Up the WINS Database

The database can be backed up automatically when WINS shuts down. You can also schedule backups or manually start a backup. All these backups are copied to the backup directory specified in the Advanced Configuration options. You can manually start a WINS backup from the Mappings menu in the WINS Manager. To automatically schedule backups, configure the path for a backup directory. After you set this path, the WINS server automatically backs itself up every 24 hours.

You should also back up the WINS subkey in the Registry. This subkey has the configuration settings for WINS, but does not contain any entries from the WINS database. The regular backup for WINS makes a copy of the database itself.

Restoring the WINS Database

You can restore the WINS database from the backups you made previously. To restore the database, from the Mappings menu in WINS Manager, choose Restore Database.

WINS can also automatically restore the database. If the WINS service starts and detects a corrupted database, it automatically restores a backup from the specified backup directory. If you suspect the database is corrupt, you can stop and start the WINS service from Control Panel, Services to force this automatic restoration.

Compacting the WINS Database

You can compact the WINS database to reduce its size. WINS under Windows NT 4.0 is designed to automatically compact the database, however, so you shouldn't have to compact it. To force a manual compaction of the database, use the JETPACK utility in the `\WINNT\SYSTEM32\WINS` directory. (The WINS database is a JET database, so this utility packs that database.) To pack the database, you must first stop the

WINS service. You cannot pack an open database. Then type the following command:

```
jetpack WINS.mdb temp.mdb
```

This command compacts the database into the file temp.mdb, and then copies the compacted database to WINS.mdb. Then, the temporary file is deleted. After the database is compacted, you can restart the WINS service from Control Panel, Services.

Understanding DNS

The Domain Name System is one way to resolve hostnames in a TCP/IP environment. In non-Microsoft environments, hostnames are typically resolved through HOST files or DNS. In a Microsoft environment, WINS and broadcasts are also used. DNS is the primary system used to resolve hostnames on the Internet. In fact, DNS had its beginning in the early days of the Internet.

In its early days, the Internet was a small network established by the Department of Defense for research purposes. This network linked computers at several government agencies with a few universities. The hostnames of the computers in this network were registered in a single HOSTS file located on a centrally administered server. Each site that needed to resolve hostnames downloaded this file. Few computers were being added to this network, so the HOSTS file was not updated too often and the different sites only had to download this file periodically to update their own copies. As the number of hosts on the Internet grew, it became more and more difficult to manage all the names through a central HOSTS file. The number of entries was increasing rapidly, changes were being made frequently, and the server with the central HOSTS file was being accessed more and more often by the different Internet sites trying to download a new copy.

DNS was introduced in 1984 as a way to resolve hostnames without relying on one central HOSTS file. With DNS, the hostnames reside in a database that can be distributed among multiple servers, decreasing the load on any one server and also allowing more than one point of administration for this naming system. The name system is based on hierarchical names in a tree-type directory structure. DNS allows more types of registration than the simple hostname-to-TCP/IP address mapping used in HOSTS files and allows room for future-defined types. Because the database is distributed, it can support a much larger database than can be stored in a single HOSTS file. In fact, the database size is virtually unlimited because more servers can be added to handle additional parts of the database. The Domain Name System was first introduced in 1984.

History of Microsoft DNS

DNS was first introduced in the Microsoft environment as part of the Resource Kit for NT Server 3.51. It was not available as part of the Windows NT source files. With version 4.0, DNS is now integrated with the Windows NT source files. Although DNS is not installed by default as part of a Windows NT 4.0 Server installation, you can specify that DNS be included as part of a Windows NT installation or you can add DNS later, just as you would any other networking service that is part of Windows NT.

Microsoft DNS is based on RFCs 974, 1034, and 1035. A popular implementation of DNS is called BIND (Berkeley Internet Name Domain), developed at UC Berkeley for their version of UNIX. However, BIND is not totally compliant with the DNS RFCs. Microsoft's DNS does support some features of BIND, but Microsoft DNS is based on the RFCs, not on BIND.

> **NOTE**
> You can read these RFCs, or any other RFC, by going to the InterNIC Web
> site at `http://ds.internic.net/ds/rfc-index.html`.

Structure of DNS

Some hostname systems, like NetBIOS names, use a flat database. With a flat database, all names exist at the same level, so there can't be any duplicate names. These names are like Social Security numbers: Every participant in the Social Security program must have a unique number. Social Security is a national system that encompasses all workers in the United States, so it must use an identification system to distinguish all the individuals in the United States.

DNS names are located in hierarchical paths, like a directory structure. You can have a file called TEST.TXT in c:\ and another file called TEST.TXT in c:\ASCII. In a network using DNS, you can have more than one server with the same name, as long as each is located in a different path.

DNS Domains

The Internet Network Information Center (InterNIC) controls the top-level domains. These have names such as "com" (for businesses), "edu" (for educational institutions such as universities), "gov" (for government organizations), and "org" (for nonprofit organizations). There are also domains for countries. You can visit the InterNIC Web site at http://www.internic.net/. Table 2.1 summarizes common Internet domains.

TABLE 2.1

COMMON INTERNET DOMAINS.

Name	Type of Organization
com	Commercial organizations
edu	Educational institutions
org	Nonprofit organizations
net	Networks (the backbone of the Internet)
gov	Non-military government organizations
mil	Military government organizations
num	Phone numbers
arpa	Reverse DNS
xx	Two-letter country code

DNS Hostnames

To refer to a host in a domain, use a fully qualified domain name (FQDN), which completely specifies the location of the host. An FQDN specifies the hostname, the domain or subdomain the host belongs to, and any domains above that in the hierarchy until the root domain in the organization is specified. On the Internet, the root domain in the path is something like "com," but on a private network the top-level domains may be named according to some internal naming convention. The FQDN is read from left to right, with each hostname or domain name specified by a period. The syntax of an FQDN follows:

```
hostname.subdomain. ... .domain
```

An example of an FQDN is www.microsoft.com, which refers to a server called "www" located in the subdomain called "microsoft" in the domain called "com." Referring to a host by its FQDN is similar to referring to a file by its complete directory path. However, a complete filename goes from general to specific, with the filename at the rightmost part of the path. An FQDN goes from specific to general, with the hostname at the leftmost part of the name. Fully qualified domain names are more like addresses. An address starts with the most specific information: who is to receive the letter. Then the address specifies the house number in which the recipient lives, the street on which the house is located, the city where the street is located, and finally the most general location, the state where that city is located.

Zone Files

The DNS database is stored in files called *zones*. It is possible, even desirable, to break the DNS database into a number of zones. Breaking the DNS database into zones was part of the original design goals of DNS. With multiple zones, the load of providing access to the database is spread among a number of servers. Also, the administrative burden of managing the database is spread out, because different administrators manage only the parts of the DNS database stored in their own zones. A zone can be any portion of the domain name space; it does not have to contain all the subdomains for that part of the DNS tree. Zones can be copied to other name servers through replication. With multiple zones, smaller amounts of information are copied when zone files are replicated than would be if the entire domain were located in one zone file.

Reverse Lookup

Looking up an IP address to find the hostname is exactly the same as the process of looking up an FQDN using a DNS server (only backward). An FQDN starts with the specific host and then the domain; an IP address starts with the network ID and then the host ID. Because you want to use DNS to handle the mapping, both must go the same way, so the octets of the IP address are reversed. That is, 148.53.66.7 in the inverse address resolution is 7.66.53.148.

Now that the IP address is reversed, it is going the same way as an FQDN. Now you can resolve the address using DNS. Just like resolving www.synergy.com, you need to create a zone. This zone must have a particular name. To find the name, take the assigned portion of the address—for example, in 148.53.66.7 the portion that was assigned is 148.53, and for 204.12.25.3 it is 204.12.25. Now, create a zone in which these numbers are reversed and to which you add in-addr.arpa— that is, 53.148.in-addr.arpa or 25.12.204.in-addr.arpa, respectively.

Installing TCP/IP

Installation of the TCP/IP protocol and support on a Windows NT Server computer is a very straightforward operation. To do so, follow these steps:

1. Open the Network Settings dialog box (double-click the Network icon in the Control Panel).

2. Click Add in the Protocols tab to open the Select Network Protocol dialog box.

3. Select TCP/IP Protocol in the Network Protocol list and click OK.

4. The next prompt asks, Do you wish to use DHCP? If this computer will obtain its IP address from DHCP, choose Yes. If this computer will be configured with a static IP address, choose No.

5. When prompted, supply the path where Setup can locate the driver files.

6. Choose Close to exit the Network Settings dialog box. After recalculating the bindings, Setup will show you a Microsoft TCP/IP Properties dialog box which will, at first, be blank.

7. If more than one adapter has been installed, select the adapter to be configured in the Adapter list. (Note: You should configure each adapter with a valid IP address for the subnet it is on.)

8. If this computer will obtain its address configuration from DHCP for any of the network adapters, click the Obtain an IP Address from a DHCP Server radio button.

9. If this computer will be configured with static addresses, click the Specify an IP Address radio button and complete the following fields:

IP Address (Required)

Subnet Mask (Required. Setup will suggest the default subnet mask appropriate for the IP address you enter.)

Default Gateway

10. Click OK and restart the computer to activate the settings.

CONFIGURING SCOPES

For a DHCP server to lease IP addresses to the DHCP clients, a range of valid IP addresses for those clients must be configured on the DHCP server. Each range of IP addresses is called a *scope*. One scope must be configured on the server for each subnet the DHCP server provides IP address leases to. The DHCP server is normally configured with a scope for the local subnet (the subnet the DHCP server is on) and, optionally, with a scope for each remote subnet that it will provide addresses for. The benefits of configuring scopes for remote subnets on a DHCP server are as follows:

♦ The DHCP server can provide IP address leases to clients on remote subnets. This feature is especially useful as a backup in case another DHCP server is not available. If no DHCP server is available with an IP address lease for a DHCP client, the client cannot initialize TCP/IP. To prevent this, you may want to have more than one DHCP server that can provide a DHCP client with a lease. You must ensure, however, that the scopes on each DHCP server have unique IP address ranges so that no duplicate IP addresses are on the internetwork.

♦ You can create separate scope options for each subnet. Each subnet would have a different default gateway that can be configured individually for each scope, for example. After installing the DHCP server and restarting the computer, you must create an IP address scope. The following list demonstrates the creation of a scope. To perform this exercise, you must have the DHCP Server service installed and running as previously shown. You should also know a range of IP addresses that you can use to create a DHCP scope, as well as the IP addresses that should be excluded out of that range.

The following list provides the steps that are required to configure a scope on the DHCP server:

1. Start the DHCP Manager (Start, Programs, Administrative Tools, DHCP Manager).

2. Select the local DHCP server "Local Machine" by clicking the entry, and then choose Create from the Scope menu item. The Create Scope dialog box appears. (Note: The first time you run the DHCP Manager, this will happen automatically.)

3. Type the starting and ending IP addresses for the first subnet in the Start Address and the End Address fields of the IP Address Pool.

4. Type the subnet mask for this scope in the Subnet Mask field.

5. If required, type a single IP address or a range of IP addresses to be excluded from the IP. The IP address that is not used in the Address Pool in the Exclusion Range Start Address scope is added to the Excluded Addresses list. Choose Add. Repeat if required.

NOTE

If any hosts are not using DHCP but have an IP address that falls within the IP address pool, the IP addresses of these hosts must be excluded from the scope. If the IP address is not excluded, DHCP does not know that the IP address is already in use and might assign the IP address to a DHCP client, causing a duplicate IP address on the network. If you want certain DHCP clients to use a specific IP address out of the scope, you can assign this address from the Add Reservations dialog box as described later in this section.

6. If you do not want the IP address leases to expire, select the Unlimited option under Lease Duration. (If you do this, the configuration of the client will never be updated.) If you want to force the DHCP clients to renew their leases periodically (to ensure that the client is still using the IP address), choose the Limited To

option and type the lease duration in days, hours, and minutes. By default, the lease duration is three days. If you have a large ratio of available IP addresses to hosts on the network, you may want to use a longer lease duration to reduce broadcast traffic. If hosts are regularly coming and going and changing subnets on the network, such as with laptops and docking stations, you want relatively short lease duration so that the DHCP server recovers previously used IP addresses fairly quickly.

7. In the Name field, type the name to be used for referring to the scope in the DHCP Manager (for example, **subnet 200.20.1.0**).

8. In the Comment field, type an optional descriptive comment for the scope (for example, **Third floor – west side**).

Scope Options

Each DHCP scope can have several options set that are configured on the client along with the IP address, such as default gateway and WINS server addresses. DHCP Manager includes many scope options that can be configured and sent to the DHCP clients; it should be noted that if TCP/IP configuration has been manually entered, the options (other than IP address and subnet mask) will be ignored by the client.

The following two types of DHCP scope options are available:

- *Global options*, which are set for all scopes in the DHCP Manager

- *Scope options*, which are set for a selected scope in the DHCP Manager

The value set in a Scope option overrides a value set for the same DHCP option in a Global option. Any values manually configured on the DHCP client—through the Network Control Panel applet, Microsoft TCP/IP Configuration dialog box, for example—override any DHCP-configured options.

The following list outlines how to view and define global options for a DHCP server:

1. Start the DHCP Manager tool.

2. Choose either Scope or Global from the DHCP Options menu.

3. Configure the DHCP options required by following these steps:

   1. From the unused Options list, select an option and click Add. The option is added to the Active Options list.

   2. Choose Value, the value for the option will now be displayed.

   3. You can now edit the value. Three types of values can be edited: strings (such as domain name), which you can just enter; hexadecimal values (such as NetBIOS node type), which you can enter; and finally IP address ranges, for which you click Edit Array and another dialog box appears, enabling you to enter one or more IP addresses.

4. When all the required options are entered, click OK and exit the DHCP manager.

Address Reservations

If a DHCP client requires a specific IP address to be assigned to it each time it renews its IP address lease, that IP address can be reserved for the DHCP client through the DHCP Manager tool. Following are examples of clients that should have an IP address reservation:

- Servers on a network with non-WINS–enabled clients. If a server on such a network does not always lease the same IP address, the non-WINS clients might not be able to connect to the servers using NetBIOS over TCP/IP (NetBT).

- Any other host that is expected to have a specific IP address that hosts use to connect to.

The following list outlines how to reserve an IP address from a scope for a specific DHCP client:

1. Determine the hardware address for the DHCP client with the IP address to be reserved from the scope. This can be done by typing **ipconfig/all** at a client's command prompt. A sample `ipconfig/all` output is shown here:

```
Ethernet adapter NDISLoop1:
        Description . . . . . . . . : MS LoopBack Driver
        Physical Address. . . . . : 20-4C-4F-4F-50-20
        DHCP Enabled. . . . . . . : No
```

```
IP Address. . . . . . . . . : 200.20.1.30
Subnet Mask . . . . . . . . : 255.255.255.0
Default Gateway . . . . . . : 200.20.1.1
```

2. Start the DHCP Manager, and select the DHCP server to be configured.

3. Select the scope containing the IP address to be reserved.

4. Choose Add Reservations from the Scope menu. The Add Reserved Clients dialog box appears.

5. In the IP Address field, type the IP address to be reserved for the DHCP client.

6. In the Unique Identifier field, type the hardware address of the network card for the IP address used. The hardware address should be typed without hyphens (-).

7. In the Client Name field, type a name for the client to be used only in DHCP Manager. This value is purely descriptive and does not affect the client in any way.

8. In the Client Comments field, optionally type any comments for the client reservation.

9. Choose Add. The reservation is enabled.

10. Choose Active Leases from the Scope menu of DHCP Manager. The Active Leases dialog box appears and the reservations are shown.

DHCP Clients

For a client to use DHCP to obtain IP address information, automatic DHCP configuration must be enabled at the client. The procedure is slightly different for Windows NT and Windows for Workgroups clients.

Windows NT and Windows 95 as DHCP Clients

You can enable automatic DHCP configuration either before or after Microsoft TCP/IP is installed. To ensure that the DHCP TCP/IP parameters are used rather than configured manually on the host, you should preferably enable automatic DHCP configuration before Microsoft TCP/IP is installed.

To enable automatic DHCP configuration after TCP/IP is installed, follow these steps:

1. Double-click the Network icon in Control Panel. The Network Settings dialog appears.

2. Select the Protocols tab. From the list of installed protocols, select TCP/IP and choose the Properties button. The TCP/IP Configuration dialog box appears.

3. Select the Enable Automatic DHCP Configuration check box. The previous IP address and subnet mask values disappear. Ensure that all other configuration parameters you want DHCP to supply are cleared.

4. Close the TCP/IP Configuration dialog box and the Network Settings dialog box. Restart the system if prompted. (If this is your only change, Windows NT won't require you to reboot when just switching from a static to a dynamic IP address.)

Windows for Workgroups as a DHCP Client

Configuring Windows for Workgroups as a DHCP client is simple, just complete the following steps:

1. Double-click the Network Setup icon in the Network program group of the Windows for Workgroups client.

2. Choose the Drivers button, select Microsoft TCP/IP, and choose the Setup button. The TCP/IP Configuration dialog box appears.

3. Select the Enable Automatic DHCP Configuration check box, and choose Continue. The dialog box closes and you are prompted to restart the computer.

4. Do not configure any other parameters unless you want to override the options set in the DHCP scope—which is not recommended.

Using Scope Options

Each time a DHCP client initializes, it requests an IP address and subnet mask from the DHCP server. The server is configured with one or more scopes, each containing a range of valid IP addresses, the subnet mask for the internetwork, and additional optional DHCP client configuration information, known as Scope options. The default gateway for a subnet is often configured as a Scope option for a given subnet, for example. If any Scope options are configured on the DHCP server, these are given to the DHCP client along with the IP address and subnet mask to be used by the client. Table 2.2 shows the common Scope options supported by Microsoft DHCP clients.

TABLE 2.2

SCOPE OPTIONS SUPPORTED BY MICROSOFT DHCP CLIENTS.

Scope Option	Option Number
Router	3
DNS server	6
DNS domain name	15
NetBIOS name server (for example, WINS)	44
NetBIOS node type	46
NetBIOS scope ID	47

The Scope Options Configuration dialog box in the DHCP Manager application contains many other Scope options (such as Time Server) that can be sent to the clients along with the other TCP/IP configuration information. The Microsoft DHCP clients, however, ignore and discard all the Scope option information except for the options listed in Table 2.2.

Compacting the DHCP Database

Entries in the DHCP database are continually being added, modified, and deleted throughout the IP address leasing process. When entries are deleted, the space is not always completely filled with a new entry because of the different sizes of each entry. After some time, the database contains unused space that can be recovered by compacting the database. This process is analogous to defragmenting a disk drive.

Microsoft recommends compacting the DHCP database from once every month to once every week, depending on the size of the internetwork. This compaction increases transaction speed and reduces the disk space used by the database.

The jetpack utility compacts the DHCP database (DHCP.mdb) into a temporary database, which is then automatically copied to DHCP.mdb and deleted. The command used is jetpack DHCP.mdb temp_name.mdb, where temp_name.mdb is any filename specified by the user, with extension .mdb.

The following list shows how to compact the DHCP database:

1. Stop the DHCP Server service by using the Control Panel, Server Manager, or a command prompt.

2. To stop the service from a command prompt, type **net stop dhcpserver** service. This stops the DHCP server.

3. Type **cd *systemroot*\\system32\\dhcp**, where systemroot is WINNT35. This changes to the DHCP directory.

4. Type **jetpack dhcp.mdb temp.mdb**. This compacts DHCP.mdb into temp.mdb, and then copies it back to DHCP.mdb, and automatically deletes temp.mdb.

5. Type **net start dhcpserver**. This restarts the DHCP Server service.

Backing Up the DHCP Database

By default, the DHCP database is automatically backed up at a specific interval. You can change the default interval by editing the DHCP server BackupInterval parameter value contained in the Registry:

```
HKEY_LOCAL_MACHINE\SYSTEM\current\currentcontrolset\services\
DHCPServer\Parameters
```

Backing up the DHCP database enables recovery from a system crash or DHCP database corruption.

You can change the default backup interval of 15 minutes by performing the following steps:

1. Stop the DHCP Server service from a command prompt by typing **net stop dhcpserver**.

2. Start the Registry Editor (REGEDT32.EXE or Regedit.exe).

3. Open the `HKEY_LOCAL_MACHINE\SYSTEM\CurrentControlSet\Services\` `DHCPserver\Parameters` key, and select `BackupInterval`.

4. In the right pane, make a selection, and configure the entry to the desired value. Close the Registry Editor.

5. Restart the DHCP Server service from a command prompt by typing **net start dhcpserver**.

Restoring a Corrupt DHCP Database

If the DHCP database becomes corrupt, it can be restored from a backup in one of the following ways:

- It can be restored automatically.

- You can use the `RestoreFlag` key in the Registry.

- You can manually replace the corrupt database file by copying from a backup.

Automatic Restoration

The DHCP Server service automatically restores the backed-up copy of the database if it detects a corrupt database. If the database has become corrupt, stop and restart the DHCP Server service. You can do this by typing **net stop dhcpserver** and then **net start dhcpserver** at a command prompt.

Registry RESTOREFLAG

If a corrupt DHCP database is not automatically restored from a backup when the DHCP Server service is started, you can force the database to be restored by setting the `RestoreFlag` key in the Registry. To do this, follow these steps:

1. Stop the DHCP Server service from a command prompt by typing **net stop dhcpserver**.

2. Start the Registry Editor (`REGEDT32.EXE`).

3. Open the `HKEY_LOCAL_MACHINE\SYSTEM\CurrentControlSet\Services\` `DHCPserver\Parameters` key, and select `RestoreFlag`.

4. Change the value to 1 in the data field, and choose OK. Close the Registry Editor.

5. Restart the DHCP Server service from a command prompt by typing **net start dhcpserver**. The database is restored from the backup, and the `RestoreFlag` entry in the Registry automatically resets to 0.

Copying from the Backup Directory

To manually replace the corrupt database file with a backed-up version, follow these steps:

1. Stop the DHCP Server service from a command by typing **net stop dhcpserver**.

2. Change to the DHCP directory by typing `cd \systemroot\system32\ dhcp\backup\jet`, where `systemroot` is `WINNT`, for example.

3. Copy the contents of the directory to the `\systemroot\system32\DHCP` directory.

4. Type **net start dhcpserver** from a command prompt to restart the DHCP Server service.

INSTALLING AND CONFIGURING A WINS SERVER

WINS must be installed on a Windows NT Server version 3.5x or 4.0. WINS servers on any version are compatible with the others—that is, you can mix a Windows NT 3.51 WINS server with an NT 4.0 WINS server, including using them as replication partners. You can install WINS on any configuration of Windows NT Server—a member server, a backup domain controller, or a primary domain controller. The WINS server should have a static TCP/IP address with a subnet mask and default gateway along with any other TCP/IP parameters required for your network (such as a DNS server address). You can assign a DHCP address to the WINS server (the address should be reserved so that the WINS server always receives the same address), but using a static address is the recommended option. Also, you should specify a WINS server address; in this case, the address would be the same machine.

The WINS service is installed as a network service. After it is installed, it is immediately available for use. Until WINS clients are configured with the TCP/IP address of the WINS server, however, they can neither register their names nor use the WINS server for name resolution. In fact, if there weren't any clients configured with this WINS server's address, the WINS database would remain empty unless you add static entries or set up replication with another WINS server.

WINS Clients

Any Microsoft client capable of networking can be a WINS client:

- Windows NT Server 3.5x, 4.0
- Windows NT Workstation 3.5x, 4.0
- Windows 95
- Windows for Workgroups with TCP/IP-32
- Microsoft Network Client 3.0 for MS-DOS
- LAN Manager 2.2c for MS-DOS

Only the Windows-based clients can register their names with the WINS server, however. The DOS-based clients can use the WINS server for name resolution, but you must add static entries for DOS clients to the WINS server so that their names can be resolved.

To enable these clients for WINS, the address of the primary WINS server must be specified on the client. The client can also have the address of a secondary WINS server configured. The client can either have this configuration information manually entered at the client or it can receive the configuration information with its TCP/IP address from a DHCP server.

Configuring WINS to be Used by Non-WINS Clients

A WINS server interacts in two ways with WINS clients. First, it registers the names of those clients. Second, it answers requests for name resolutions (name queries). You can enable both functions for non-WINS clients through additional configuration.

IMPORTING LMHOSTS FILES TO WINS

The LMHOSTS file is a static file that can be used in place of WINS for NetBIOS name resolution. It is discussed in greater detail later in this chapter. If you have been using LMHOSTS files and decide to implement WINS, you can copy entries from an LMHOSTS file to a WINS server. Any entries copied this way are considered static entries. To do so, follow these steps:

1. Choose Start, Programs, Administrative Tools.

2. From the Administrative Tools menu, choose WINS Manager.

3. From the Mappings menu in WINS Manager, choose Static Mappings.

4. Choose the Import Mappings button.

5. Browse to find the LMHOSTS file you modified, and then choose that file.

6. Choose Open.

7. Note the names from the LMHOSTS file have been added to the static mappings.

8. Close the Static Mappings dialog box.

9. From the Mappings menu, choose Show Database.

10. Note the mappings you added from the LMHOSTS file are now in the WINS database.

RUNNING WINS ON A MULTIHOMED COMPUTER

A *multihomed* computer is one containing more than one network card (NIC) that participates on more than one network. A Windows NT Server can have two NIC cards installed in it, for example. One NIC card can have the address of 192.2.2.1 and communicate with the network of hosts from 192.2.2.2 to 192.2.2.254. The other NIC card can have the address 160.2.2.1 and communicate with the network of hosts from 160.2.2.2 to 160.2.2.254.

The common object between these two networks is the multihomed host, and as such, it can act as a quasi-router between the two networks. This proves most useful when you have two different physical types of networks, such as Ethernet and token ring.

Normally, the WINS service should not be run on a computer that is multihomed (has two or more network cards). This is because the WINS server always registers its names in the local database. This is a problem if you will run DOS clients because they will always try the first address that they receive from the WINS server. Because the WINS server registers all of its cards in order, the DOS client might not be able to reach resources on the WINS server from networks other than the one on which the first card is located.

Configuring WINS Replication

Because WINS clients are configured to communicate only with specified WINS servers, the database on each WINS server may not have entries for all the WINS clients in the network. In fact, many TCP/IP implementations divide WINS clients among different WINS servers to balance the load. Unfortunately, WINS clients cannot resolve addresses registered with another WINS server unless the registrations from that server are somehow copied to the client's WINS server. *WINS replication* is the process used to copy one WINS server's database to another WINS server.

You can configure a WINS server so that it replicates its database with another WINS server. This way, clients registered with one WINS server can be added to the database of another server. Static mappings entered on one server are also replicated to replication partners. In fact, you can enter static entries on only one WINS server and yet these entries can be propagated to any number of WINS servers through replication.

After you enable replication, clients seeking name resolution can see not only entries from their server but entries of the replication partners. Remember that clients register their names with the WINS server for which the clients are configured. WINS registrations are not done through broadcasts. (In fact, one of main benefits of WINS is the reduction of broadcast traffic.) Because one WINS server is collecting registrations just for its clients, the only way for its clients to resolve names registered with another WINS server is for replication to be configured between the servers.

To set up replication, you must configure a WINS server as a push partner or a pull partner. A *push partner* sends its entries to another server, such as if you want to send a copy of the database from this WINS server to the other WINS server. A *pull partner* receives entries from another server, such as if you want this server to receive a copy of the database from another WINS server. You must always configure WINS servers in pairs; otherwise, replication won't work.

At the very least, one WINS server must be a push partner to send its entries out; the other WINS server must be a pull partner to receive the entries. Replication does not occur unless both WINS servers are properly configured. If both WINS servers are configured as push and pull partners, each server ends up with entries from the other server. In theory, the combined database on each WINS server should be the same. Because of the lag time in replication, however, this doesn't always happen.

Deciding which WINS server will be a push partner and which will be a pull partner is often driven by performance considerations. You often use a pull partner across slow WAN links because you can configure a pull partner to replicate only at certain times, such as at night when the WAN link is not as heavily used. In this case, you could make the WINS server on each side of the WAN link a pull partner with the other WINS server. This is known as pull-pull replication.

On faster links, you can use push partners. Push partners replicate when a specified number of changes are made to the database. These updates can happen fairly frequently, but are not too large because you are not waiting to replicate a whole day's worth of changes. If you want two WINS servers to have identical databases, you must configure each WINS server to be a push and a pull partner for the other server.

You can configure a replication partner to start replication in several ways:

- ◆ **When the WINS server starts up.** You can configure this startup replication for either a push or a pull partner.

- ◆ **At a specified interval, such as every 24 hours.** This applies to pull replication.

♦ **When a push partner reaches a specified number of changes to the database.** These changes include name registrations and name releases. When this threshold is reached, the push partner notifies all its pull partners that it has changes for replications.

♦ **Manually.** You can force replication from the WINS Manager.

WINS can automatically replicate with other WINS servers if your network supports multicasting. By default, every 40 minutes, each WINS server sends a multicast to the address 224.0.1.24. Any servers found through this multicast are automatically configured as push and pull partners, with replication set to occur every two hours. If the routers on your network do not support multicasting, the WINS servers see only other servers on the same subnet.

You can turn off this multicasting feature by editing the Registry in the following location:

```
HKEY_LOCAL_MACHINE\System\CurrentControlSet\Services\NetBT\
Parameters
```

Change the value of UseSelfFndPnrs to 0.

Change the value of McastIntvl to a large number.

Understanding the Replication Process

A WINS server replicates only its active and extinct entries; released entries are not replicated. A replication partner can have entries that are marked active even though they have been released by its partner. Released entries are not replicated, to reduce the traffic from computers booting and shutting down each day. If a registration changes, it is considered a new entry and it is replicated. The following example shows how records are replicated between replication partners.

Using the WINS Manager

As you install WINS, a WINS Manager tool is added to the Administrative Tools group. You can use this tool to manage the local WINS server and remote WINS servers as well. You can use WINS Manager to view the WINS database, add static entries to the database, configure push and pull partners for replication, and back up and restore the WINS database.

You can use the WINS Manager configuration dialog box to configure how long entries stay in the WINS database. The following four parameters control the life of entries:

- **Renewal Interval.** This is the interval given to a WINS client after it successfully registers its name. The client begins renewing the name registration when half this time has expired. The default is six days.

- **Extinction Interval.** This is the amount of time that must pass before the WINS server marks a released entry as extinct. An extinct entry is not immediately deleted. The default is six days. The time until removal is controlled by the following parameter.

- **Extinction Timeout.** This is the amount of time WINS waits before removing (scavenging) entries that have been marked extinct. The default is six days.

- **Verify Interval.** This parameter applies if WINS servers are set up for replication. This is the interval at which the WINS server verifies that names in its database that came from other servers are still valid. The default is 24 days, and cannot be set below this value.

Initial Replication Configuration

You can configure whether the WINS server replicates with its replication partners when it starts. Check the Initial Replication option under Pull Parameters on the WINS Server Configuration dialog box to have a pull replication partner replicate on start up. You can also specify the number of times the pull partner tries to contact the other WINS server as the pull partner does the startup replication.

For a push partner, you can also configure it to replicate upon startup by checking the Initial Replication option under Push Parameters. You can also specify that the push partner replicates when it has an address change.

Advanced Configuration Options

You can turn on or turn off the logging of entries to the WINS database. This log file records changes made to the WINS database before they are made. By default, logging is on, which gives the WINS server a backup via the log file. If you turn off the logging, the WINS server registers names more quickly, but you lose the backup support of the log file. These settings are configured through the WINS Advanced Configuration dialog box.

The following are the advanced settings you can configure:

*   **Log Detailed Events.** If you turn this on, the logging of WINS events in Event Viewer is more verbose. This means that you get more useful troubleshooting information from the log file. Some performance degradation occurs when verbose logging is turned on.

*   **Replicate Only with Partners.** By default, WINS replicates only with other WINS servers that are specifically configured as push or pull partners. If you want the WINS server to replicate automatically, you must turn off this setting.

*   **Backup on Termination.** If you set this option, the WINS database is automatically backed up when the WINS service is stopped. The database is not backed up, however, when the Windows NT Server is shut down.

*   **Migrate On/Off.** If this switch is on, static entries that have the same address as a WINS client requesting registration are overwritten. This option is helpful if you are converting a computer from a non-Windows NT machine to a Windows NT machine with the same TCP/IP address. To have addresses resolved for this non-Windows NT machine in the past, you may have added a static entry to the WINS database. With the option on, the new dynamic entry can overwrite the old static entry. It is usually best to turn off this switch after you have migrated (upgraded) the new Windows NT machine. This switch is off by default, so static entries are not overwritten.

*   **Starting Version Count.** This specifies the largest version ID number for the database. Each entry in the database is assigned a version ID. Replication is based on the version ID. A replication partner checks its last replicated entries against the version IDs of the records in the WINS database. The replication partner replicates only records with a later version ID than the last records it replicated from this partner. Usually, you don't need to change this parameter. If the database becomes corrupted, however, you may

need to adjust this number so that a replication partner replicates the proper entries.

◆ **Database Backup Path.** When the WINS database is backed up, it is copied to a local hard drive. This specifies the path to a directory on a local drive where the WINS backups are stored. This directory can also be used to automatically restore the WINS database. You must specify a local drive path.

CONFIGURING STATIC MAPPINGS IN THE WINS DATABASE

You can register a non-WINS client with a WINS server by adding a static entry to the WINS database. With entries added for non-WINS clients, a WINS client can resolve more names without resorting to looking up the entries in an LMHOSTS file. In fact, by adding entries for all non-WINS clients, you can eliminate the need for an LMHOSTS file. Static entries are added through the WINS Manager.

There are several types of static mappings. Table 2.3 summarizes the types that you can add.

TABLE 2.3

TYPES OF STATIC MAPPINGS.

Type of Mapping	Explanation
Normal Group	Group names don't have an address; instead, the WINS server returns FFFFFFFF (the broadcast address). This forces the client to broadcast on the local subnet to resolve the name.
Multihomed	A multihomed name is used to register a computer with more than one network card. It can contain up to 25 addresses.
Domain Name	In Windows NT 3.51, the domain name mapping was known as an Internet group. The domain name mapping contains up to a maximum of 25 IP addresses for the primary or backup domain controllers in a domain. This enables client computers and servers to locate a domain controller for logon validation and pass thru authentication.
Internet Group	An Internet group mapping name is a user-defined mapping used to store addresses for members of a group other than a domain (such as a workgroup).

CONFIGURING SUBNET MASKS

Communication in a TCP/IP network is based on sending messages back and forth between computers and network devices. The messages contain a sender and a recipient address, known as IP addresses. The IP addresses are in an octet-based form such as 100.34.192.212. The first octet dictates the "class" of network being referred to, and as such, there are three classes:

- 01–126, Class A
- 128–191, Class B
- 192–223, Class C

Therefore, an address of 100.34.192.212 is clearly a Class A address, and one of 220.34.192.212 is a Class C address. The class is important because it indicates the maximum number of hosts that a network can have. The breakout follows:

- Class A—16,777,214
- Class B—65,534
- Class C—254

Although the existing shortage of addresses has made it impossible to obtain a Class A address for some time, imagine the difficulties inherent in trying to network 16 million hosts at a single site: It is virtually impossible. At the same time, networking 254 hosts, although not impossible, is rarely done at a single site either. Typically, hosts are spread out across several physical locations, often within the same building, campus, or other geographical area.

For that reason, and to make routing practical and possible, subnets are used to divide the network (and network numbers) into smaller portions. This discussion assumes some familiarity with the basics of TCP/IP and addressing, and concentrates on looking at subnetting— one of the most misunderstood components of addressing.

Simply put, subnetting is a mechanism for using some bits in the host ID octets as a subnet ID. Without subnetting, an IP address is interpreted as two fields:

netid + hostid

With subnetting, an IP address is interpreted as three fields:

netid + subnetid + hostid

Subnet Masks, Host IDs, and Network IDs

Subnets are created in a TCP/IP internetwork by choosing the IP addresses and subnet masks used, a process known as subnet addressing or subnetting. The term network is used when it is not necessary to distinguish between individual subnets and internetworks. A *subnet* is simply a subdivision of a network. The term subnetworking or subnetting is used when a single network ID is subdivided into multiple network IDs by applying a custom subnet mask.

The subnet mask, like the IP address, is a 32-bit number often shown in dotted decimal notation. When shown in binary notation, the subnet mask has a 1-bit for each bit corresponding to the position of the network ID in the IP address, and a 0-bit for each bit corresponding to the position of the host ID in the IP address (in binary notation). An example of a subnet mask would be:

11111111111111111100000000000000

or 255.255.0.0 in dotted decimal notation.

A binary number is made up of bits. A bit can be either a 1 or a 0, where 1 represents TRUE and 0 represents FALSE. All computer operations are performed using binary numbers because the bits are easily represented by electrical charges. Huge binary numbers are usually fairly meaningless to the average person, so the computer converts them to more human-friendly states such as decimal numbers and characters.

Any decimal number is represented in binary notation, using 1s and 0s. Each bit with a 1 represents 2 raised to the power of n-1 ($2^{\wedge}(n-1)$), where n is the position of the bit from the right. Each bit with a 0 represents a 0 in decimal notation as well. The decimal number results from adding together all the 1-bits after converting each to $2^{\wedge}(n-1)$.

The binary number 100 is $2^{\wedge}2$, for example, which means the decimal equivalent is 4.

The binary number 101 would be 2^2+0+2^0 , or 5 in decimal notation.

With TCP/IP, 8-bit binary numbers are often used in IP addresses, also called octets or bytes. An example is:

11111111

Each bit in position n from the right gives a value of $2^{(n-1)}$. Therefore the first bit represents a 1, the second bit a 2, the third a 4, the fourth an 8, and so on, so that we have the following:

11111111   (binary)

128+64+32+16+8+4+2+1 = 255   (decimal)

Keep in mind that any 0 bits do not add to the total, so the following are equal:

1 1 0 0 1 0 0 1   (binary)

128+64+0 +0 +8+0+0+1 = 201   (decimal)

Memorize the decimal equivalent number of each character in the 8-bit number.

At A Glance: Decimal to Binary Conversion

Binary	1	1	1	1	1	1	1	1
Decimal	128	64	32	16	8	4	2	1

This makes it extremely easy to convert between binary and decimal quickly. For example, the number:

01111111

should be easily recognized as 127, by taking the maximum value (255) and subtracting the missing digit (128). Likewise:

11011111

is quickly converted to 223 by subtracting the value of the missing digit (32) from the maximum value (255).

The 0-bits of the subnet mask essentially mask out, or cover up the host ID portion of an IP address. Thus, the subnet mask is used to determine on which network or subnet the address being referred to is found. When one host sends a message to another host, the TCP/IP protocol must determine whether they are on the same subnet and can communicate by broadcasts, or whether they are on different subnets and the message should be sent via a router to the other subnet. It is impossible to determine whether two IP addresses are on the same subnet just by looking at the IP addresses without the subnet mask. If the host at 192.20.1.5 sends a message to the host at 192.20.6.8, for example, should it be sent by broadcast or to a router connecting to another subnet?

The answer depends on the subnet mask being used on the network. If the subnet mask was 255.255.255.0, the network ID of the first host would be 192.20.1 and the network ID of the second host would be 192.20.6, which are on different subnets and therefore they must communicate via a router. On the other hand, if the subnet mask was 255.255.0.0, both hosts would be on subnet 192.20 and could communicate by using local broadcasts and local address resolution.

When the subnet mask is one of 255.0.0.0, 255.255.0.0, or 255.255.255.0, it is fairly obvious which part of the IP address is the network ID. (These are the defaults for Class A, B, and C networks, respectively.) Yet, it becomes less apparent which part of the IP address is the network when other subnet masks are used (such as 255.255.248.0). In this case, if both the IP address and subnet mask are converted to binary, it becomes more apparent (the 1-bits of the subnet mask correspond to the network ID in the IP address).

By figuring out what subnet a host is on from the IP address and subnet mask, it becomes easier to route a packet to the proper destination. Fortunately, all you have to do is supply the proper IP addresses with one subnet mask for the entire internetwork and the software determines which subnet the destination is on. If the destination address is on a different subnet than the sender, it is on a remote network and the packet is routed appropriately, usually by being sent to the default gateway.

If a network has a small number of hosts all on the same segment without any routers, they are likely given the same network ID (the network portion of an IP address). If the network is larger, however, with remote segments connected by routers (an internetwork), each individual subnet needs a different network ID. Therefore when assigning IP addresses and subnet masks, the network administrator must know how many subnets are required and the maximum number of hosts on each subnet.

Depending on the subnet mask chosen, the internetwork can either have a lot of different network IDs with a smaller number of hosts on each subnet, or a smaller number of network IDs with a larger number of hosts on each subnet. Although it will become clearer why the results are the way they are as you read further, the following table shows the maximum number of hosts and subnets available per the number of bits used.

Additional Bits Required	Number of Possible Subnets	Maximum C Hosts	Maximum B Hosts	Maximum A Hosts	Subnet Mask
0	0	254	65,534	16,777,214	0
1	Invalid	Invalid	Invalid	Invalid	Invalid
2	2	62	16,382	4,194,302	192
3	6	30	8,190	2,097,150	224
4	14	14	4,094	1,048,574	240
5	30	6	2,044	524,286	248
6	62	2	1,022	262,142	252
7	126	Invalid	510	131,070	254
8	254	Invalid	254	65,534	255

Purpose of Subnet Masks

By specifying the correct subnet mask for addresses, you are letting the TCP/IP software know which part of the address refers to the host and which part refers to the specific subnet the host is located on. As mentioned previously, the IP address and subnet mask are made up of four 8-bit octets that are most often shown in decimal rather than binary format for ease of reading. As an example, an IP address and subnet mask in binary format could be:

IP address: 11001000 00010100 00010000 00000101

Subnet mask: 11111111 11111111 11111111 00000000

Network ID: 11001000 00010100 00010000 00000000

Host ID: 00000000 00000000 00000000 00000101

Notice that the network ID is the portion of the IP address corresponding to a bit-value of 1 in the subnet mask.

In the preceding example, you could have a maximum of 254 different hosts on the network 192.20.16 (192.20.16.1 through 192.20.16.254). If you want to have more hosts on one network, you have to use a different addressing scheme. Using a subnet mask of 255.255.0.0, for example, gives the following results:

IP address   192.20.16.5

Subnet mask   255.255.0.0

Network ID   192.20

Host ID   16.5

> **NOTE**
> It is common in TCP/IP to omit the trailing 0 octets in a network ID and the leading 0 octets in a host ID. Therefore, the network ID 192.20 really represents 192.20.0.0, and the host ID 16.5 really represents 0.0.16.5.

By virtue of the host ID in this example being a 16-bit value, it enables you to have (256*256)-2 hosts on the network 192.20. The two addresses that must be subtracted from the possibilities are 0 (consisting of all 0s) and 255 (consisting of all 1s)—both reserved addresses. 0 is used to define the network, and 255 is a broadcast address for all computers in the network.

A host ID cannot have all bits set to either 1 or 0, because these addresses would be interpreted to mean a broadcast address or "this network only," respectively. Therefore, the number of valid addresses will be $(2^n)-2$, where n is the number of bits used for the host ID.

> **NOTE**
> Common law dictates that address bits cannot be all 1s or 0s. In reality, if—and *only* if—the routers on the network support extended prefixing addressing, it is possible to have addresses of all 1s or 0s. Both the software, and the routers, must support RIP V2, and you must disallow the possibility of traffic over any older (noncompatible) routers.

Cisco routers, NetWare 4.x, and Windows NT all support the extended pre-fixing address (although they often call it a "zero network"). Although against the principles of RFC 950, they permit the use of the all 0s and all 1s subnets. Just one NetWare 3.x system anywhere on your network, or any older router, means that the zero network option cannot be used. For all practical purposes, however, you should consider 0s and 1s off limits.

You may also notice that the second scheme allows for fewer combinations of network IDs than the first scheme. Although the second example scenario might seem preferable for most networks, you may often not have the freedom to use such a scheme. If the hosts are on the Internet, however, you must assign a certain set of IP addresses by the Internet address assignment authority, InterNIC. Because the number of IP addresses available today are limited, you usually do not have the luxury to choose a scheme that gives so many combinations of available host addresses. Suppose you were assigned the network ID 192.20.5 and had a total of 1,000 hosts on three remote networks. A Class#C network using the default subnet mask of 255.255.255.0 only has one network (192.20.5) and 254 hosts (192.20.5.1 through 192.20.5.254).

Now look at how a subnet mask is used to determine which part of the IP address is the network ID and which part is the host ID. TCP/IP does a binary calculation using the IP address and the subnet mask to determine the network ID portion of the IP address.

The computation TCP/IP performs is a logical bitwise AND of the IP address and the subnet mask. The calculation sounds complicated, but all it means is that the octets are converted to binary numbers and a logical AND is performed whose result is the network ID. To make it simpler, recall that in the preceding example, the network ID is the portion of the IP address corresponding to a bit-value of 1 in the subnet mask.

Performing a bitwise AND on two bits results in 1 (or TRUE), if the two values are both 1. If either or both of the values are not 1, the result is 0 (or FALSE).

Any logical AND with a 0 will result in 0.

At A Glance: Logical Addition

Number	AND	Results In
1	1	1
1	0	0
0	1	0
0	0	0

In the first example of this section, the IP address 192.20.16.5 is AND'ed with the subnet mask 255.255.255.0 to give a network ID of 192.20.16. The calculation performed is illustrated here and is an example of a bitwise AND operation.

	Decimal Notation:	*Binary Notation:*
IP address:	192 20 16 5	11000000 00010100 00010000 00000101
Subnet mask:	255 255 255 0	11111111 11111111 11111111 00000000
IP address AND subnet mask:	192 20 16 0	11000000 00010100 00010000 00000000

Determining the network ID is very easy if the subnet mask is made up of only 255 and 0 values. Just "mask" or cover up the part of the IP address corresponding to the 0 octet of the subnet mask. If the IP address is 15.6.100.1 and the subnet mask is 255.255.0.0, for example, the resulting network ID is 15.6. You are not able to use a subnet mask with only 255 and 0 values if you need to subdivide your network ID into individual subnets.

Default Subnet Masks

There are default masks, usually assigned by the vendor, based on the class network in question. Table 2.4 shows the subnet mask that appears in the subnet mask field when an IP address is selected.

TABLE 2.4

DEFAULT SUBNET MASKS.

Class	IP Address	Default Subnet Mask
A	001.y.z.w to 126.y.z.w	255.0.0.0
B	128.y.z.w to 191.y.z.w	255.255.0.0
C	192.y.z.w to 223.y.z.w	255.255.255.0

Thus, using the default mask, the emphasis is on the number of hosts available, and nothing more, as Table 2.5 illustrates.

TABLE 2.5

MAXIMUM NUMBER OF NETWORKS AND HOSTS PER NETWORK IN TCP/IP.

Class	Default Subnet Mask	Number of Networks	Number of Hosts per Network
A	255.0.0.0	126	16,777,216
B	255.255.0.0	16,384	65,534
C	255.255.255.0	2,097,152	254

If the hosts on your internetwork are not directly on the Internet, you are free to choose the network IDs that you use. For the hosts and subnets that are a part of the Internet, however, the network IDs you use must be assigned by InterNIC (the Internet Network Information Center).

It must be noted that if you are using network IDs assigned by InterNIC, you do not have the choice of choosing the address class you use (and you can bet you will be given Class C addresses). In this case, the number of subnets you use is normally limited by the number of network IDs assigned by InterNIC, and the number of hosts per subnet is determined by the class of address. Fortunately, by choosing the proper subnet mask, you can subdivide your network into a greater number of subnets with fewer possible hosts per subnet.

Many companies today with Internet requirements are avoiding the addressing constraints and security risks of having hosts directly on the Internet by setting up private networks with gateway access to the Internet. Having a private network means that only the Internet gateway host needs to have an Internet address. For security, a firewall can be set up to prevent Internet hosts from directly accessing the company's network.

Subdividing a Network

Internetworks are networks comprised of individual segments connected by routers. The reasons for having distinct segments are as follows:

- They permit physically remote local networks to be connected.

- A mix of network technologies are connected, such as Ethernet on one segment and token ring on another.

- They allow an unlimited number of hosts to communicate, whereas the number of hosts on each segment are limited by the type of network used.

- Network congestion is reduced because broadcasts and local network traffic are limited to the local segment.

Each segment is a subnet of the internetwork, and requires a unique network ID. If you only have one network ID that is used, for example, if you have an InterNIC assigned Internet network ID, you have to subdivide this network ID into other network IDs—a process known as subnetting or subnetworking.

The steps involved in subnetting a network are as follows:

1. Determine the number of network IDs required for planning future growth needs.

2. Determine the maximum number of host addresses that are on each subnet, again allowing for future growth.

3. Define one subnet mask for the entire internetwork that gives the desired number of subnets and allows enough hosts per subnet.

4. Determine the resulting subnet network IDs that are used.

5. Determine the valid host IDs and assign IP addresses to the hosts.

The following section shows each of these steps in detail.

Step 1: Determine the Number of Network IDs Required

The first step in subnetting a network is to determine the number of subnets required while planning for future growth. A unique network ID is required for the following:

◆ Each subnet

◆ Each wide area network (WAN) connection

Step 2: Determine the Number of Host IDs per Subnet Required

Determine the maximum number of host IDs that are required on each subnet. A host ID is required for the following:

◆ Each TCP/IP computer network interface card

◆ Each TCP/IP printer network interface card

◆ Each router interface on each subnet. If a router is connected to two subnets, for example, it would require two host IDs and therefore two IP addresses.

N O T E

When determining the number of subnets and hosts per subnet that are needed in your internetwork, it is very important to plan for growth! The entire internetwork should the same subnet mask, therefore the maximum number of subnets and hosts per subnet is set when the subnet mask is chosen.

To illustrate the need for growth planning, consider an internetwork with two subnets with 50 hosts on each subnet connected by a router. The network administrator is authorized by InterNIC to use the network ID 192.20.16 to

continues

continued
put all the hosts on the Internet. As will be explained in the following sections, subnet mask of 255.255.255.192 would create two logical subnets on the internetwork, each allowing a maximum of 62 valid host IDs. In the future, if another segment were added or more than 62 hosts were needed on one segment, the network administrator needs to do the following: choose a new subnet mask, shut down every computer on the network to reconfigure the subnet mask, reconfigure a lot of the network software, and probably look for another job.

Step 3: Define the Subnet Mask

The next step is to define one subnet mask for the entire internetwork that gives the desired number of subnets and allows enough hosts per subnet.

As shown previously, the network ID of an IP address is determined by the 1-bits of the subnet mask shown in binary notation. To increase the number of network IDs, you need to add more bits to the subnet mask.

Assume, for example, that you are assigned a Class B network ID of 192.20 by InterNIC. Using the default Class B subnet mask 255.255.0.0, you have one network ID (192.20) and about 65,000 valid host IDs (192.20.1.1 through 192.20.255.254). Suppose you wanted to subdivide the network into four subnets.

First, consider the host 192.20.16.1 using the subnet mask 255.255.0.0. In binary notation, it is represented as:

IP address:	11000000	00010100	00010000	00000001
Subnet mask:	11111111	11111111	00000000	00000000
Network ID:	11000000	00010100		

Remember that the subnet mask 1 bits correspond to the network ID bit in the IP address.

By adding additional bits to the subnet mask, you increase the bits available for the network ID and thus create a few more combinations of network IDs.

Suppose in the preceding example that you added three bits to the subnet mask. The result increases the number of bits defining the network

ID and decreases the number of bits that define the host ID. Therefore you have more network IDs, but fewer hosts on each subnet. The new subnet mask is as follows:

Subnet mask: 11111111   11111111   11100000   00000000

Now, as you have three extra bits in the Network ID, you now have six different Network IDs. All 0s or all 1s is not allowed, because this is reserved for the broadcast address. The former implies "this network only," and the latter would be the same as the subnet mask.

Network IDs:

11000000 00010100 001

11000000 00010100 010

11000000 00010100 011

11000000 00010100 100

11000000 00010100 101

11000000 00010100 110

To summarize the preceding example using decimal notation:

By applying the new subnet mask of 255.255.224.0 to the network ID 192.20, you create six new network IDs: (192.20.32, 192.20.64, 192.20.96, 192.20.128, 192.20.160, 192.20.192).

Note that if you used only two additional bits in the subnet mask, you would only be able to have two subnets. The network IDs that result in the preceding example are as follows:

11000000   00010100   01   (192.20.64)

and

11000000   00010100   10   (192.20.128)

Therefore you must use enough additional bits in the new subnet mask to create the desired number of subnets, although still allowing for enough hosts on each subnet.

Next is a look at calculating the subnet mask after the number of subnets required is known.

After you determine the number of subnets you need to create, calculate the subnet mask required as follows:

1. Convert the number of subnets to binary format. You may want to use the Windows Calculator in Scientific view.

2. The number of bits required to represent the number of subnets in binary is the number of additional bits that you need to add to the default subnet mask.

3. Convert the subnet mask back to decimal format.

Suppose, for example, that you are assigned a Class B network ID of 192.20 and you need to create five subnets.

Converting 5 into binary format gives 00000101 or just 101. By ignoring the 0 bits to the left of the leftmost 1, the required number of bits is 3.

Therefore you need to add 3 bits to the default subnet mask. The default subnet mask for a Class B network is 255.255.0.0.

In binary notation, this is as follows:

Default subnet mask: 11111111 11111111 00000000 00000000

Adding 3 bits gives the following subnet mask:

11111111   11111111   11100000   00000000

or 255.255.224.0 in decimal notation.

Step 4: Determine the Network IDs to Use

The next step is to determine the subnet network IDs that are created by applying the new subnet mask to the original assigned network ID. Any or all of the resulting subnet network IDs are used in the internetwork.

Three different methods in this discussion are given for determining the network IDs. The first is a manual computation, the second is a shortcut for the first method, and the third uses tables with the values already calculated. As noted previously, you should become familiar with the manual calculations to understand the fundamentals of subnetting.

Step 5: Determine the Host IDs to Use

The final step in subnetting a network is to determine the valid host IDs and assign IP addresses to the hosts.

The host IDs for each subnet start with the value .001 in the last octet, and continue up to one less than the subnet ID of the next subnet. Keep in mind that the last octet cannot be .000 or .255; these are reserved for broadcast addresses.

Finally, the valid IP addresses for each subnet are created by combining the subnet network ID with the host ID.

CONFIGURING WINDOWS NT TO FUNCTION AS AN IP ROUTER

Routers have built-in tables used to determine where to send a packet destined for a particular network. By default, routers know only about networks to which they are physically attached, and depend on tables to inform them about networks to which they are not physically attached— either through manual configuration or dynamic configuration.

Static routers are routers that are not able to discover networks other than those to which they have a physical interface. If this type of router is to be able to route packets to any other network, it has to be told manually what to do, through either the assignment of a default gateway on the router, or by manually editing the route table. Microsoft Windows NT enables the user to build a static router, or multihomed router, using multiple network cards and IP addresses. In a static router environment, new changes are not reflected in the routing tables on these routers.

Dynamic routers, on the other hand, utilize inter-routing protocols. These protocols just provide a language for routers to communicate changes to their route tables to other routers in their environment. In this way, routing tables are built dynamically and the administrator does not have to manually edit route tables to bring up a new network segment.

Dynamic routers cannot provide this function without routing protocols, however. The most popular routing protocols are the Routing Information Protocol (RIP) and Open Shortest Path First protocol (OSPF). RIP is a broadcast-based protocol used primarily on small- to medium-sized networks. The more sophisticated OSPF protocol is used for medium to large networks.

Microsoft Windows NT 4.0 supports the installation and use of RIP to provide dynamic routing for multihomed computers using Windows NT as the operating system. In this way, routing tables can be updated whenever any additions to a network occur. If RIP or OSPF is used in a routed environment, it should help eliminate the need to have to manually edit route tables in your environment.

Static Routing Environment

A typical small network environment can have two routers dividing three subnets. Each router has a standard routing table consisting of the networks to which they are attached. Router A would be connected to subnet 1 and 2 and have a routing table that reflects this information. Router B would be connected to subnet 2 and 3 and its routing table would reflect the networks on which it is currently configured.

Assume a Ping (echo request) packet is initiated by a machine on subnet 1. From the command prompt, or possibly a specific application on subnet 1, a Ping command is issued to an IP address on subnet 3 (from IP address 131.107.32.10 to 131.107.96.20, for example). First, IP takes the destination address and compares it to the source address using the subnet mask of that machine. After the comparison is done, IP determines that this destination address is on a remote network. IP checks its internal route table to determine where it is supposed to send packets destined for a remote network. Whenever a destination address is remote, IP knows to ask ARP for the physical address of the default gateway specified in the internal route table. ARP then either returns the physical address from the ARP cache or does a local ARP broadcast for the router's physical address. At this point, the Ping request has not yet left the sending machine. IP gathers the physical address of the router, inserts the destination address into the Ping packet, and finally transmits the packet on to the wire of subnet 1.

Because IP very smartly sends the packet on the wire in such a way that only the router would not discard the packet, the packet safely arrives at the router. The network interface on the router passes the data up its network stack to IP, where IP discovers that this packet is not destined for it. Normally, IP on a machine would discard the packet. But this is a special kind of machine, a router, which has additional responsibilities including trying to forward packets it receives to the necessary network. Router A reads the IP address of the destination and compares this destination to its own source address using its subnet mask. At this point, IP determines the network to which this packet is supposed to be sent and checks its internal route table to see what to do with packets destined for the 131.107.96.0 network. Unfortunately, this router has no entries for this network and therefore drops this packet. ICMP reports an error to the machine on subnet 1, indicating that the destination address cannot be reached.

This seems like an awful lot of work to get an error message, especially if you know that the destination machine is working. There are two ways to get around this kind of scenario:

- Add a default gateway to the router's configuration
- Add a manual entry in the router's internal table

See what happens if you utilize one or both of these solutions on router A, picking up right where router A decided to drop the packet. Router A has just figured out that the packet's destination address does not match its own IP address. It therefore checks its route table, looking for either a path to the 131.107.96.0 network or for the IP address of its default gateway. By configuring a default gateway, an administrator indicates to the router that if it handles a packet destined for a network that it has no idea about, the router should send it to the default gateway specified and hope for the best. This can be useful if you don't want to configure 37 route table entries on a network. Merely specifying default gateways can minimize the size of your route tables and minimize the number of manual entries you have to maintain. This, of course, comes with the possibility of making your network a little more inefficient. There are always tradeoffs when configuring a network.

Router A now figures out that it needs to send the Ping request to the IP address of the other router based on its route table, in this case 131.107.64.2. Here is yet another conceptual gap. Router A really doesn't know whether the IP address represents a router or just another machine on the network. For that matter, it might be sending this packet into bit-space. Router A trusts that the administrator was wise enough to specify an IP address of a device that will help get the packet to its final destination. As an aside, this means that if you enter a route table entry incorrectly, the router just merrily starts sending packets to wherever you specified.

IP on router A now asks ARP to find the physical address of the next router in line. Just as on another machine, ARP either already has the physical address in cache or initiates an ARP broadcast to get it. After IP has the physical address, it reformulates the packet, addressing it to router B's physical address but leaving the original source address intact. It does not insert its own IP address as the source. If it did this, the destination address would never respond back to the original machine. The packet is transmitted on to the wire destined for router B.

Router B hears the transmission, goes through basically the same process, determines the destination address, and discovers that it can send the packet directly to the destination machine. Utilizing the same ARP and IP procedures, the packet finally arrives at the destination machine on subnet 3. The ICMP echo request is acknowledged and ICMP formulates the ICMP echo response packet that must be sent back. Remember that up to this point, the original sending machine is just patiently waiting for a response. The destination machine looks at the source address (131.107.32.10), figures out that it's remote, finds the physical address of router B to send the message back, and transmits it on to the wire.

> **NOTE** For routing to work in a static routing environment, be sure that each router is aware of all relevant networks; otherwise, packets will be dropped unexpectedly on their return to a destination.

Router B receives the packet, breaks it down, and tries to figure out what to do with a packet destined for the 131.107.32.0 subnet. And, after all this work, router B drops the packet. Why? You made all the changes to router A in terms of a default gateway and route table entries, but you didn't do anything to router B.

To make static routing work, each router has to be updated and configured to know about other networks in the environment. Only after a default gateway or manual entry in router B's route table is configured will the packets be successfully transmitted between these two networks.

Default Gateways

You can easily identify default gateways on a machine. The two easiest ways to identify default gateways for a machine or multihomed router is through manual configuration through the IP properties sheet, or as a DHCP option. You can specify more than one default gateway on a machine. Remember, however, that dead gateway detection will work only for machines initiating a TCP connection. In a routing table, the default gateway(s) is identified by the entry 0.0.0.0.

Route Tables

Route tables are used by machines/hosts on the network and by routers to determine where packets should be sent to reach their final destination. Each router builds an internal route table every time IP is loaded during system initialization. Take a closer look at a route table.

The following five columns of information are provided within the route table:

- **The Network Address.** This column represents all networks that this machine or router knows about, including entries for the default gateway, subnet and network broadcasts, the universal loopback address, and the default multicast address. In a route table, you can use names rather than the IP addresses to identify networks. If you use names rather than IP addresses, the names are resolved using the networks file found in the `\%system drive%\system32\drivers\etc` directory.

- **The Netmask.** This column just identifies the subnet mask used for a particular network entry.

- **The Gateway Address.** This is the IP address to which packets should be sent to route packets to their final destination. Each network address may specify a different gateway address in which to send packets. This may be particularly true if more than one router is connected to one network segment. This column may also have self-referential entries indicating the IP address to which broadcasts should be sent, as well as the local loopback entries. You can also use names to identify these IP addresses. Any names used here will be resolved using the local HOSTS file on the machine.

♦ **Interface.** This IP address is used primarily to identify the IP address of the machine and to identify this IP address as the interface to the network. On a machine with one network card, only two entries appear. For any network address that is self-referential, the interface is 127.0.0.1, meaning that packets are not even sent on to the network. For all other communications, the IP address represents the network card interface used to communicate out on to the network. For multihomed machines, the interface IP address changes depending on which network address is configured on each network card. In this case, the interface identifies the IP address of the card connected to a particular network segment.

♦ **The Metric.** The metric indicates the cost or hops associated with a particular network route. The router's job is to find the path representing the least cost or effort to get the packet to its destination. The lower the cost or hop count, the better or more efficient a particular route. On a static router, the metric for any network address will be one, indicating that the router thinks every network is only one router hop away. This is obviously not true, indicating that on static routers, this column is fairly meaningless. On dynamic routers, however, this column indicates to a router the best possible route to send packets.

Viewing the Route Table

To view the route table of a Windows NT machine/router, two utilities can be used: the Netstat utility and the route utility. To view the route table through Netstat, go to the command prompt and type the following:

```
netstat -r
```

This brings up the route table on your machine. All you can do is view the table. To view and manage the route table, including adding or changing entries, use the route utility. To view the route table using the route command, type the following:

```
route print
```

This shows you the same table as before. When you type **route print** from the command prompt, the same table that displays with `netstat -r` is shown. In both cases, the route table appears.

The entries in a route table on Windows NT 4.0 by default include the following:

- **0.0.0.0.** This entry identifies the IP address of the default gateway, or the IP address to which packets will be sent if no other specific route table entry exists for a destination network. If multiple gateways are defined on a Windows NT machine, you may notice more than one entry that looks like this, specifying each of the default gateways that is defined.

- **127.0.0.1.** This is the local loopback address used for diagnostic purposes, to make sure that the IP stack on a machine is properly installed and running.

- **Local network.** This is the identifier indicating the local network address. It indicates the gateway and interface, such as the machine's IP address, that is used whenever a packet needs to be transmitted to a local destination.

- **Local host.** This is used for self-referential purposes and points to the local loopback address as the gateway and interface.

- **Subnet broadcast.** This is a directed broadcast and is treated as a directed packet by routers. Routers support the transmission of directed broadcasts to the network that is defined by the broadcast. The packet is forwarded to the network, where it is broadcast to the machines on that network. In this case, the default entry specifies the IP address of the current machine for sending out subnet broadcasts to the network this machine is on.

- **224.0.0.0.** This is the default multicast address. If this machine is a member of any multicast groups, this and other multicast entries indicate to IP the interface used to communicate with the multicast network.

- **255.255.255.255.** This is a limited broadcast address for broadcasts destined for any machine on the local network. Routers that receive packets destined for this address may listen to the packet as a normal host, but do not support transmission of these types of broadcasts to other networks.

When a router looks for where to send a particular packet, it searches through the route table. After a route has been determined, meaning that an IP address has been found to send the data to, IP asks ARP for the physical address of that IP address. As soon as ARP replies, the frame can be constructed and transmitted on to the wire.

Building a Static Routing Table

The route command has a number of other switches that can be used to manage a route table statically. Up to this point, the print command is the only parameter that has been used. To manage a route table, however, an administrator must be able to add, delete, change, and clear route table entries. Each of these options is available and the following table shows each respective command:

To Add or Modify a Static Route	Function
route add [net id] mask [netmask][gateway]	Adds a route
route -p add [net id] mask [netmask][gateway]	Adds a persistent route
route delete [net id][gateway]	Deletes a route
route change [net id][gateway]	Modifies a route
route print	Displays route table
route -f	Clears all routes

Notice the entry that utilizes a -p (persistent) before the add parameter. By default, route table entries are kept only in memory. After a machine is rebooted, any entries that were manually added are gone and must be re-entered. You can use batch files, startup scripts—or the persistent switch—to re-enter static routes. The persistent entry switch writes route entries into the Registry so that they survive a reboot of the machine. Naturally, this removes the need to create batch files or scripts, but requires manual deletion of the routes if they should change.

> NOTE
>
> Route table entries are kept only in memory and will not survive a reboot unless the -p switch is used.

The TRACERT Utility

Windows NT includes the TRACERT utility, which is used to verify the route a packet takes to reach its destination. To use this utility, just go to the command prompt and type the following:

```
tracert <IP address>
```

The result of running this utility for a destination address will probably look similar to the following output:

```
C:\>tracert www.learnix.com

Tracing route to www.learnix.com [199.45.92.97]
over a maximum of 30 hops:

  1   156 ms   156 ms   141 ms   annex.intranet.ca [206.51.251.5]
  2   157 ms   156 ms   156 ms   cisco2.intranet.ca [206.51.251.10]
  3   172 ms   156 ms   172 ms   spc-tor-6-Serial3-3.Sprint-Canada.Net
                                 [206.186.248.85]
  4   156 ms   172 ms   187 ms   204.50.128.17
  5   171 ms   172 ms   157 ms   205.150.206.97
  6   172 ms   172 ms   297 ms   h5.bb1.tor2.h4.bb1.ott1.uunet.ca
                                 [205.150.242.70]
  7   172 ms   171 ms   172 ms   max1.ott1.uunet.ca [205.150.233.2]
  8   188 ms   203 ms   218 ms   router.learnix.ca [199.71.122.193]
  9   203 ms   218 ms   235 ms   evan [199.45.92.97]

Trace complete.
```

The result shows each route traversed to get to a destination, as well as how long it took to get through each particular router. The time it takes to get through a particular router is calculated using three algorithms, which are displayed for each router hop. The IP address of each router traversed also displays. If a FQDN is available, this displays as well.

The TRACERT utility is useful for two primary diagnostic purposes:

- ◆ It detects whether a particular router is not functioning along a known path. Assume, for instance, that a user knows that packets on a network always go through Texas to get from Florida to California, but communication seems to be dead. A TRACERT to a California address shows all the hops up to the point where the router in Texas should respond. If it does not respond, the time values are marked with asterisks (*), indicating a nonfunctioning path.

◆ This utility also determines whether a router is slow and possibly needs to be upgraded or helped by adding additional routes on the network. You can determine this just by looking at the time it takes for a packet to get through a particular router. If a particular router is deluged by packets, its return time may be significantly higher than that of any of the other hops, indicating it should be upgraded or helped in some way.

Dynamic Routing

Discussion to this point has focused on how to manually edit the route table to notify routers of the existence of networks to which they are not physically connected. This would be an enormously difficult task on large networks, where routes and networks may change on a frequent basis. It also makes redundant pathways horribly complex to manage, because you have to rely on each host to manage multiple default gateways and utilize dead gateway detection. Even utilizing these features on the client side does not guarantee timely reactions to failure of links between routers.

These problems led to the development of routing protocols, used specifically by routers to dynamically update each other's tables. Two of the most common protocols used by dynamic routers are RIP and OSPF protocol. These protocols notify other routers that support these protocols of the networks they are attached to and of any changes that occur due to links being disconnected or becoming too congested to efficiently pass traffic. The standard rule of thumb when considering the use of either protocol is that RIP works well for small- to medium-sized networks and OSPF works well for medium to large networks. The characteristics of RIP are discussed here because Windows NT supports RIP on its multihomed routers, but the characteristics of OSPF are left to other reference sources. Windows NT multihomed routers do not support the OSPF protocol out of the box.

To understand the Routing Internet Protocol (RIP) better on routers, first consider static routing, where routing tables had to be built manually. To pass packets from one network to another, each router had to be told where to send packets destined for a specific network (route table entry) or where to send packets it had no idea what to do with (default gateway). By default, routers know about the networks to which they are physically attached, because their IP addresses on each of those networks give them the necessary information. The problem of remote networks is encountered almost immediately, however. For this reason, it became apparent that as networks grew in size, a more sophisticated way to update route tables would be necessary. From this need arose routing protocols, which enable routers to communicate with each other. The protocols enable one router to send information about the networks it knows about to any other router physically connected to the wire, and enable the router to receive information about other networks dynamically from other routers that also are able to communicate.

The RIP procedure for communicating between routers is through broadcasts over UDP port 520. RIP routers broadcast their route tables over this port and listen on this port for broadcasts from other routers that may be connected to the network. In this way, eventually all routers that are physically connected have up-to-date route tables and know where to send data for any network in the environment.

Not only do routers communicate the networks to which they are attached, but they also communicate how far away remote networks are from their particular location. This distance to another network is called a *hop*, or metric, and each router keeps track of this value within the route table. Each router along the path to a destination network represents a hop. For this reason, RIP is considered a distance-vector routing protocol. In this fashion, RIP can determine the route with the least number of hops necessary to get a packet to its final destination.

As RIP was being developed, it was decided that routers would need to keep track of a maximum of 15 hops between networks. Therefore, any network address that has a hop count of 16 is considered unreachable. If a router's route table has two different hop counts for a particular network, the router sends the data to the route that has the least number of hops to the destination network.

Initially, it doesn't seem to make sense to limit the number of hops to a destination address, but this limitation is based primarily on how the RIP protocol works. Because RIP routers broadcast the networks they know about and how far away they are from those networks, certain precautions must be made in case any of these connections fail. After a router determines that a connection has failed, it must find a better route to that network from other route tables. This could create circular and upward-spiraling loops between routers, where the hop count continues to increase, ad infinitum.

If a redundant connection to that network exists with a higher hop count, eventually each router's tables increase to the point that the redundant route is chosen over the connection that died. But if no redundant route is available, the hop count could continue to increase indefinitely. To reduce this risk, several algorithms have been written to successfully react to connection failures, including the maximum hop count of 16, indicating an unreachable network. Administrators also have the ability to alter the hop count between routers, to encourage the use of some network routers over others that may be used purely for redundancy. Broadcasts between routers occur every 30 seconds, whether the route table has changed or not.

Because RIP is the oldest routing protocol on the block and is widely used throughout the industry, several well-known problems exist when trying to implement this protocol in larger networks. These protocol deficiencies result in RIP being useful only in small to medium networks. RIP falls short in the following basic categories:

- Because RIP keeps track of every route table entry, including multiple paths to a particular network, routing tables can become large rather quickly. This can result in multiple RIP packets having to be broadcast to send a complete route table to other routers.

- Because RIP can allow hop counts only up to 15, with 16 representing an unreachable network, the size of networks on which RIP can be successfully implemented is necessarily restricted. Any large enterprise may need to achieve hop counts over and above this value.

- Broadcasts are sent by default every 30 seconds. This results in two fundamental problems. First, significant time delays occur between the times when a route goes down and all routers in the environment are notified of this change in the network. If a network goes down nine routers (hops) away, it can take up to 4 ½ minutes before that change makes it to the other end of the network. Meanwhile, packets sent in that direction can be lost and connections dropped. Second, while on a LAN, these broadcasts may not be significant in terms of bandwidth; but on an expensive WAN connection, these broadcasts may become bothersome, especially if the network is stable and the route tables are large. These broadcasts transmit redundant route table entries every 30 seconds without regard to whether it is necessary.

But these problems should not discourage the administrator of a small to medium network from using the RIP protocol. As long as you understand the benefits and limitations of the protocol, you should be able to use it quite successfully on a network.

Building a Multihomed Router

Windows NT enables an administrator to convert a machine into either a static or dynamic IP router. Static routers work well for extending a small network segment, and dynamic routers using RIP work well on small to medium networks. A multihomed computer would probably not work well on large networks, however, based on RIP's limitations and the significant overhead associated with maintaining large route tables. Other considerations aside, however, building a Windows NT router is fairly simple and easy to do.

Before continuing, however, it is important for you to understand the terms multihomed computer and multihomed router. A multihomed router is simply a computer with more than one network card, which has been configured to route packets from one network segment to another. The defining characteristic between a hardware router and a multihomed router is that on a multihomed computer, the operating system is the one that performs the routing. A hardware router is a device specifically manufactured and designed for routing only. You could think about it in more simple terms. You can run any Windows application, including Freecell on a multihomed router, for example, but you can't do that on a hardware router.

The first step toward building a Windows NT router is to install two or more network cards in the machine. Anyone who has ever tried to do so will tell you this can often sound much easier than it is. Each network card has to have its own IRQ and I/O address to use on the machine. These must be independent of other hardware cards you may be using in your machine, including video cards, sound cards, modems, hard-disk controller cards, and so on. Basically, the machine needs to be stripped of any bells and whistles and other functions so that enough resources are available. Any resource conflicts result in significant headaches, because your network cards don't appear and protocol drivers fail to load. The typical machine built for Windows NT seminars and classes uses a Windows NT router with three network cards and little else. After the machine successfully identifies the network cards, be careful of installing any additional third-party utilities. Sometimes they decide to steal the I/O addresses your network cards are using. Bottom line is that after this machine is built, try to leave it alone. Getting your machine stable will be the toughest part. Afterward, everything else is easy.

After you install your network cards, make sure to assign separate IP addresses to each card. To do this, follow these steps:

1. In the Network section of Control Panel under the Protocol tab, select TCP/IP and choose Properties. Notice that where the network card is identified, the drop-down box reveals all the network cards you have installed, enabling you to choose a different IP address scheme for each network card.

2. After you give each network card its own IP address, indicating which network it is on, the machine can respond to packets coming from the networks to which it is attached. However, the machine is still not a router.

3. To turn the machine into a router, go back to TCP/IP Properties and choose the Routing tab. Select the Enable IP Forwarding check box. After you select this box and have chosen OK to exit this configuration and the network configuration, you are asked to reboot your machine.

4. Reboot the machine. After the machine is rebooted, it is officially a router that can pass packets from one network to another.

The administrator then needs to decide whether the router will be static or dynamic. After IP forwarding is enabled, the router is a static router. If this is what is desired, no more configuration is necessary. If the administrator wishes to make this a dynamic router, the RIP protocol needs to be installed.

This can be installed in the Services tab through the Network icon. After RIP is installed, this router listens for other RIP broadcasts, and broadcasts its own route table entries.

Although Windows NT supports the capability to create a static or dynamic router, the most important consideration for an administrator is probably whether he or she should spend the money to upgrade a machine for occasional routing of packets or spend the money for a hardware router. If the administrator plans to spend over $1,000 for a machine to route packets on a network, he may be better off spending it on hardware optimized for that purpose. Think of Windows NT routing versus hardware routing in much the same way as you would think about Windows NT RAID versus hardware RAID. Hardware implementation is usually a little more expensive, but is optimized for that specific task; whereas Windows NT implementations work well and are cheaper, but are not designed for constant pounding by a large network.

INSTALLING AND CONFIGURING THE DHCP RELAY AGENT

Essentially, the job of the DHCP Relay Agent is to forward DHCP broadcast messages between DHCP-enabled clients and DHCP servers, across IP routers. The Relay Agent can be configured on any Windows NT Server computer and adds very little load.

NOTE The DHCP Relay Agent that comes with Windows NT 4.0 is a new service that will listen for DHCP broadcasts and forward them to one or more configured DHCP servers. This is different from an RFC1542-compliant router in that the system running the Relay Agent is not a router.

To install the DHCP agent, follow these steps:

1. Open the Network Configuration dialog box and select the Services tab.

2. Select Add and, from the list that appears, select the DHCP Relay Agent. Click OK and, when prompted, enter the path to the distribution files.

3. Click the Protocols tab and double-click the TCP/IP protocol.

4. On the DHCP Relay tab, enter the IP address of a DHCP server and the maximum number of hops and seconds that the relay can take.

5. Close the TCP/IP Configuration dialog box and the Network Configuration dialog box.

6. Restart the computer when prompted.

INSTALLING AND CONFIGURING DNS

The system on which you install the DNS service must be running Windows NT Server and needs to have a static IP configuration. Installing the DNS server is simple, given that installing it is the same as installing any other network service. The steps are as follows:

1. Open the Network Settings dialog box (right-click the Network Neighborhood and choose Properties).

2. On the Services tab, click Add and select the Microsoft DNS Server.

3. Click OK to add the service. When prompted, enter the directory in which your Windows NT source files are located.

4. Choose Close from the Network Settings dialog box and, when prompted, restart your system.

You have now installed the DNS server. To verify that the service is correctly installed, check the Services icon in Control Panel to ensure the Microsoft DNS server is listed and has started.

Enabling DNS on the Client

Now that you have a DNS server, you need to have your clients use the DNS server. To enable Windows clients to use the DNS server, you can add the address of the DNS server to each station (manually), or you can set the DNS server option on the DHCP server.

For Windows NT, you can use the following procedure to set the DNS server address (setting the address on Windows 95 is the same):

1. Open the TCP/IP Settings dialog box. (Open the Network Settings dialog box, and from the Protocol tab, double-click TCP/IP.)

2. On the DNS tab, enter the required information. As a minimum, you need to enter the IP address of a DNS server. The other options on this tab are described as follows:

   ♦ **Hostname.** This is the name of the local host. This is the same as the NetBIOS name by default; however, you can change it. (If you select a different name, you are warned that if the NetBIOS name is ever changed, the hostname is set to the new NetBIOS name. If you use WINS to create a Dynamic DNS, the NetBIOS name and the hostname must be the same.)

   ♦ **Domain**. This is the Internet domain to which the system belongs. This is combined with the hostname to create the FQDN name that this system is known as.

   ♦ **DNS Service Search Order.** This is the IP address of one or more DNS servers that you use. They are tried in the order given.

   ♦ **Domain Suffix Search Order.** When you search for another host—for example, if you enter **FTP evan**—the system first looks for "evan" as the name in the DNS server. If "evan" is not in your current domain, that system will not be found and you would have to enter **FTP evan.synergy.com**. If you work with servers at synergy.com frequently, you can add the domain synergy.com into this area, and if the address is not resolved from "evan," a second query for evan.synergy.com is automatically sent.

3. Click OK to close the TCP/IP settings. (If you are installing TCP/IP, you will need to enter the path to the Windows NT source files.)

4. Choose Close from the Network Settings dialog box and restart your system. (This is not absolutely required, but generally it is recommended to ensure that the values are correctly set.)

You can also use the DNS server in place of the WINS server for resolving the hostnames. To do this, you need to change the settings on the WINS tab in the TCP/IP configuration. Specifically, you need to select the option to use DNS to resolve hostnames.

Using Existing BIND Files

If you already have a series of BIND files set up on an existing DNS server, you can use these files to configure the Microsoft DNS server. The following are the steps you need to follow to configure Microsoft DNS server to use these files:

1. Install the Microsoft DNS service (see the preceding section for instructions).

2. Stop the DNS service (from the Control Panel, choose the Services icon, click on Microsoft DNS, and click the Stop button).

3. Copy the BIND files to the `%winroot%\System32\DNS` directory.

4. Start the DNS service (from the Control Panel, choose the Services icon, click Microsoft DNS, and click the Start button).

5. Use the DNS Manager to verify that your entries are there.

Reinstalling Microsoft DNS Server

A quick note should be made here in case you need to reinstall the DNS server. When you start adding zones to a Microsoft DNS server, it by default switches to starting from the Registry rather than the DNS files discussed earlier. It makes a note of this in the boot file. When you remove the server (before you reinstall), it does not remove this file; therefore, when you install the DNS server again, it assumes the boot file is valid and tries to read it. This causes several errors in the Event Log and causes the DNS not to start.

Therefore, if you need to remove the DNS server, you should remove the boot file from the DNS directory. The original file is in the directory `%winroot%\system32\dns\backup` and you can copy the files back from there; however, the server continues to boot from the Registry.

If you need to enable the system to boot from files, you must use the Registry Editor to open `HKEY_LOCAL_MACHINE\SYSTEM\CurrentControlSet\ Services\DNS\Parameters` and delete the value `EnableRegistryBoot`.

DNS Administration Tool

Adding the DNS server adds the DNS Administration tool. This tool makes configuring and maintaining the DNS server very simple. And because you can add several DNS servers, it also provides single-seat administration.

First, you need to add the DNS server that you wish to manage. This is done by following these simple steps:

1. Start the DNS Manager by choosing Start, Programs, Administrative Tools, DNS Manager.

2. In the left pane of the DNS Manager, right-click Server List.

3. Choose New Server from the menu.

4. In the DNS Server box, enter the name or IP address of the server you wish to add.

Now that you have added the server, you can configure it and add entries. The DNS Server needs to be configured for the role that it plays in the overall system, and you should know what the server you are configuring will be used for.

Creating a Subdomain

Many organizations are broken down into smaller groups that focus on one area of the business. Or perhaps the organization is dispersed geographically. In either case, the company may decide that they want break down their main domain into subdomains. This is simple in Microsoft's DNS server. Choose the parent domain (synergy.com, for example) and then right-click. Choose New Domain and enter the subdomain name in the dialog box that appears.

If the subdomain is handled on another server, enter NS records for each of the other servers. If it is handled locally, just add the required records.

Updating DNS Startup Files

After you have added several records to the DNS server, you need to update the information in the files on the system. Even if the server boots from the Registry, the database (zone) files are stored. To do this, choose DNS from the menu, and then choose Update Server Data Files. This is done automatically when the server is shut down or when you exit the DNS Manager.

DNS Manager Preferences

As a final note, you can set the following three options under Options, Preferences that affect the way the DNS Manager itself will behave:

- **Auto Refresh Statistics.** Enables you to configure the Statistics screen to automatically update information.

- **Show Automatically Created Zones.** Shows the zones that are automatically created. These are used for internal purposes only.

- **Expose TTL.** Enables you to expose the TTL for entries in your cache. (You can view these by double-clicking cache and then double-clicking the subfolders.)

NSLOOKUP

Along with the addition of a DNS server, Windows NT 4.0 also has a tool that uses the DNS and enables you to verify that it is working. The NSLOOKUP command line is as follows:

```
nslookup [-option ...] [computer-to-find | - [server]]
```

You can use NSLOOKUP to query the DNS server from the command line (see Table 2.6 for a list of switches) or you can start an interactive session with the server to enable you to query the database. For the purposes here, only look at the command line.

TABLE 2.6

COMMAND-LINE SWITCHES FOR THE **NSLOOKUP** COMMAND.

Switch	Description
-option	Enables you to enter one or more commands from the command line. A list of the commands follows. For each option you wish to add, enter a hyphen (-) followed immediately by the command name. Note that the command-line length needs to be less than 256 characters.
Computer-to-find	This is the host or IP address about which you wish to find information. It is processed using the default server or, if given, using the specified server.

The following list provides the options available with the NSLOOKUP command:

- `-t querytype` Lists all records of a given type. The record types are listed under Querytype.

- `-a` Lists all the CNAME entries from the DNS server.

- `-d` Dumps all records that are in the DNS server.

- `-h` Returns information on the DNS server's CPU and operating system.

- `-s` Returns the well-known services for hosts in the DNS domain.

INTEGRATING DNS WITH OTHER NAME SERVERS

The other name server that DNS can integrate with is WINS. During the installation process, the last tab in the Zone Configuration dialog box is the WINS tab. You can use WINS to resolve DNS queries by telling the server to use the WINS server. Remember, for this to work, the hosts must use the same name for both their NetBIOS name and the hostname, and they must register with the WINS server.

Only the following three options are available:

- **Use WINS Resolution.** Check this box to enable the DNS server to query the WINS server for queries it receives that it cannot resolve from its own database.

- **Settings Only Affect Local Server.** Normally a temporary entry is added to the domain when this resolution method is used. Selecting this option only allows the current server to see these entries.

- **WINS Servers.** Here you need to enter the address of at least one WINS server. This server is queried in the order entered.

From the WINS tab, you can also open the Advanced Options dialog box. You may need to use a couple of other settings in this dialog box.

The following options are available:

- **Submit DNS Domain as NetBIOS Scope.** In some organizations, the NetBIOS scope ID is used to limit the number of hosts you can see using NetBIOS. The WINS server only responds with the address if matching scope IDs are used. Therefore, this option enables you to use the domain name as the NetBIOS scope.

- **Cache Timeout Value.** Length of time the DNS server keeps the information that it gets from the WINS server.

- **Lookup Timeout Value.** Length of time the DNS server waits for a resolution from the WINS server.

Adding HOSTS

Now that the domain has been created, and the WINS resolution is set up, you need to add the records that the WINS resolution cannot handle. Essentially, this is any non-WINS client that you have on your network, as well as any host that has an alias (discussed in the next section).

Adding a host record (or any record) is simple. All you need to do is right-click the domain (or subdomain) to which you want to add the record. A menu appears from which you can choose New Host.

When you choose New Host, you see a dialog box. Enter the hostname and the IP address in this dialog box. You need only the hostname because the domain or subdomain you clicked on is assumed.

An option to Create Associated PTR Record also exists. This enters the required information for the reverse lookup zone for this host. You need to create the reverse lookup zone before you can do this.

Adding Other Records

The main purpose of a DNS server is to resolve a hostname to an IP address. Other organizations may want other types of information, however, such as the address of your mail server. You can add several types of records to the DNS server. The following list describes these other records:

- A   This is a host entry, exactly the same as was entered in the preceding section.

- AAAA   This is also a host entry; the difference is that you can enter an IPng address (the new version of TCP/IP that will use 128-bit addresses rather than 32-bit).

- AFSDB   The AFSDB record gives the address of an AFS (Andrew File System) database server, or a DCE (Distributed Computing Environment) authenticated name server.

- CNAME   The canonical name is an alias that points one name such as WWW to another such as Web. This is one of the most common records that you need to enter.

- HINFO   Enters machine information about a host, which allows other hosts on the network to find out CPU (central processing unit) type and operating system information.

- ISDN   Integrated Services Digital Network enables you to map an entry to an ISDN phone number rather than an IP address. This is used in conjunction with an RT (Route Through; see the RT entry in this list) record to automate routing over dial-up ISDN.

- MB   This is an experimental record type used to associate an email ID with a particular host ID.

- MG   Like an MB record, the MG is experimental; this associates an MB record with a mail group that could be used for mailing lists.

- MINFO   Another experimental record, MINFO enables you to enter the mail information about the person responsible for a given mail record.

- MR   This is another experimental record. This provides for the mail records the same service that CNAME entries provide for hostnames—aliases.

- MX   You must have at least one MX record. The MX record takes incoming connections for mail and directs them to a mail server. You can enter more than one MX record. If you do, the system uses the preference number to determine the order in which to try them (lowest first).

- NS   This is a name server record. It is used to find the other name servers in the domain.

- PTR   The Pointer record is part of the reverse lookup zone and is used to point the IP address at the hostname.

- RP   This is where you enter the name (or names) of those people who are responsible for the domain that the server provides resolution for. There can be multiple entries of this type.

- RT   This points at another record in the DNS database. The Route Through provides information on how to get to a host using dial-up ISDN or X.25.

- SOA   As already discussed, the Start of Authority record provides the basic configuration for a zone.

- TXT   The Text record is a way of associating text information with a host. This can provide information about the computer (in addition to the information in an HINFO entry) or other information such as the location.

- WKS   Provides the ability to indicate which Well Known Services are running on a particular host. These match the service and protocols that are listed in the services file (%winroot%\System32\drivers\ etc) below port 256.

- X25   Similar to the ISDN entry, this provides the capability to map a name to an X.121 name.

Adding these records is similar to adding a host record. Right-click the domain or subdomain and choose New Record.

CONNECTING A DNS SERVER TO A DNS ROOT SERVER

A cache file that has entries for top-level servers of the Internet domains is included with DNS. If a hostname cannot be resolved from local zone files, DNS uses the cache file to look for a higher-level DNS server to resolve the name. If your organization has only an intranet without any Internet access, you should replace this file with one that lists the top-level DNS servers in your organization. This file is called `cache.dns` and is located at `\winnt\system32\dns`.

The latest version of this file can be downloaded from InterNIC at `ftp://rs.internic.net/domain/named.cache`.

CONFIGURING DNS SERVER ROLES

The roles that a server can take on include that of a primary and secondary DNS server, as well as an IP forwarder, or a caching-only server—that is, a server that can only resolve addresses, but which does not host any domains or subdomains (zones).

In the next few sections, each of these is examined, in order from the simplest to the most complicated.

Configuring for Caching-Only

There is just about nothing you need to do to run a server as a caching-only server. The caching-only server does not host any zones. If this is all you need, stop here.

Configuring as an IP Forwarder

An IP forwarder is also a caching-only server; however, you need to configure it with the address of another DNS server (another Microsoft

DNS server or any other DNS—for example, the one from your ISP). This configuration is fairly simple and the only information you require is the IP address of the server to use. Follow these steps:

1. Right-click the server in the Server list and select Properties.

2. On the Forwarders tab, check the Use Forwarders box.

3. If the server is to only use the services of the other system, select Operate As Slave Server. (If you don't select this, the server attempts to resolve through the forwarder; however, it then uses an iterative query if that fails.)

4. Enter the address or addresses of the DNS servers to which this one should forward queries.

5. If desired, set a time-out for the request.

6. Click OK to close the dialog box.

Creating a Primary DNS Server

The purpose of DNS is to resolve hostnames to IP addresses. Therefore you need to enter the addresses into the DNS server so that other users can find your hosts. You do this by creating a zone in the DNS server and entering the information that you wish to make available to the world. The following list covers the steps required to create a zone:

1. Right-click the server that hosts the zone in the Server list.

2. Choose New Zone.

3. From the dialog box that appears, choose Primary. Then choose Next.

4. Enter the name of the domain (or subdomain) for which you are creating a zone on the next screen. Then press Tab (this automatically enters a zone filename; if you are adding an existing zone file, enter the name of the file that has the information—it must be in the `%winroot%\System32\DNS` directory). When the information is in, click Next.

5. On the next screen, choose Finish.

That is all there is to creating a zone. Now you can configure the zone and add the host (and other) records.

Setting Up and Reviewing the SOA Record

Configuring a zone is straightforward. Essentially, the information that you are entering here includes details for the Start of Authority (SOA) record and information about using WINS.

Setting up the information is easy. The following steps outline the process:

1. Right-click the zone you want to configure. Choose Properties from the menu. The Properties dialog box appears, presenting the basic zone information.

2. Click the SOA Record tab to bring up the information about the SOA.

3. Edit the information in the SOA record. You can change the following fields:

   ◆ **Primary Name Server DNS Name.** The name of the primary name server that contains the files for the domain. Note that only the hostname is entered, and then a period (.) that means this domain (for example, NS1 is NS1.Synergy.com).

   ◆ **Responsible Person Mailbox DNS Name.** The email address of the person who is in charge of the DNS. (Note, as in the primary name server, you need to enter only the email username—followed by a period—if the email address is within this domain.)

   ◆ **Serial Number.** A version ID assigned to the zone. The number is updated whenever you make changes to the database, so the secondary servers know that changes were made and can retrieve the new information.

   ◆ **Refresh Interval.** Tells the secondary servers how often they should check their version number with the primaries to see whether they need to transfer the zone information again.

♦ **Retry Interval.** Tells how long the secondary server should wait before retrying the primary server if it could not connect at the time given in Refresh Interval.

♦ **Expire Time.** Sets how long a secondary server continues to give out information on this zone after not being able to connect with the primary server.

♦ **Minimum Default TTL.** When a DNS server performs an iterative query to resolve a name, the name is cached. This value sets how long other DNS servers are allowed to keep the information about records that your DNS server resolves for them.

4. Click the Notify tab. (This is not really part of the SOA; however, it is added here because it deals with the secondary servers.)

5. Enter the IP addresses of all the secondary servers that should be notified when a change is made.

6. If desired, you can choose Only Allow Access from Secondaries Included on Notify List, which restricts which servers can retrieve your zone information.

7. Click OK to accept the changes you have made (the WINS tab is covered in the next section.)

Setting Up the Secondary DNS Server

After you configure your server, you need to add a secondary server. Adding this server provides redundancy and also splits the workload among the servers (you can have several secondary servers if you wish). The following list outlines the steps involved:

1. In the DNS Manager, right-click the server to be configured as a secondary server.

2. Choose New Zone from the context menu. From the New Zone dialog box, choose Secondary.

NOTE On this screen, you are asked for the zone name and the server from which to get zone files. A handy option is the ability (as seen here) to drag the hand over another server listed in the DNS Manager to automatically pick up the information.

If the primary DNS server is not a Microsoft DNS server, you will need to enter the information manually.

3. Click the Next button, and you can enter the information for the file. This should already be entered, and you should click Next to accept the defaults.

4. The next screen asks you to identify the IP master for the zone. This should already be filled in for you.

5. The last screen tells you that you are finished. Click Finish to close this screen.

CONFIGURING HOSTS AND LMHOSTS FILES

The HOSTS file is used for static hostname mapping to IP addresses (in place of DNS); LMHOSTS provides static mapping to NetBIOS names (in place of WINS).

Configure HOSTS Files

The HOSTS file is an ASCII text file that statically maps local and remote hostnames and IP addresses. It is located in \\`systemroot`\\System32\\ Drivers\\etc.

It is case sensitive in Windows NT versions prior to 4.0, and on other operating systems. It is limited to 255 characters per entry, and is used by Ping and other utilities to resolve hostnames locally and remotely. One HOSTS file must reside on each host, and the file is read from top to bottom. As soon as a match is found for a hostname, the file stops being read. For that reason, when there are duplicate entries, the later ones are always ignored, and the most commonly used names should be near the top of the file.

The following is an example of the default HOSTS file:

```
# Copyright© 1993-1995 Microsoft Corp.
#
# This is a sample HOSTS file used by Microsoft TCP/IP for Windows NT.
#
# This file contains the mappings of IP addresses to hostnames. Each
# entry should be kept on an individual line. The IP address should
# be placed in the first column followed by the corresponding
# hostname.
# The IP address and the hostname should be separated by at least one
# space.
#
# Additionally, comments (such as these) may be inserted on individual
# lines or following the machine name denoted by a '#' symbol.
#
# For example:
#
#      102.54.94.97      rhino.acme.com          # source server
#      38.25.63.10       x.acme.com              # x client host

127.0.0.1       localhost
```

You should notice several things in this file. The first is that the pound sign (#) indicates a comment. When the file is read by the system, every line beginning with a comment is ignored. When a # appears in the middle of a line, the line is only read up to the sign. If this were in use on a live system, the first 17 lines should be deleted or moved to the end of the file to keep them from being read every time the file is referenced.

The second thing to note is the entry:

```
127.0.0.1       localhost
```

This is a "loopback" address in every host. It references the internal card, regardless of the actual host address and can be used for diagnostics to verify that things are working properly internally, before testing that they are working properly down the wire.

Within the HOSTS file, fields are separated by white space that can be either tabs or spaces. As mentioned earlier, a host can be referred to by more than one name. To do so, separate the entries on the same line with white space, as shown in the following example:

127.0.0.1   me loopback localhost

199.9.200.7   SALES7 victor

199.9.200.4   SALES4 nikki

199.9.200.3   SALES3 cole

199.9.200.2   SALES2 victoria

199.9.200.1   SALES1 nicholas

199.9.200.5   SALES5 jack

199.9.200.11   ACCT1

199.9.200.12   ACCT2

199.9.200.13   ACCT3

199.9.200.14   ACCT4

199.9.200.15   ACCT5

199.9.200.17   ACCT7

The *aliases* are other names by which the system can be referred. Here, me and loopback do the same as localhost; nicholas is the same as SALES1. If an alias is used more than once, the search stops at the first match because the file is searched sequentially.

Configure LMHOSTS Files

The HOSTS file contains the mappings of IP addresses to hostnames, but the LMHOSTS file contains the mappings of IP addresses to Windows NT computer names. When speaking of Windows NT computer names, the inference is to NetBIOS names, or the names that would be used in conjunction with NET USE statements.

An example of the default version of this file follows:

```
# Copyright© 1993-1995 Microsoft Corp.
#
# This is a sample LMHOSTS file used by the Microsoft TCP/IP for
# Windows NT.
#
# This file contains the mappings of IP addresses to NT computernames
# (NetBIOS) names.  Each entry should be kept on an individual line.
# The IP address should be placed in the first column followed by the
# corresponding computername. The address and the comptername
# should be separated by at least one space or tab. The "#" character
# is generally used to denote the start of a comment (see the
# exceptions below).
#
# This file is compatible with Microsoft LAN Manager 2.x TCP/IP
# lmhosts files and offers the following extensions:
#
```

```
#        #PRE
#        #DOM:<domain>
#        #INCLUDE <filename>
#        #BEGIN_ALTERNATE
#        #END_ALTERNATE
#        \0xnn (non-printing character support)
#
# Following any entry in the file with the characters "#PRE" will
# cause the entry to be preloaded into the name cache. By default,
# entries are not preloaded, but are parsed only after dynamic name
# resolution fails.
#
# Following an entry with the "#DOM:<domain>" tag will associate the
# entry with the domain specified by <domain>. This affects how the
# browser and logon services behave in TCP/IP environments. To preload
# the hostname associated with #DOM entry, it is necessary to also add
# a #PRE to the line. The <domain> is always preloaded, although it
# will not be shown when the name cache is viewed.
#
# Specifying "#INCLUDE <filename>" will force the RFC NetBIOS (NBT)
# software to seek the specified <filename> and parse it as if it were
# local. <filename> is generally a UNC-based name, allowing a
# centralized lmhosts file to be maintained on a server.
# It is ALWAYS necessary to provide a mapping for the IP address of
# the server prior to the #INCLUDE. This mapping must use the #PRE
# directive. In addtion, the share "public" in the example below must
# be in the LanManServer list of "NullSessionShares" in order for
# client machines to be able to read the lmhosts file successfully.
# This key is under
# \machine\system\currentcontrolset\services\lanmanserver\parameters\
# nullsessionshares in the registry. Simply add "public" to the list
# found there.
#
# The #BEGIN_ and #END_ALTERNATE keywords allow multiple #INCLUDE
# statements to be grouped together. Any single successful include
# will cause the group to succeed.
#
# Finally, non-printing characters can be embedded in mappings by
# first surrounding the NetBIOS name in quotations, then using the
# \0xnn notation to specify a hex value for a non-printing character.
#
# The following example illustrates all of these extensions:
#
# 102.54.94.97     rhino       #PRE #DOM:networking  #net group's DC
# 102.54.94.102    "appname  \0x14"                  #special app
                                                      server
# 102.54.94.123    popular           #PRE           #source server
# 102.54.94.117    localsrv          #PRE           #needed for the
                                                      include
#
```

```
# #BEGIN_ALTERNATE
# #INCLUDE \\localsrv\public\lmhosts
# #INCLUDE \\rhino\public\lmhosts
# #END_ALTERNATE
#
# In the above example, the "appname" server contains a special
# character in its name, the "popular" and "localsrv" server names are
# preloaded, and the "rhino" server name is specified so it can be
# used to later #INCLUDE a centrally maintained lmhosts file if the
# "localsrv" system is unavailable.
#
# Note that the whole file is parsed including comments on each
# lookup, so keeping the number of comments to a minimum will improve
# performance. Therefore it is not advisable to simply add lmhosts
# file entries onto the end of this file.
```

Once more, the pound sign (#) indicates comments, and the file is read sequentially on each lookup. Therefore, limiting the size of the comment lines at the beginning of the file is highly recommended.

A number of special commands can be used in the file to load entries into a name cache which is scanned on each lookup prior to referencing the file. (By default, entries are not preloaded, but are parsed only after dynamic name resolution fails.) Using these commands will decrease your lookup time and increase system efficiency.

CONFIGURING A WINDOWS NT SERVER TO SUPPORT TCP/IP PRINTING

Printing within Windows NT is a remarkably complex process. The same is true of remote host systems, such as UNIX platforms. The Windows NT and host system print models can interact to a large extent. The following sections describe how clients and servers on Windows NT and remote host systems can interact.

Windows NT Client Printing to a Remote Host System

You can use two methods to print to a remote host from a Windows NT client: using the LPR command from the Windows NT client computer, or creating an LPR printer on a Windows NT client computer.

Using the LPR Command-Line Utility

One of the utilities included with Microsoft TCP/IP is the LPR utility. This program allows a Windows NT computer to send a print job to a remote host printer. The remote host system must be running the LPD daemon, and you must know the name of the remote host and the printer. This utility has the following command-line options:

```
Sends a print job to a network printerUsage: lpr -S server -P
printer [-C class] [-J job] [-o option] [-x] [-d] filename

Options:
      -S server   Name or IP address of the host providing lpd service
      -P printer   Name of the print queue
      -C class    Job classification for use on the burst page
      -J job      Job name to print on the burst page
      -o option   Indicates the type of file (by default assumes a
                  text file)
                  Use "-o l" for binary (for example, postscript)
                  files
      -x          Compatibility with SunOS 4.1.x and prior versions
      -d          Sends data file first
```

Creating an LPR Printer on a Windows NT Computer

By creating an LPR printer on the Windows NT client computer, a higher degree of transparency is provided. If the printer is shared, the Windows NT client can act as a print gateway for other Windows NT computers.

To create an LPR printer under Windows NT, follow these steps:

1. Select Settings/Printers, and then click Add Printer. Select My Computer, because you need to add a new printer port.

2. At this point, select Add Port, and select LPR Port.

3. You are then prompted to provide the hostname (or IP address) of the remote host system, along with the printer name.

4. If you choose to share the printer, any client computer that can print to your Windows NT computer can also print to the LPR printer on the remote host system.

Remote Host Client Printing to a Windows NT Server

Remote hosts can also print to a Windows NT printer, because Windows NT can provide an LPD service. The LPD service (`lpdsvc`) provides the same service as an LPD daemon on a UNIX host. Because it is implemented as a service, it is controlled through Control Panel, Services. This service automatically installs when you opt to install TCP/IP print services.

Remote host systems use different commands for printing. One command that works on most systems is the `lpr` command. A sample command line that would work on most systems is as follows:

```
lpr -s NTSYSTEM -p NTPRINTER filename
```

For the `lpr` command on the remote system, specify the DNS name (or IP address) of your Windows NT system, along with the printer name. Windows NT internally directs the print job to the specified printer.

CONFIGURING SNMP

SNMP (Simple Network Management Protocol) is part of the TCP/IP protocol suite. It corresponds to the Application layer in the Internet Protocol suite.

SNMP enables network administrators to remotely troubleshoot and monitor hubs and routers. Much of SNMP is defined within RFCs 1157 and 1212, although there are many more RFCs on SNMP. SNMP can be found, along with other RFCs, on various Web sites, including `http://ds.internic.net`. You can also do a search on SNMP or RFC to find more specific information related to a specific part of SNMP—for example, on just Ethernet and SNMP.

Using SNMP, you can find out information about these remote devices without having to physically be at the device itself. This can be a very useful tool if understood and used properly. You can find a wide variety of information about these devices, depending on the device itself, of course. Some examples include the following:

- IP address of a router
- Number of open files
- Amount of hard drive space available
- Version number of a Windows NT host

Before you set up SNMP, you need the IP address or hostnames of the systems that will either be the initiators or those that will respond to the requests. Microsoft's SNMP service uses the regular Windows NT hostname resolution, such as HOSTS, DNS, WINS, and LMHOSTS. Therefore if you are using one of these resolution methods, add the correct hostname to IP address resolution for the computers that you are setting up with SNMP.

The types of systems on which you can find data include the following:

- Mainframes
- Gateways and routers
- Hubs and bridges
- Windows NT servers
- LAN Manager servers
- SNMP agents

SNMP uses a distributed architecture design to facilitate its properties. This means that various parts of SNMP are spread throughout the network to complete the task of collecting and processing data to provide remote management.

Because SNMP is a distributed system, you can spread out the management of it in different locations so as not to overtax any one PC, and for multiple management functionality.

SNMPv1 does not provide tiered management. The various versions of SNMPv2 do provide for tiered management. For purposes of the exam, consider the latter.

An SNMP service by Microsoft enables a machine running Windows NT to transfer its current condition to a computer running an SNMP management system. However, this is only the agent side, not the management tools. Various third-party management utilities are available, including the following:

+ IBM NetView

+ Sun Net Manager

+ Hewlett-Packard OpenView

The management utilities are a product of their own. They are *not* included on the Microsoft exam.

SNMP Agents and Management

There are two main parts to SNMP: the agent and the management side.

+ The management station is the centralized location from which you can manage SNMP.

+ The agent station is the piece of equipment from which you are trying to extract data.

The following sections discuss each part.

The SNMP Management System

The management system is the key component for obtaining information from the client. You need at least one management system to even be able to use the SNMP service. The management system is responsible for "asking the questions." As mentioned earlier, there are a certain number of questions it can ask each device, depending on the type of device. The management system is a computer running one of the various software components mentioned earlier.

Certain commands can also be given specifically at the management system. These are generic commands not specific to any type of management system directly:

- `get`   Requests a specific value. It can query how many active sessions are open, for example.

- `get-next`   Requests the next object's value. You, for example, can query a client's ARP cache and then ask for each subsequent value.

- `set`   Changes the value on an object that has the properties of read-write. This command is not often used due to security, and the fact that the majority of objects have a read-only attribute.

Usually, you have only one management system running the SNMP service per group of hosts. This group is known as a *community*. Sometimes, however, you may want to have more. Some of these reasons are discussed in the following list:

- You may want to have multiple management systems inquire different queries to the same agents.

- There might be different management sites for one community.

- As the network grows and becomes more complex, you may need to help differentiate certain aspects of your community.

The SNMP Agent

You have seen so far what the SNMP management side is responsible for and can specifically do. For the most part, the management side is the active component for getting information. The SNMP agent, on the other hand, is responsible for complying with the requests and responding to the SNMP manager accordingly. Generally, the agent is a router, server, or hub. The agent is usually a passive component responding only to a direct query.

In one particular instance, however, the agent is the initiator, acting on its own without a direct query. This special case is called a *trap*. A trap is set up from the management side on the agent. But the management does not need to go to the agent to find out whether the trap information has been tripped. The agent sends an alert to the management system telling it that the event has occurred. Most of the time, the agent is passive except in this one occasion. A trap is similar to a father and son fishing with a net on a stream. The dad sets up the net on the stream. The net has certain sized holes in it, just the right size for catching a certain type and size of fish. The dad then goes downstream to set up more, leaving his son to tend to the net. When the fish comes along, it gets caught in the net and the son runs to tell his father.

The stream is the traffic going through the router. The net is the trap set by the management system. The son is the one responding to the trap and running to tell his father that they have caught the fish without the father having to go back and check on his trap. The special fish that is caught might be an alert that a particular server's hard drive is full or a duplicate IP address. Although this is a rough analogy, it gets the basic idea across. What happens, however, if a spare tire comes down the stream and gets caught in the trap? Sometimes invalid packets can set off the trap without being what you are looking for. These are rare events, and the traps set are very specific in what they are looking for.

Management Information Base

Now that you have learned a little about the management system and agents, you can delve into the different types of query databases.

The data that the management system requests from an agent is contained in a *Management Information Base* (MIB). This is a list of questions that the management system can ask. The list of questions depends on what type of device it is asking. The MIB is the database of information that can be queried against. What specifically can be queried depends on the type of system it is. The MIB defines what type of objects can be available and what type of information is available about the network device.

A variety of MIB databases can be established. The MIB is stored on the SNMP agent and is similar to the Windows NT Registry in its hierarchical structure. These MIBs are available to both the agents and management system as a reference from which both can pull information.

The Microsoft SNMP service supports the following MIB databases:

- Internet MIB II
- LAN Manager MIB II
- DHCP MIB
- WINS MIB

The following sections discuss these databases.

Internet MIB II

Internet MIB II defines 171 objects for fault troubleshooting on the network and configuration analysis. It is defined in RFC 1212, which adds to, and overwrites, the previous version, Internet MIB I.

LAN Manager MIB II

LAN Manager MIB II defines about 90 objects associated with Microsoft Networking, such as the following:

- Shares
- Users
- Logon
- Sessions
- Statistical

The majority of LAN Manager MIB II's objects are set to read-only mode due to the limited security function of SNMP.

DHCP MIB

The DHCP MIB identifies objects that can monitor the DHCP server's actions. It is set up automatically when a DHCP Server service is installed and is called DHCPMIB.DLL. It has 14 objects that can be used for monitoring the DHCP server activity, including items such as the following:

- The number of active leases
- The number of failures
- The number of DHCP discover requests received

WINS MIB

WINS MIB (`WINSMIB.DLL`) is a Microsoft-specific MIB relating directly to the WINS Server service. It is automatically installed when WINS is set up. It monitors WINS server activity and has approximately 70 objects. It checks such items as the number of resolution requests, success and failure, and the date and time of last database replication.

MIB Structure

As mentioned previously, the name space for MIB objects is hierarchical. It is structured in this manner so that each manageable object can be assigned a globally unique name. Certain organizations have the authority to assign the name space for parts of the tree design.

The MIB structure is similar to TCP/IP addresses. You get only one address from the InterNIC and then subnet it according to your needs. You do not have to contact them to inquire of each address assignment. The same applies here. Organizations can assign names without consulting an Internet authority for every specific assignment. For example, the name space assigned to Microsoft's LAN Manager is 1.3.6.1.4.1.77. More recently, Microsoft Corporation has been assigned 1.3.6.1. 4.1.311; any new MIB would then be identified under that branch.

The object identifier in the hierarchy is written as a sequence of labels beginning at the root and ending at the object. It flows down the chart, starting with the International Standards Organization (ISO) and ending with the object MIB II. Labels are separated by periods. The following is an example of this labeling technique:

The object identifier for a MIB II is as follows:

Object Name	Object Number
Iso.org.dod.internet. management.mibii	1.3.6.2.1

The object identifier for LAN Manager MIB II is as follows:

Object Name	Object Number
iso.org.dod.internet.private. enterprise.lanmanger	1.3.6.1.4.77

> **NOTE** The name space used here for the object identifiers is completely separate from that used with UNIX domain names.

Microsoft SNMP Service

The SNMP service is an additional component of Windows NT TCP/IP software. It includes the four supported MIBs; each is a dynamic link library and can be loaded and unloaded as needed. It provides SNMP agent services to any TCP/IP host running SNMP management software. It also performs the following:

- Reports special happenings, such as traps, to multiple hosts

- Responds to requests for information from multiple hosts

- Can be set up on any system running Windows NT and TCP/IP

- Sets up special counters in Performance Monitor that can be used to monitor the TCP/IP performance related to SNMP

- Uses hostnames and IP addresses to recognize which hosts it receives, and requests information

SNMP Architecture

The MIB architecture can be extended to enable developers to create their own MIB libraries, called *extension agents*. Extension agents expand the list of objects that an MIB can report on, making it not only more expansive, but also directed to be specifically related to network setup and devices.

Although the Microsoft SNMP service does not have management software included, it does have a Microsoft Win32 SNMP Manager API that works with the Windows Sockets. The API can then be used by developers to create third-party SNMP management utilities.

The Microsoft SNMP uses User Datagram Protocol (UDP port 161) to send and receive messages, and IP to route messages.

SNMP Communities

A *community* is a group of hosts running the SNMP service to which they all belong. These usually consist of at least one management system and multiple agents. The idea is to logically organize systems into organizational units for better network management.

Communities are called by a *community name*. This name is case sensitive. The default community name is public and generally all hosts belong to it. Also by default, all SNMP agents respond to any request using the community public name. By using unique community names, however, you can provide limited security and segregation of hosts.

Agents neither accept requests nor respond to hosts not from their configured community. Agents can be members of multiple communities at the same time, but they must be explicitly configured as such. This enables them to respond to different SNMP managers from various communities.

Security

There really is no established security with SNMP. The data is not encrypted, and there is no setup to stop someone from accessing the network, discovering the community names and addresses used, and sending fake requests to agents.

A major reason most MIBs are read-only is so that unauthorized changes cannot be made. The best security you can have is to use unique community names. Choose Send Authentication Trap and specify a Trap Destination, and stipulate Only Accept SNMP Packets from these Hosts.

You might also set up traps that let you know whether the agents receive requests from communities or addresses not specified. This way, you can track down unauthorized SNMP activity.

Installing and Configuring SNMP

The SNMP service can be installed for the following reasons:

- ♦ You want to monitor TCP/IP with Performance Monitor.

◆ You want to monitor a Windows NT-based system with a third-party application.

◆ You want to set up your computer as an SNMP agent.

You perform the following steps to install the SNMP service, assuming you already have TCP/IP installed and set up. These steps also assume you have administrative privileges to install and utilize SNMP.

1. Click Start, Settings, Control Panel.

2. Double-click Network to bring up the Network Properties dialog box.

3. On the Network Settings dialog box, click Add.

4. Click the Services tab and click Add.

5. The Select Network Service dialog box appears.

6. Click SNMP Service, and then click OK.

7. Specify the location of the Windows NT distribution files.

8. After the files are copied, the SNMP Service Configuration dialog box appears. Table 2.7 shows the parameters that need to be configured.

TABLE 2.7

SNMP CONFIGURATION OPTIONS.

Parameter	Definition
Community Name	The community name to which traps are sent. Remember, it is public by default. There must be a management system in that community to receive and request information.
Trap Destination	The IP addresses of hosts to which you want the SNMP service to send traps. Note that you can use IP addresses, hostnames (as long as they are resolved properly), and IPX addresses.

9. Now choose OK to close the SNMP Properties dialog box. Then choose Close to exit the Network Properties dialog box. When prompted, restart your computer.

SNMP Security Parameters

You can set several options that affect the security of the SNMP agent. By default the agent will respond to any manager using community name "public." Because this can be inside or outside your organization, you should at the very least change the community name.

Table 2.8 describes the available options.

TABLE 2.8

SECURITY OPTIONS FOR THE **SNMP** AGENT.

Parameter	Description
Send Authentication Trap	Sends information back to the trap initiator responding that the trap failed. This could be because of an incorrect community name or because the host is not specified for service.
Accepted Community Names	When a manager sends a query, a community name is included; this is a list of community names that the agent will respond to.
Accept SNMP Packets from Any Host	Responds to any query from any management system in any community.
Only Accept SNMP Packets from These Hosts	Responds to only the hosts listed.

SNMP Agent

In some cases you will configure other aspects of the SNMP agent. These set the type of devices that you will monitor and who is responsible for the system.

The following options are available on this screen:

- ◆ The contact name of the person you want to be alerted about conditions on this station—generally, this is the user of the computer.

- ◆ The location is a descriptive field for the computer to help keep track of the system sending the alert.

- The last part of the screen identifies the types of connections/ devices this agent will monitor. These include the following:

  - **Physical.** You are managing physical devices such as repeaters or hubs.

  - **Applications.** Set if the Windows NT computer uses an application that uses TCP/IP. You should check this box every time, because just by using SNMP you should have TCP/IP setup.

  - **Datalink/Subnetwork.** For managing a bridge.

  - **Internet.** Causes the Windows NT computer to act as an IP gateway and monitors the router functionality of the Windows NT server.

  - **End-to-End.** Causes the Windows NT computer to act as an IP host. You should check this box every time because you are most likely an IP host.

Any errors with SNMP will be recorded in the System Log. The log records any SNMP activity. Use Event Viewer to look at the errors and to find the problem and possible solutions.

Using the SNMP Utility

The SNMP utility does not come with Windows NT. It is included in the Windows NT Resource Kit and called SNMPUTIL.EXE. Basically, it is a command-line management system utility. It checks that the SNMP service has been set up and is working correctly. You can also use it to make command calls. You cannot do full SNMP management from this utility but, as you will see, you would not want to because of the complex syntax.

The following is the general syntax structure:

```
snmputil command gent community object_identifier_(OID)
```

You can use the following commands:

- walk   Moves through the MIB branch identified by what you have placed in the object_identifer.

- get   Returns the value of the item specified by the object_identifier.

- getnext   Returns the value of the next object after the one specified by the get command.

To find out the time the WINS Server service began, for example, providing WINS is installed and the SNMP agent is running, you query the WINS MIB with the following command:

```
c:\>snmputil getnext localhost public .1.3.6.1.4.1.311.1.1.1.1
```

In this example, the first part refers to the Microsoft branch: .1.3.6.1.4.1.311 (or iso.org.dod.internet.private.enterprise.microsoft). The last part of the example refers to the specific MIB and object you are querying—.1.1.1.1 (or .software.Wins.Par.ParWinsStartTime). A returned value might appear like the following:

```
Value = OCTET STRING - 01:17:22 on 11:23:1997.<0xa>
```

What SNMP Is Really Doing

The following example tracks a sample of SNMP traffic between a manager and an agent. Remember, in real life you will use management software (such as HP's OpenView that will enable you to see the MIBs and query without knowing all the numbers).

1. The SNMP management system makes a request of an agent using the agent's IP address or hostname.

   1. Request sent by the application to UDP port 161.

   2. Hostname resolved to an IP address, if hostname was used, using hostname resolution methods: localhost, HOSTS file, DNS, WINS, broadcast, LMHOSTS file.

2. SNMP packet gets set up with the listed information inside, and routes the packet on the agent's UDP port 161:

   1. The command for the objects: get, get-next, set.

   2. The community name and any other specified data.

3. An SNMP agent gets the packet and puts it into its buffer.

   1. The community name is checked for validity. If it is not correct or is corrupted, the packet is rejected.

2. If the community name checks out, the agent checks to see whether the originating hostname or IP address is correct as well. If not, it is thrown out.

3. The inquiry is then passed to the correct DLL as described in the preceding section on MIBs.

4. The object identifier gets mapped to the specific API and that call gets made.

5. The DLL sends the data to the agent.

4. The SNMP packet is given to the SNMP manager with the requested information.

WHAT IS IMPORTANT TO KNOW

The following bullets summarize the chapter and accentuate the key concepts to memorize for the exam:

- IP addresses are 32-bit binary numbers, most often written in four octets of decimal numbers. An example of an address in decimal form would be 192.14.200.2, or in binary form:

  `11000000.00001110.11001000.00000010`

- The following table illustrates binary to decimal converting:

Binary	1	1	1	1	1	1	1	1
Decimal	128	64	32	16	8	4	2	1

- Within the octets, the first set of number identifies the class of network; the last set identifies the host. Those in between essentially form the network ID. There are three possible classes:

Address	Class	Number of Possible Hosts	Default Subnet Mask
01–126	A	16,777,214	255.0.0.0
128–191	B	65,534	255.255.0.0
192–223	C	254	255.255.255.0

- Address 127 is reserved for a "loopback" address.

- The subnet mask, however, enables you to decrease the number of hosts and increase the number of sites (subnets) that you can have. The tradeoff is shown in the following table.

VALID SUBNET ADDRESSES

Subnet Address	Additional Bits Required	Maximum Number of Subnets	Maximum Number of Hosts C Network	Maximum Number of Hosts B Network	Maximum Number of Hosts A Network
0	0	0	254	65,534	16,777,214
192	2	2	62	16,382	4,194,302
224	3	6	30	8,190	2,097,150
240	4	14	14	4,094	1,048,574
248	5	30	6	2,046	524,286
252	6	62	2	1,022	262,142
254	7	126	Invalid	510	131,070
255	8	254	Invalid	254	65,534

◆ IP addresses can be manually assigned to every machine on your network, or a DHCP server can issue them. DHCP—an extension of the BOOTP protocol (for diskless workstations)—eliminates configuration problems and simplifies IP administration by issuing clients an address from a pool of addresses (called a scope).

◆ The issuing of a DHCP address is called leasing, and the address is given for a period of time called a lease period. Approximately halfway through that period, the client will try to renegotiate the lease to keep it longer. If the lease expires, the client will try to get another one from that or another DHCP server. A DHCP server cannot be a DHCP client (it must have its own static IP address, subnet mask, and default gateway address), and it must have at lease one scope.

◆ Multiple DHCP servers should have portions of each other's scopes so that they can serve their clients in the event the other server is down.

◆ Client reservation means that a DHCP client will always get the same IP address from the DHCP server.

◆ The HOSTS file is a static, ASCII-readable file that can be used to map hostnames (common system names) to IP addresses for address resolution. The LMHOSTS file is similar, but used to map NetBIOS names (MS computer names) to IP addresses. The LMHOSTS file (which should at a minimum contain each domain controller on the local domain and the PDC of every remote domain) also enables you to choose to load portions of the file in memory so that the file does not need to be read each time a name resolution takes place. Both HOSTS and LMHOSTS are static files. DNS and WINS servers can perform these same functions, with WINS being a dynamic version.

◆ DNS servers map hostnames given in the format of FQDNs (fully qualified domain names, such as iquest.net) to IP addresses. There should be two DNS servers in each zone: one primary and one secondary.

◆ WINS servers map NetBIOS names to IP addresses and make the need for LMHOSTS files unnecessary. WINS servers work with Microsoft clients, but cannot integrate with Macintosh clients (for which you would need DNS).

◆ TCP/IP printing can take place between UNIX and Windows NT hosts. The UNIX host can send print jobs to the Windows NT server, or the Windows NT server can send print jobs to the UNIX host.

◆ SNMP allows events to be trapped and sent across a network for network management. To do so, the SNMP service must be installed on the server, and the trap messages must be configured for a destination they are to be sent to.

OBJECTIVES

Connectivity Objectives:

▶ Given a scenario, identify which utility to use to connect to a TCP/IP-based UNIX host

▶ Configure a Remote Access Service (RAS) server and Dial-Up Networking for use on a TCP/IP network

▶ Configure and support browsing in a multiple-domain routed network

CHAPTER 3

Connectivity

CONNECTIVITY

Windows NT includes TCP/IP utilities that provide many options for connecting to foreign systems using the TCP/IP protocol. In cases where it is impossible to connect to remote host systems by using Microsoft networking, these utilities provide a variety of network services.

These utilities enable Microsoft clients to perform remote execution, data transfer, printing services, and much more. The following sections examine these utilities in more detail.

Remote Execution Utilities

At A Glance: Remote Execution

Utility	Usefulness
REXEC	Remotely start a process
RSH	Remotely start a shell
Telnet	Begin an interactive session

Windows NT includes a series of remote execution utilities that enable a user to execute commands on a UNIX host system. These utilities provide varying degrees of security. Note that varying subsets of these utilities are available with Windows NT Server and Workstation. The Resource Kit includes all these utilities.

> **NOTE**
>
> All of these utilities that require passwords transmit the password as plain text. Unlike the Windows NT logon sequence, the logon information is not encrypted before being transmitted. Any unscrupulous user with access to network monitoring software could intercept the username and password for the remote host. If you use the same username and password on the remote host and on your Windows NT system, your Windows NT account could be compromised.

Windows NT provides three remote execution utilities. The following sections discuss each of these in more detail.

The REXEC Utility

REXEC enables a user to start a process on a remote host system, using a username and password for authentication. If the host authenticates the user, REXEC starts the specified process and terminates. Command-line options are as follows:

```
D:\>rexec /?
Runs commands on remote hosts running the REXEC service. REXEC
authenticates the user name on the remote host before executing the
specified command.

REXEC host [-l username] [-n] command

   host            Specifies the remote host on which to run command
   -l username     Specifies the user name on the remote host
   -n              Redirects the input of REXEC to NULL
   command         Specifies the command to run
```

You can specify the remote host as an IP address or as a hostname. After REXEC connects to the specified host, it prompts for a password. If the host authenticates the user, the specified command is executed, and the REXEC utility exits. REXEC can be used for command-line programs—interactive programs such as text editors would not be usable with REXEC.

This utility provides a reasonable degree of security because the remote host authenticates the user. The down side is that the username and password are not encrypted prior to transmission.

The RSH Utility

RSH provides much the same function as REXEC, but user authentication is handled differently. Unlike with REXEC, you do not need to specify a username. The only validation performed by RSH is to verify that the username is in a hidden file on the UNIX system (the .rhosts file). If the remote host is configured to allow any user to use RSH, no username needs to be provided.

NOTE   On UNIX systems, the .rhosts and the hosts.equiv files are used for authentication. Because these files can be used to grant access to either all users on a computer or some users on a computer, be careful with their use.

It is extremely unlikely that a system would be configured in this way; however, the RSH utility provides the logged-on username if no username is provided. This can be overridden if desired. What follows are the Runs commands on remote hosts running the RSH service:

```
C:\>rsh /?
rsh: remote terminal session not supported

Runs commands on remote hosts running the RSH service.

RSH host [-l username] [-n] command

   host          Specifies the remote host on which to run command.
   -l username   Specifies the user name to use on the remote host.
                 If omitted, the logged on user name is used.
   -n            Redirects the input of RSH to NULL.
   command       Specifies the command to run.
```

After you start RSH, it connects to the remote system's RSH daemon (UNIX-speak for a service). The RSH daemon ensures that the username is in the .rhosts file on the remote host, and if authentication succeeds, the specified command is executed.

Like REXEC, RSH provides a certain degree of security insofar as the remote host validates the access.

The Telnet Utility

Telnet is defined in RFC 854 as a remote terminal emulation protocol. It provides terminal emulation for DEC VT100, DEC VT52, and TTY terminals. Telnet uses the connection-oriented services of the TCP/IP protocol for communications.

The remote host system must be running a Telnet daemon. After you start Telnet, you can connect to a remote host by using the Connect/Remote System option. You are prompted for the information required for a Telnet session:

- **Hostname.** The IP address or hostname of the remote host

- **Port.** One of the ports supported by the Telnet application—telnet, daytime, echo, quotd or chargen

- **Terminal type.** One of VT100, ANSI (TTY), or VT52

As with REXEC and RSH, Telnet provides some security, insofar as access to the remote system requires a username and password.

Telnet does not encrypt any information whatsoever. The password and username are sent as clear text, as is your entire terminal session. If you are using Telnet to perform remote administration on a UNIX system, your root password could be intercepted by an unscrupulous user.

Data Transfer Utilities

At A Glance: Data Transfer

Utility	Usefulness
RCP	Remotely copy a file with few options
FTP	Remotely copy a file with many options
TFTP	Same as FTP only unattended and with few options
HTTP and Web browsers	Interactively—and visually—copy files

Several utilities are available to allow file transfer between Windows NT systems and remote hosts. As with remote execution utilities, the same caveat applies when dealing with usernames and passwords. These utilities are examined in greater detail in the following sections.

RCP

The RCP command copies files from a Windows NT system to a remote host, and handles authentication in much the same way as RSH. To communicate with the RCP daemon on the remote system, the username provided must be in the remote host's .rhosts file. The following command-line options are available:

The current user account is used when issuing the RCP command. If the current user logged on to the Windows NT system doesn't have a corresponding account in the .rhosts file, access won't be granted. Also, in many cases, the RCP daemon requires the RSHD daemon as well at the UNIX server.

```
C:\>rcp ?

Copies files to and from computer running the RCP service.

RCP [-a | -b] [-h] [-r] [host][.user:]source [host][.user:]
path\destination
```

-a	Specifies ASCII transfer mode. This mode converts the EOL characters to a carriage return for UNIX and a carriage return/line feed for personal computers. This is the default transfer mode.
-b	Specifies binary image transfer mode.
-h	Transfers hidden files.
-r	Copies the contents of all subdirectories; destination must be a directory.
host	Specifies the local or remote host. If host is specified as an IP address, you must specify the user.
.user:	Specifies a user name to use, rather than the current user name.
source	Specifes the files to copy.
path\destination	Specifies the path relative to the logon directory on the remote host. Use the escape characters (\ , ", or ') in remote paths to use wildcard characters on the remote host.

As with RSH, RCP provides security by matching the username provided with a username in the .rhosts file. Unlike RSH, RCP does not prompt for a password.

FTP

FTP, or the File Transfer Protocol, provides a simple but robust mechanism for copying files to or from remote hosts using the connection-oriented services of TCP/IP. FTP is a component of the TCP/IP protocol, and is defined in RFC 959. To use FTP to send or receive files, the following requirements must be met:

- The client computer must have FTP client software, such as the FTP client included with Windows NT.

- The user must have a username and password on the remote system. In some cases, a username of *anonymous* with no password suffices.

- The remote system must be running an FTP daemon.

◆ Your system and the remote system must be running the TCP/IP protocol.

You can use FTP in either a command-line mode or in a command-interpreter mode. The following options are available from the command line:

```
Transfers files to and from a computer running an FTP server service
(sometimes called a daemon). Ftp can be used interactively.

FTP [-v] [-d] [-i] [-n] [-g] [-s:filename] [-a] [-w:windowsize]
[host]
```

```
-v              Suppresses display of remote server responses.
-n              Suppresses auto-login upon initial connection.
-i              Turns off interactive prompting during multiple
                file transfers.
-d              Enables debugging.
-g              Disables filename globbing (see GLOB command).
-s:filename     Specifies a text file containing FTP commands; the
                commands will automatically run after FTP starts.
-a              Use any local interface when binding data
                connection.
-w:buffersize   Overrides the default transfer buffer size of 4096.
host            Specifies the hostname or IP address of the remote
                host to connect to.
```

If you use FTP in a command-interpreter mode, some of the more frequently used options are as follows:

◆ open   Specifies the remote system to which you connect.

◆ close   Disconnects from a remote system.

◆ ls   Obtains a directory listing on a remote system, much like the dir command in DOS. Note that the ls -l command provides file size and time stamps.

◆ cd   Changes directories on the remote system. This command functions in much the same way as the DOS cd command.

◆ lcd   Changes directories on the local system. This command also functions in much the same way as the DOS cd command.

◆ binary   Instructs FTP to treat all files transferred as binary.

◆ ascii   Instructs FTP to treat all files transferred as text.

◆ get   Copies a file from the remote host to your local computer.

◆ put   Copies a file from your local computer to the remote host.

◆ debug   Turns on debugging commands that can be useful in diagnosing problems.

Because remote host systems typically are based on UNIX, you encounter a number of nuances relating to UNIX, such as the following:

◆ The UNIX operating system uses the forward slash in path references, not the backward slash. In Windows NT, the filename `\WINNT40\README.TXT` would be `/WINNT40/README.TXT`.

◆ UNIX is case sensitive at all times—the command `get MyFile` and the command `get MYFILE` are not the same. Usernames and passwords are also case sensitive.

◆ UNIX treats wildcard characters, such as the asterisk and the question mark, differently. The `glob` command within FTP changes how wildcard characters in local filenames are treated.

You can also install a Windows NT FTP server, which can provide FTP file transfer services to other systems.

TFTP

Trivial File Transfer Protocol is the connectionless communication feature (UDP) of TCP/IP. TFTP provides similar functions as FTP. Unlike FTP, TFTP uses the connectionless communication features of TCP/IP. The features available in FTP are complex; those in TFTP are simpler. Unlike FTP, TFTP can be used only in a command-line mode—no command-interpreter mode is available. For command-line mode, the following options are available:

```
C:\>tftp /?

Transfers files to and from a remote computer running the TFTP
service.

TFTP [-i] host [GET | PUT] source [destination]

     -i              Specifies binary image transfer mode (also called
                     octet). In binary image mode the file is moved
                     literally, byte by byte. Use this mode when
                     transferring binary files.
```

```
host              Specifies the local or remote host.
GET               Transfers the file destination on the remote host
                  to the file source on the local host.
PUT               Transfers the file source on the local host to
                  the file destination on the remote host.
source            Specifies the file to transfer.
destination       Specifies where to transfer the file.
```

There is no TFTP server included with Windows NT; however, third-party TFTP servers are available.

Why use TFTP rather than FTP? Some platforms don't support FTP, notably devices that require firmware updates. Routers typically require the use of TFTP to update firmware information, such as micro-kernels.

> **NOTE** Many network devices such as routers and concentrators use an operating system stored in firmware. As such, upgrades are usually handled by using TFTP—the process is known as a firmware update.

HTTP and Web Browsers

The explosive growth of the Internet in recent years is largely due to its flexibility. One of the Internet's building blocks is the Hypertext Transfer Protocol, HTTP. It defines a way of transferring hypertext data across TCP/IP networks. The hypertext data is formatted in HTML (Hypertext Markup Language). An HTML document can have a link to any other HTML document. This enables Web page designers to include text, audio files, graphics, and video within the same page.

HTTP and HTML are comprehensive standards, and a full discussion is outside the scope of this exam. However, a discussion of Web browsers is in order. Web browsing software is used to download and view HTML documents using the HTTP protocol, but can also be used to download documents using FTP, Gopher, or other protocols.

Unlike the other file transfer utilities mentioned in this section, HTTP does not use a username or password. Information on the World Wide Web is typically destined for access by any user, and therefore usually does not require authentication.

Many Web browsers are available; however, they all function in much the same way.

RAS SERVERS AND DIAL-UP NETWORKING

Essentially, RAS enables users to connect to your network and act as if they are directly connected to it. There are two main components to RAS: the server (Remote Access Service) and the client (Dial-Up Networking). The RAS server can be Windows NT Server, Workstation, or Windows 95 (with the Plus! Pack), and will enable users to connect to the network from a remote location. The Microsoft RAS server will always use the PPP (Point-to-Point Protocol) when users are dialing in to the network as the line protocol.

In addition to connecting to a Microsoft RAS server, Windows Dial-Up Networking can connect with other forms of RAS (other dial-in servers such as UNIX terminal servers) using either SLIP (Serial Line Internet Protocol) or PPP. All that is required is a communications device.

PPP Versus SLIP

When clients connect to a server by using a modem, they must do so through something other than the frames that normally traverse a network (such as IEEE802.3). Some other transport method is needed. In the case of dial-up servers (or terminal servers), there are two popular line protocols. Serial Line Internet Protocol (SLIP) is used frequently in UNIX implementations. SLIP is the older of the two line protocols and is geared directly for TCP/IP communications. Windows NT can use the services of a SLIP server. However, it does not provide a SLIP server. Microsoft's RAS server uses Point-to-Point Protocol (PPP) because SLIP requires a static IP address and does not provide facility for secured logon (passwords are sent as clear text).

PPP was developed as a replacement for SLIP and provides several different advantages over the earlier protocol. PPP can automatically provide the client computer with an IP address and other configuration. It provides a secure logon and has the capability to transport protocols other than TCP/IP (such as AppleTalk, IPX, and NetBEUI).

There are two important extensions to the PPP protocol. These extensions are the Multilink Protocol (MP) and Point-to-Point Tunneling Protocol (PPTP). Windows NT supports both of these extensions to the original PPP protocol.

Multilink Protocol allows a client station to connect to a remote server by using more than one physical connection. This capability provides better throughput over standard modems. You will, however, need multiple phone lines and modems to enable this protocol. This can be an easy interim solution if you need to temporarily connect to offices and don't have time or budget to set up a leased line or other similar connection.

Point-to-Point Tunneling Protocol facilitates secure connections across the Internet. Using PPTP, users can connect to any Internet service provider (ISP) and can use the ISP's network as a gateway to connect to the office network. During the session initialization, the client and server negotiate a 40-bit session key. This key will then be used to encrypt all packets that will be sent back and forth over the Internet. The packets will be encapsulated into PPP packets as the data. PPTP is predominantly used in a virtual private network.

Modems

Modems have been around for years and provide a cheap and relatively reliable method of communication over the Public Switched Telephone Network (PSTN). Installing a modem in a computer is a straightforward process. This section covers the configuring and testing of modems and what can go wrong with them.

There are two main types of modems: internal and external. Internal modems are slightly cheaper, but require you to open the computer to install it and will require a free interrupt (IRQ). If you elect to go with an external modem, you should check that you have a communications (COM) port available, and that it will be able to handle the speed of the modem.

Ports

Whether you have an internal or external modem, you will need to install the modem as a communications port. Normally, this is no problem;

however, there are cases (notable with internal modems) where you will need to change the settings for the port. This can also cause problems with an external modem; if you cannot talk to the modem, you should also check the port settings.

To check the port settings, open the Control Panel (Start, Settings, Control Panel) and double-click on the Ports icon. This brings up the Ports dialog box.

Select the port that you wish to check the settings for and click Settings. Another dialog box will appear showing you the settings for the port.

Five settings are available. These are general settings, however, and only deal with applications that don't set these parameters. The following list provides a brief description of the parameters.

- **Baud Rate.** This is the rate at which the data will flow. Serial communications moves your data one bit at a time. In addition, for every byte that is sent, there are (normally) 4 bits of overhead. Therefore, to find the transfer rate in bytes, divide this number by 12.

- **Data Bits.** Not all systems will use 8 bits to store one character. Some systems use only 7. This setting will allow the computer to adjust the number of bits used in the transfer.

- **Parity.** Parity is used to verify that information being transferred is getting across the line successfully. The parity can be Even, Odd, Mark, or Space—or you can use No Parity (which is what is normally used).

- **Stop Bits.** In some systems, these are used to mark the end of the transmission.

- **Flow Control.** This option can be set to XON/XOFF, Hardware, or None. Flow control, as the name implies, is used to control the movement of the data between the modem and your computer. Hardware flow control uses Request to Send (RTS) and Clear to Send (CTS). The system will send a signal through the RTS wire in the cable, telling the modem it wants to send. After the modem has finished transmitting what is in its buffer and has space, it will signal the computer that it can send the data using the CTS wire. XON/XOFF is a software form of flow control where the modem will send XON (ASCII character 17) when it is ready for data from the computer, and XOFF (ASCII character 19) when it has too much data. (This type of flow control does not work well with binary transfers, because the XON and XOFF characters can be part of a file.)

In most cases, you can ignore these settings. They will be set and reset by the application that you will use. If you click the Advanced button, however, you will find some settings of which you need to be aware.

NOTE
If you make changes in this dialog box, the system will no longer be a standard system. Many applications can be affected if you make changes here.

The options that you can set here will affect all applications that use the communications port. The following list provides an overview of the options that you can set:

- **COM Port Number.** Here you will select the port that you wish to configure.

- **Base I/O Port Address.** When information is received from a hardware (physical) device, the information is placed in RAM by the BIOS. This setting changes where in RAM you will place the information. Unless your hardware requires a different address, do not change this.

- **Interrupt Request Line (IRQ).** After the BIOS places the information in RAM, it will alert the CPU to the presence of the data. This is done using a hardware interrupt. Interrupts are a prime source for conflicts and one of the main causes of system failures. As stated previously, unless your hardware requires it, do not change this option.

- **FIFO Enabled.** This will enable the on-chip buffering available in 16550 UARTs. Note that on some of the older revisions of the 16550, there were problems with random data loss when using FIFO. If you are experiencing unexplained problems, try disabling FIFO. With FIFO enabled, there can be a slight increase in throughput.

When you are attempting to troubleshoot a serial problem, you should always check that these settings are correct. Making sure that the port options are correct will enable you to communicate with the modem.

Configuring Modems

There are many means by which users can connect to the office network or to the Internet. The most common method is to connect by using a modem. This section deals with installing and troubleshooting modems.

Installing a Modem

Installing a modem is simple in Windows NT. After the hardware is connected, go to the Control Panel and double-click the Modems icon. If no modem is installed, the Modem Installer will start automatically. This wizard will step you through the installation of the modem. If you have a modem already, you will need to click Add.

If you have already used the installer once and it could not detect the modem, you probably have one of two problems: Either the modem cannot be detected and you will have to install it manually, or the system can't see the modem, in which case you should check the port. If you need to install the modem manually, check the box Don't detect my modem, I will select it from a list. This brings up a screen that enables you to select the modem.

After you have the modem installed, you can check modem properties by using the Modems icon in the Control Panel. When you open the icon, you will see a dialog box that lists all the available modems.

From here you can check and set the properties for the modems installed in the computer. Several different options are of interest. Select Modem, Properties to bring up the General properties for the modem.

You need to set only a couple of settings on the General tab. The following list provides the properties and what you should check for.

- ◆ **Port.** Displays the port that the modem was installed on. You should check this if the hardware has been changed, and also check the port settings if the modem is not working.

- ◆ **Speaker Volume.** Determines the volume of the speaker during the connection phase. This should be turned up to enable you to verify that you are getting a dial tone and that the other end is in fact a modem.

- **Maximum Speed.** Sets the fastest rate that the system will attempt to communicate with the modem. If this is set too high, some modems will not be able to respond to the system. If this is the case, try lowering the rate.

- **Only connect at this speed.** Instruct the modem that it must connect to the remote site at the same speed you set for communications with the modem. If the other site cannot support this speed, you will not be able to communicate.

The other tab in the Modem Properties dialog box is the Connections tab. This tab deals with the way that the modem will connect. There are a couple of settings that you can check here when you attempt to troubleshoot modems.

There are two sections for Connection properties. These are the Connection preferences and the Call preferences. The Connection preferences are the communications settings (which were discussed earlier in the Ports section). These settings will override the port settings. The three items from the Call preferences are as follows:

- **Wait for tone before dialing.** Normally this should be selected; however, there are some phone systems in the world that do not have a dial tone. Make sure that this is set correctly for your area.

- **Cancel the call if not connected within.** This option sets the maximum amount of time that it will take for the call to be established. If the line conditions are very bad, you may have to bump up this number to allow the modem more time to establish a connection and negotiate the line speed that will be used.

- **Disconnect a call if idle for more than.** This option enables you to set the maximum amount of time that a call can sit idle. Windows NT 4 provides an autodial service. This will automatically call back a server if you have become disconnected and then attempt to use a network service. This feature reduces the amount of time a user will tie up a line and can prevent massive long-distance charges. The users need to be made aware of the time limit, however. If they are required to enter information for a terminal logon, they should be told, because otherwise the terminal screen will appear unexpectedly when the system tries to autoconnect.

  And if the user is not aware and is using an ISP for email, he or she needs to be told that setting the email program to check for new mail at periodic intervals will cause the system to automatically dial the server and check—possibly using up the allowed number of hours with their ISP.

The final thing to check when doing modem configurations and when troubleshooting is the Advanced Connection information. These settings can adversely affect communications.

You will want to verify a few options in the advanced modem options. The following list describes the different options and things that you should look for:

- **Use Error Control.** This will turn on or off some common settings that affect the way the system will deal with the modem. The specific options are as follows:

  - **Required to Connect.** This will force the modem to establish that an error-correcting protocol (such as MNP class 5) be used before the connection will be established. This should not be used by default. If the modem on the other end of the connection does not support the same class of error detection, the connection will fail.

  - **Compress Data.** This will tell the modem to use data compression. Microsoft RAS will automatically implement software compression between the client and workstation if both are Microsoft. This option should be turned on only if you will be talking to a non-Microsoft server; otherwise, the modem will try to compress data that is already compressed.

  - **Use Cellular Protocol.** Lets the system know that the modem you will be using is a cellular modem.

- **Use Flow Control.** This will override the flow control setting for the port. Both types of flow control are available. In most cases, you should choose to use hardware flow control. Using flow control will enable you to set the speed of the transmission between the computer and the modem. The choices are XON/XOFF and hardware.

- **Modulation Type.** This will enable users to set the type of frequency modulation for the modem to that of the phone system they are using. The modulation is either standard or Bell, and deals with the sound frequency that will be used for the send and receive channels for the communicating hosts.

♦ **Extra Settings.** This will enable you to enter extra modem initialization strings that you wish to have sent to the modem whenever a call is placed.

♦ **Record a Log File.** This probably is the most important setting from the perspective of troubleshooting. This will enable you to record a file that will then enable you to see the communications that take place between the modem and the computer during the connection phase of the communications.

Dialing Properties

From the Modem Properties dialog box, you can also click the Dialing Properties button. This enables you to configure the system so that it knows where you are dialing from. This information is used in conjunction with Dial-up Networking to allow the system to determine whether your call is long distance, if it should use a calling card, how to disable the call-waiting feature, and so on.

When you click the Dialing Properties dialog box, a dialog box will appear. You can create a single location or multiple locations.

Several different items are available, and if this information is not set correctly, the client computer may attempt to connect to a local server as a long-distance call (or vice versa). The following list describes the entries that you can make here:

♦ **I am dialing from.** This is the name of the location. To create a new entry, click the New button, and enter a name in this box. The user will need to know which entry to use when dialing.

♦ **The area code is.** The computer can use this information to determine whether it is required to dial the number as a long-distance number or a local number.

♦ **I am in.** Sets the country code for dialing purposes so that the system can connect to international numbers.

♦ **To access an outside line, first dial.** Set the access code for dialing out from a location. There is an entry for local calls and one for long distance.

- **Dial by using calling card.** Enables you to have the computer enter the calling-card information to make the connection with the remote host. Click the Change button to review or change calling-card information.

- **This location has call waiting.** The call-waiting tone will often cause a connection to be dropped. You can enter the information here to disable call waiting for the location that you are dialing from.

- **The phone system at this location uses.** Enables you to select whether the system that you are calling from will use tone or pulse dialing.

If there are problems trying to connect, you should always verify the information in the Dialing Properties.

Other Communications Technologies

As stated previously, there are other ways in which you can connect to the Windows NT Server. There are two principal ways that you can connect: ISDN (Integrated Services Digital Network) and X.25 (which is a wide area networking standard).

ISDN

One of the most common choices for connecting remote sites or even for individuals or small organizations to connect to the Internet, ISDN is becoming a very common method of communication.

Whereas a standard phone line can handle transmission speeds of up to 9,600 bits per second (compression makes up the rest of the transmission speed in most modems, such as those that transfer data at 33.6Kbps), ISDN transmits at speeds of 64 or 128 kilobits per second, depending on whether it is one or two channels.

ISDN is a point-to-point communications technology, and special equipment must be installed at both the server and at the remote site. You will need to install an ISDN card (which will act as a network card) in place of a modem in both computers. As you will have guessed by now, ISDN connections are more expensive than modems. If there is a requirement for higher speed, however, the cost will most likely be justified. Be aware that in some parts of the world, this is a metered service: The more you use, the more you pay.

X.25

The X.25 protocol is not an actual device, but rather a standard for connections. It is packet-switching communication protocol that was designed for WAN connectivity.

RAS supports X.25 connections using packet assemblers/disassemblers (PADs) and X.25 smart cards. These will be installed as a network card, just like ISDN.

Dial-In Permissions

As with all other aspects of Windows NT, security is built in to the RAS server. At a minimum, a user will require an account in Windows NT, and that account will need to have dial-in permissions set.

You can grant users dial-in permission by using the User Manager (or User Manager for Domains) or through the Remote Access Admin program. If you are having problems connecting to the RAS server, this is one of the first things you will want to check. Following are the steps to set or check dial-in permissions:

1. Open the User Manager (Start, Programs, Administrative Tools, User Manager).

2. Select the account that you are using and choose User, Properties. You will see the User Properties sheet.

3. Click the Dial In button. This brings up the Dial In Permissions dialog box.

4. Check the Grant Dial In Permission to User box to allow the user to dial in.

You can also check the permissions from the Remote Access Admin utility. To do so, follow these steps:

1. Start the Remote Access Admin (Start, Programs, Administrative tools, RAS Admin).

2. From the menu, choose Users, Permissions.

3. In the Permissions dialog box, select the user and ensure that dial-in permission is granted.

You probably noticed in both of the methods that there was a setting for Call Back. Call Back means that the server will do just that, call the user back. This can be set to one of the following three options:

- **No Call Back.** This is the default, and means that the Call Back feature is disabled.

- **Set by Caller.** Using this option, the user can set the number that should be used when the server calls back. This is useful if you have a large number of users who will be traveling and wish to centralize long distance.

- **Preset To.** This enhances the security of the network by forcing the user to be at a set phone number. If this is set, the user can call from that one location only.

PPP Problems

As mentioned earlier, Windows NT acts as a PPP server. This means that the client station and the server will undergo a negotiation during the initial phase of the call.

During the negotiation, the client and server will decide on the protocol that will be used, and the parameters for the protocol. If there are problems attempting to connect, you may want to set up PPP logging to actually watch the negotiation between the server and client.

This is set up on the server by changing the Logging option under the following:

```
HKEY_LOCAL_MACHINE\SYSTEM\CurrentControlSet\Services\RASMAN\PPP\
Parameters
```

The log file will be in the system32\RAS directory and, like the modem log, can be viewed using any text editor.

Some of the problems that you may encounter include the following:

- You must ensure that the protocol you are requesting from the RAS client is available on the RAS server. There must be at least one common protocol or the connection will fail.

- If you are using NetBEUI, ensure that the name you are using on the RAS client is not in use on the network that you are attempting to connect to.

- If you are attempting to connect using TCP/IP, the RAS server must be configured to provide you with an address.

Dial-Up Networking

This section goes through the configuration of the client computer and points out important areas. The component used to connect to the RAS server is Dial-Up Networking. Before you can configure Dial-Up Networking, you need to install a modem or other means of communication.

Using Dial-Up Networking, you will create a phonebook entry for each of the locations that you will call. To create an entry, follow these steps:

1. Click the My Computer icon, and from there open Dial-Up Networking. (If you do not have an entry, a wizard will appear and step you through creating a phonebook entry.)

2. Click the New button to create an entry. You can also select an entry in the list and click More, and then choose Edit the Entry.

   If you choose New, the New Entry Wizard appears. You can choose to enter the information manually (which this section covers).

3. The New (or Edit) Phonebook Entry dialog box appears. By default it will open to the Basic tab. The options for this tab are discussed in the following list. Enter or verify the information.

   - **Entry name.** The name of the entry.

   - **Comment.** Any comment you wish to make about the entry.

   - **Phone number.** This is the phone number for the entry; you should verify this. You can enter multiple entries by selecting the Alternates button. These numbers will be tried in the sequence that they are entered; you also have the option to move the successful number to the top of the list.

   - **Use telephony-dialing properties.** This tells the system to use the properties that you set for your location when dialing the number. When you are troubleshooting, you should try turning this off.

   - **Dial using.** Informs the system which modem you wish to use when dialing. Verify that the modem exists, and if Multilink is selected, choose configure and verify the phone numbers that are entered for each of the listed modems.

◆ **Use another port if busy.** This tells the system to dial using another modem if the specified modem is busy.

4. Select the Server tab and enter or verify the information. The entries are as follows:

◆ **Dial-up server type.** Tells the system what type of server you are trying to connect to. You can use three different types of servers: PPP (such as Windows NT), SLIP, and Windows NT 3.1 RAS. Make sure the correct type is selected, or your computer will attempt to use the wrong line protocol.

◆ **Network protocols.** Here you can select the protocols that you wish to be able to use. If the client computer will be using the Internet, TCP/IP must be selected. If the client is going to use the services of a remote NetWare server, IPX/SPX must be selected. If you will be using only the services from a Windows NT network, you can choose any of the protocols (remembering that the server must also use this protocol).

◆ **Enable software compression.** If you are working with a Windows NT Server, you can select this to turn on the software compression. For troubleshooting purposes, you should turn this off.

◆ **Enable PPP LCP extensions.** Tells the system that the PPP server will be able to set up the client station and will be able to verify the username and password. This also should be turned off when you are troubleshooting.

5. If you are using TCP/IP for this connection, you should also set or verify the TCP/IP settings. The TCP/IP Settings screen will appear. The screen will be different, depending on the type of server you selected. Options that appear include the following:

◆ **Server assigned IP address.** Tells the computer that the server will assign the IP address for this station. The server must have some means of assigning IP address to use this option.

◆ **Specify an IP address.** Enables you to give the station an IP address. The address needs to be unique, and must be correct for the server's network. The server must also allow the client to request an IP address.

- **Server assigned name server addresses.** Tells the system that the server will assign the IP addresses for DNS and WINS servers.

- **Specify name server addresses.** Enables you to set the addresses for DNS and WINS servers. This enables you to see whether the server is giving you correct addresses.

- **Use IP header compression.** Using IP header compression reduces the overhead transmitted over the modem. For troubleshooting, you should disable this.

- **Use default gateway on the remote network.** If you are connected to a network and dialed in to a service provider, this will tell Windows NT to send information bound for a remote network to the gateway on the dial-in server.

6. Set the script options on the Script tab. You have the following options:

- **After dialing (login).** You can choose three different settings here. Make sure the correct one is used. For NT-to-NT communications, you can select None. For other connections, you may have to enter information. For troubleshooting, you should try the terminal window. In this window, you can enter the information manually rather than using the script. If this works, you should verify the script.

- **Before dialing.** If you click this button, you will be presented with basically the same options. This can be used to bring up a window or run a script before you dial the remote host.

7. Check or enter the security information on the Security tab. This should be set to the same level as the security on the server, or the connection will probably fail. Your security options are as follows:

- **Authentication and encryption policy.** Here you can set the level of security that you wish to use. For troubleshooting, you can try Accept Any Authentication Including Clear Text. This setting should be set to match the setting on the server.

- **Require data encryption.** If you are using Microsoft-encrypted authentication, you will have the option to encrypt all data that is being sent over the connection. This should be set the same as the server.

◆ **Current username and password.** Allows Windows to send the current username and password as your logon information. If you are not using the same name and password on the client as you do on the network, do not check this box. You will be prompted for the username and password to log on as when you attempted to connect.

◆ **Unsave password.** If you told the system to save the logon password for a connection, you can clear it by clicking this button. You should do this in the case of a logon problem.

8. Finally, you can enter or check the information for X.25 connections.

Because you can configure a lot of different options, there is great potential for errors. Client errors tend to be either validation problems or errors in the network protocols. Remember that you may need to check the configuration of the server.

The RAS Server

This section covers the RAS server and the configuration of that server. Probably the best place to start is the installation of the RAS server. After a short description of the installation, this section moves on to the configuration of the server.

Installing the RAS Server

The following steps describe the process of installing RAS:

1. Open the Network Setting dialog box (Start, Settings, Control Panel, Network).

2. From the Services tab, choose Add.

3. From the list that appears, choose Remote Access Service, and then click OK.

4. When prompted, enter the path to the Windows NT source files.

5. RAS will ask you for the device that it should use at that point. (This will include ISDN and X.25.)

6. The Remote Access Setup dialog box appears. Click Continue. (The options for this dialog box are discussed later.)

7. From the Network Settings dialog box, click Close.

8. When prompted, shut down and restart your system.

Configuring the RAS Server

If several users are all having problems connecting to your RAS server, you should check the modem first, and then check the configuration of the server. This section covers the basic configuration for a RAS server. This configuration is done when you install RAS or when you verify it after installation by going to the Network Settings dialog box and double-clicking on Remote Access Service from the Services tab.

You will see the dialog box that enables you to configure each port and set the network preferences overall. The following four buttons are concerned with the port settings:

- **Add.** Enables you to add another port to the RAS server. This could be a modem, X.25 PAD, or a PPTP virtual private network.

- **Remove.** Removes the port from RAS.

- **Configure.** This brings up a dialog box that enables you to configure how this port is to be used. You should check this if no users are able to dial in.

- **Clone.** This setting enables you to copy a port. Windows NT Server has been tested with up to 256 ports.

NOTE

Windows NT Workstation and Windows 95 (with the Plus! Pack) will only allow one client to dial in.

After the ports are configured, you need to configure the network settings. These affect what users will be able to see, how they are authenticated, and what protocols they can use when they dial in to the network. When you click the Network button, a dialog box appears.

This dialog box has three main sections. The first is dial out protocols, which will set which protocols you can use to dial in to another server. Then there are the dial-in protocols, which will set the protocols with which users can connect to you.

Finally, there are the encryption settings. The level of security that you choose must also be set on the client computer. If the client cannot use the same level of security, the client cannot be validated by the server.

Each of the server-side protocols has a configuration button. The following sections deal with the configuration of each. Before you can use a protocol with RAS, it has to be installed on the server.

Configuring TCP/IP on the RAS Server

If you run a mixed network that includes UNIX-like hosts, you should enable the TCP/IP protocol on the RAS server. This will also allow your clients to use an Internet connection on your network. The TCP/IP Configuration dialog box again includes the ability to restrict network access to the RAS server.

The other options all deal with the assignment of TCP/IP addresses to the clients that are dialing in. By default, the RAS server will use the services of a Dynamic Host Configuration Protocol (DHCP) server to assign the addresses. If your DHCP server has a long lease period, you may wish to assign the numbers from a pool of addresses given on the server. If you allow the client to request an address, you will need to configure the client stations for all the other parameters.

If your clients are having problems connecting, assign a range of addresses to the RAS server. This eliminates any problems related to the DHCP server and still enables you to prevent clients from requesting specific IP addresses.

Monitoring the RAS Connection

After you have made the RAS connection, you can monitor the connection. There is a tool for both the client side and the server side. This section looks at both of them.

Monitoring from the RAS Server

From the server, you can use the Remote Access Admin tool to monitor the ports. From the Start menu, choose Programs, Administrative tools, RAS Admin. This brings up the Admin tool.

Select the server that you wish to look at and double-click the server. A list of the communications ports appears. For every port that is available on the server, you will see the user currently connected and the time he or she connected.

From here you can disconnect users or send a message to a single user or all the users connected to the server. You can also check the port status. This shows you all the connection information for the port.

Dial-Up Networking Monitor

On the client side, there is an application called the Dial-Up Networking Monitor; you can use this to check the status of the communications. The monitor has three tabs.

Status Tab

The Status tab provides basic information about the connection. From here you have the option to Hang Up the connection or to view the Details about the connection.

Clicking the Details tab brings up another screen that gives you the details about the client's names on the network.

Summary Tab

The Summary tab summarizes all the connections that the client currently has open. This is really only useful in a case where you have multiple connections.

Preferences Tab

The Preferences tab enables you to control the settings for Dial-Up Networking. You should be aware of several options on this tab.

The options that you can set break down into two main areas. You can control when a sound is played, and how the Dial-Up Networking Monitor will look.

Common RAS Problems

There are two common problems that clients will experience with RAS. These are described in the following section.

Authentication

There are two areas where authentication can be a problem. The first is obvious. The client can attempt to connect by using the incorrect username and password. This can easily happen if the user is dialing from a home system. The RAS client may be set to attempt the connection using the current username and password.

The other authentication problem occurs if the security settings on the server and the client do not match. You can get around this by using the Allow Any Authentication Setting or possibly by using the After Dial terminal window.

Call Back with Multilink

There is currently no way in which you can configure call-back security with a multilink setup. If you attempt to do this, the initial connections will be made, and then the server will hang up. The server has only one number for the client and will therefore only call back to one port.

BROWSING IN A MULTIPLE-DOMAIN ROUTED NETWORK

The sharing of resources is the key to networking. For what other purpose does networking exist? Therefore, it is of utmost importance that there be an easy way of not only sharing a resource but of knowing what resources on the network are accessible. Microsoft has made this process of viewing network resources available through what may be referred to as *browsers*.

What these browsers do is actually collect a list (called the *browse list*) of the resources available on the network, and pass this list out to requesting clients. One main computer is designated to collect and update the browse list. Having one computer keep track of the browse list frees the other systems to continue processing without the added overhead of constantly finding where everything is. It also cuts down on the network traffic by having a single source for this list of information rather than everyone needing a separate copy.

Browsing Tools

The next question you may ask is, "How do I browse and what am I browsing for?" The answer is easier than you might think, and you have probably already used this browsing technique. One very simple example of browsing is the Network Neighborhood icon on your desktop. When you open up Network Neighborhood, it provides a list of the network resources available in your local workgroup or domain. These network resources include, but are not limited to, printers, fax, CD-ROM, and other drives or applications available on the network. This is the default list you should see when you first open it. The top icon, Entire Network, refers to just that—anything else that may be available on your network, but not necessarily in your local workgroup or domain. This implies that there may be multiple workgroups/domains in your network environment.

When you start opening up some of these remote domains or workgroups, you are in the process of browsing. This is much like window shopping. You go to the mall not knowing exactly what you need, and so you browse through the shops until you find what you want.

The same applies to the network, but now you are browsing network resources—remote files, printers, CD-ROMs. Anything you need access to can be considered a resource. After you find the resource you want, you can utilize it—such as by printing a document to a network printer or by changing to a server-based database. By using the Network Neighborhood for browsing network resources, you are using the graphical view method or GUI (graphical user interface). You can also browse network resources from the command prompt by using the Net View command. After you specify the server name, a list appears showing the resources available on that specific server. Notice that you must use the correct universal naming convention with the two backslashes (\\Server\Share).

For example:

```
C:\users\default>net view \\instructor
```

Results in the following:

```
Shared resources at \\instructor


Share name   Type          Used as  Comment

_ _ _ _ _ _ _ _ _ _ _ _ _ _ _ _ _ _ _ _ _ _ _ _ _ _ _ _ _ _
_ _ _ _ _.
cdrom        Disk
MSDOS        Disk
NETLOGON     Disk                   Logon server share
Public       Disk
SQLSETUP     Disk
WGPO         Disk
The command completed successfully.
```

System Roles

Certain predefined roles must be addressed with certain names. The computer that has the resource you are trying to access may be referred to as the *host computer*. While you are trying to access its resources, this computer is also playing the role of a server because it is providing a service: the sharing of its resources. The person trying to access the host computer is in the role of a *client*. Remember, a computer may play the roles of both client and server simultaneously. If, for example, you are trying to access a printer on a remote computer while someone is using your shared CD-ROM, you are then both client and server, because you are both sharing a resource and accessing a remote one.

Anytime a resource—drive, printer, and so forth—is shared, it will appear on the browse list, which is available to everyone. Even if you have not been given permission to use the resource, it will still appear on the list you see. This is because it is an overall list of what network resources are available, not just the network resources available to you. There are ways of limiting access to the resource to the specific clients who you want, but there is not a way to have just the resources you have access to appear in your list, because your list is not specific to you; it is the entire list for either your workgroup, domain, or network. You limit access by setting permissions directly on the resource you are sharing.

You may have noticed that sometimes the browse list appears incomplete, or things are on the list that you cannot access even though you have been given the correct permissions. If you do not have enough permissions to access this network resource, even though it appears in your browse list, you will still be denied access. The issues of proper permissions but no access and not appearing on the browse list at all happen because there is a delay on updating the browse list you are accessing. What happens is the resource you attempt to access is either not available anymore (which results in you being denied access to a resource you had previously been allowed to access) or does not appear in the browse list. Browse list timing issues are covered later in this section.

Using the Direct Approach

There is, however, a way around this problem of the browse list delay. One way is the direct approach, but this requires you to know the exact name of the network host that has the resource you desire to obtain, but not the resource itself. This is similar to the Net View command, but with a graphical interface.

To use the direct approach to access a computer, follow these steps:

1. Click the Start button.

2. Click Find.

3. Click Computer.

4. If the resources do not present themselves, type in the name of the server you are trying to find.

5. Click Find Now.

You should then see a list of resources that system has available.

The direct approach bypasses browsing and does a broadcast for that host computer. It is especially helpful when a new resource has been made available but may not have appeared on any browse list, or when you want to see whether a resource to which you are getting denied access is really currently available on the network. You can also use the Net Use command at the command prompt to specify the remote resource you are going to access. The Net Use command is usually used in conjunction with the previously described Net View command (which just lists that servers shared resources, whereas the Net Use command actually attaches you to the resource).

Browsing Roles

Now that you understand what browsing itself is and what it can do for you, the next stage is to discuss the different browsing processes and the defined roles for browsing. The following are the browsing roles available:

+ **Master browser.** Collects and maintains the master list of available resources in its domain or workgroup, and the list of names, not resources, in other domains and workgroups. Distributes the browse list to backup browsers.

+ **Backup browser.** Obtains its browse list from the master browser and passes this list to requesting clients.

+ **Domain master browser.** Fulfills the role of a master browser for its domain as well as coordinating and synchronizing the browse list from all other master browsers for the domains that reside on remote networks.

+ **Potential browser.** A computer that could be a master, backup, or domain master browser if needed, but currently does not fill a role or hold a browse list.

+ **Non-browser.** A computer that does not maintain a browse list. It may have been configured not to participate, or it may possibly be a client computer.

Filling Roles

Now that browsing roles are defined, who can fill them? Windows NT Workstation, Windows NT Server, Windows for Workgroups, and Windows 95 all can perform these browsing roles. However, only a Windows NT Server acting as a primary domain controller (PDC) may occupy the role of the domain master browser. In a LAN, the domain master browser is also the master browser.

Windows NT Workstation and Windows NT Member Servers can become backup browsers if there are at least three Windows NT server-based computers not already filling these roles for the workgroup or domain.

How do you know and control in which roles your computers are participating? Unfortunately, there is not a way to see what browsing role the computer is filling without looking in the Registry. By understanding some default rules and by a little user intervention, however, you can control the browsing environment to a certain extent. The first default to grasp is that Windows NT and Windows 95 are set to auto—meaning it potentially can fill a browsing role. The master browser is chosen through what is called an *election process*, which is based on the following criteria:

*   **A Windows NT–based computer takes precedence over a Windows 95 or Windows for Workgroups computer.** Windows 95 will take priority over Windows for Workgroups. This is at anytime. If a Windows 95 machine has been on for two years, as soon as a Windows NT computer comes online, an election will be held and the Windows NT computer will win because of its higher priority rating. Additionally, newer software versions win. (Windows NT 4.0 would win over Windows NT 3.51.)

*   **The computer that has been turned on the longest wins the election and will become the new master browser.** The idea behind this is that if it has been on the longest it has the most potential to not go down frequently, and therefore provides a more accurate and current browse list.

*   **If none of the previous criteria fit, the server with a NetBIOS name of lowest alphabetic lettering will win the election race for master browser.** A server with the name of Argyle, for example, will become the next Master Browser over a server with the name of Zot.

Controlling Your Browser Role

To control the browser role that your computer is playing for a Windows NT Server and Windows NT Workstation, you can change the IsDomainMaster Registry setting to a *true* or *yes* to force your computer to be the master browser. You find this setting in the following Registry subkey:

```
\HKEY_LOCAL_MACHINE\SYSTEM\CurrentControlSet\Services\Browser\
Parameters
```

To control your browser role for Windows 95, follow these steps:

1. Right-click Network Neighborhood.

2. Choose Properties.

3. Select the File and Print Sharing for Microsoft Networks service if you have it installed. If it is not installed, you are not currently participating in browsing. You can install it by clicking the Add button, selecting Microsoft, and then adding File and Print Sharing for Microsoft Networks.

4. Choose Properties.

5. Select Browse Master. This is set to Automatic by default; you can either enable or disable it.

These are the only controls you have for configuring the browser roles of your computers. So you could turn it off on all but the specific machines that you want to participate in browsing, enabling you to at least narrow the possibilities. If one of those goes down, however, there goes your browsing. You cannot directly control backup browsers; you can only set them to auto, with one set to `IsDomainMaster`.

Understanding the Cost of Browsing

Does being a browse master affect a computer's performance? Yes, it affects system performance. This performance degradation may be noticeable on slower systems, such as 486/66, but not as noticeable on most newer machines, such as a P5/100. Anything the computer does in some way affects its performance, but remember that being a browse master means keeping an updated list of network resources. The number of network resources with which the browse master needs to keep up obviously affects that computer's performance accordingly. The best you can do to minimize this performance degradation is to keep the number of computers sharing network resources to a minimum. Doing so allows the browse list to be short, relieving the strain on the master browser.

Windows NT Browsing Services

A lot is involved with browsing to make it do what it does—most of which happens automatically without any intervention. Sometimes, however, there are problems and it can help to understand the process involved to better understand the possible solutions to the problem.

The browsing services have three main break points, or sections, in Windows NT:

+ Collecting information for the browse list

+ Distributing the browse list itself

+ Servicing browser client requests for the list

The following sections discuss each of these break points.

Collecting the Browse List

The first important part of being able to browse network resources is the collection of the browse list itself. The master browser continually updates its browse list to include the current network resources available. This update process is continual, in that it is constantly having to revise its browse list as network resources appear and disappear. This process happens every time a computer is turned on that has something to share, and every time one that is sharing resources is turned off. The master browser obtains a list of servers in its own domain or workgroup, as well as a list of other domains and workgroups, and updates these servers with network resources to the browse list as changes are made. Much of this process has to do with browser announcements.

When a computer that is running a server service is turned on, it announces itself to the master browser, which then adds this new resource to its browse list. This happens regardless of whether the computer has resources to share. When a computer is shut down properly, it announces to the master browser that it is leaving, and again the master browser updates its list accordingly. If a master browser has an empty list, it can force domains to announce themselves so that it can add them to its list.

NOTE Additionally, the master browser also polls each machine on its subnet every 15 minutes to determine whether the server has any new resources.

Master browsers also receive what are called `DomainAnnouncement` packets that come from other domains and place these packets in their own local browse lists. These `DomainAnnouncement` packets contain the following information:

+ The name of the domain

+ The name of the master browser for that domain

+ Whether the browser is a Windows NT Server or Windows NT Workstation computer

+ If the browser is a Windows NT Server computer, it is the primary domain controller for that domain

Distributing the Browse List

The next important part of browsing is the distribution of the previously collected browse list. The extent of this distribution depends largely on the size of the network. A master browser broadcasts a message every so often to let the backup browsers know that the master browser is still around. This is important because if the master browser does not do this, the network holds an election process to elect a new master browser.

The master browser holds the list of network resources. It is the backup browser that contacts the master browser and copies the list from the master browser. Therefore the backup browsers are the active component, intermittently contacting the passive master browser for the updated list.

There can often be complications with distributing this browse list. The following sections discuss some of these difficulties and the corresponding solutions, such as browsing over subnets, announcement period timings, and domain master browser failure.

Browsing over Subnets

Within Windows NT, every local subnet—a collection of computers separated by a router—is its own browsing area. This browsing area is complete with its own master browser and backup browsers. Subnets hold browser elections for their own subnet; this demonstrates the need for a domain master browser if you have multiple subnets on your internetwork to allow for browsing over more than just one subnet. Additionally, each subnet needs at least one Windows NT controller in each subnet to register with the domain master browser. This allows for multi-subnet browsing.

Generally, broadcasts do not go through a router; the router needs to be BOOTP enabled to allow passing of broadcasts. If a domain has multiple subnets, each master browser for each subnet uses a directed datagram called a `MasterBrowserAnnouncement`. The `MasterBrowserAnnouncement` lets the domain master browser know that it is available and what it has on its Subnet list. These datagrams pass through the routers, enabling these updates to occur. The domain master browser adds all the subnet master browser lists to its own browse list, providing a complete browse list of the entire domain, including all subnets. This process occurs every 15 minutes to ensure regular list updates. The timing is not adjustable. Windows NT workgroups and Windows for Workgroups cannot send a `MasterBrowserAnnouncement` packet, and therefore cannot span these multiple subnets or have a complete list—therefore the need for Windows NT domain controllers to allow for multiple subnet browsing.

Announcement Periods

When the master browser first comes online it sends out a `DomainAnnouncement` once a minute for the first 5 minutes and then only once every 15 minutes. If the domain does not respond by sending out its own `DomainAnnouncement` for three successive announcement periods, the domain is removed from the master browser list. A resource, therefore, might appear on your browse list but actually be unavailable, because it remains on the browse list until three full announcement periods have passed. It is then possible for a domain to appear up to 45 minutes after it is originally unavailable, which may be due to the primary domain controller being off or having physical connectivity problems, such as a bad network card and or cable. You cannot change these announcement times or removal periods.

Domain Master Browser Failure

In the event of a domain master browser failure, users on the entire network are limited to their own individual subnets, assuming they have a master browser for their subnet, of course. If there is not a master browser within your subnet, you are left with no browsing capabilities whatsoever. Without a domain master browser, no complete overall browse list exists of the entire domain, and within three announcement periods all other servers not on the local subnet are removed from the browse list. You then need to either promote a backup domain controller to perform the role of domain master browser, or bring the downed domain master browser back online before the time limit expires for its three announcements. Remember that the backup domain controller does not automatically promote itself, and after a new domain master browser is elected it will take time to collect the browse list from all the different subnets. There is no way you can force the browse list.

Servicing Client Requests

The final browsing service process is the actual servicing of client requests. Now that a browse list exists and has been distributed, clients have something to access.

The process follows these steps:

1. The client uses Explorer to try to access a domain or workgroup. In doing so, it contacts the master browser of the domain or workgroup that it is trying to access.

2. The master browser gives the client a list of three backup browsers.

3. The client then asks for the network resource from one of the backup browsers.

4. The backup browser gives the list of servers in that domain or workgroup for which the client is asking.

5. The client chooses a server and obtains a list of that server's shared resources.

This process can occasionally cause some conflict (if the master browser has a resource in its list, but the backup browser has not updated itself yet, and the client connects to that backup browser and looks for the current list). The resource is not listed in the backup browse list yet. This is another reason why items that are not available may appear on the list, or may not be on the list at all.

Browsing in an IP Internetwork

Now that you have learned about browsing itself and know how it works, you are ready to learn about browsing in an IP internetwork, meaning browsing over multiple subnets. This is not as easy as it sounds. Some has already been explained through the process of domain announcement. But this only allows for master browsers to talk to the domain master browser. This requires a Windows NT domain controller to be in each subnet. It may not be feasible to put a domain controller at each subnet—therefore, no browsing. The first major obstacle is that browsing relies on broadcast packets, which means they are actually sent to everyone on the network segment. Routers do not generally forward these broadcast packets, however, creating a browsing problem for collecting, distributing, and servicing the client request for browse lists. If these packets are not forwarded, you cannot browse in an internetwork environment without a local domain controller.

If the browse list cannot get distributed properly, you have no browsing ability.

Internetwork Browsing Solutions

There are a few possible solutions to the problem of being able to browse in an IP internetwork. The following sections discuss a few of these solutions: the usefulness of the IP router, directed traffic, LMHOSTS files, and others.

IP Router

You can use a few solutions to get around the problem of routers and multiple subnets not being able to browse without a Windows NT controller on each subnet. The first solution is to have a specific router that can forward these NetBIOS name broadcasts. This makes all the broadcasts and network resource requests appear to all client computers as if the broadcasts are all on the same subnet. Master browsers have their own lists as well as those of the other domains and workgroups; therefore, when a client makes an inquiry for a browse list, the list can be provided for any domain or workgroup.

Having a BOOTP-enabled router, of course, fixes the browsing problem across routers. But this solution may not be perfect for every network layout and size. The reason having this BOOTP-enabled router is not the perfect solution is because if you do have the BOOTP-enabled router all NetBIOS traffic is broadcast over the entire network rather than just to each subnet. This adds extremely high overhead to all the nodes of the network, degrading overall performance. The subnets are no longer isolated to their own specific areas, which causes a higher potential for browser election conflicts and excessive network traffic. Therefore even though it does fix the problem of routers and multiple subnets, other problems such as the excessive traffic that is generated should be anticipated.

Directed Traffic

Additional solutions to the problem of browsing an IP internetwork without using a BOOTP-enabled router are available. The following section explains how to use directed IP traffic to service the client's browsing requests.

LMHOSTS File

An LMHOSTS file helps distribute the browsing information and service client requests. You can also use WINS to collect the browse lists and service client requests.

In the LMHOSTS file, the LM stands for LAN Manager; HOSTS is for the host computer. Its job is to resolve NetBIOS names to the corresponding IP address of remote hosts on different subnets. The purpose is to allow for communication between master browsers on remote subnets and the domain master browser. This sets up direct communication, enabling an updated list to be developed across a subnet. The one thing to remember about an LMHOSTS file is that it is your responsibility to create and maintain the file.

Using an LMHOSTS file is a workable solution, but be aware of some considerations. The LMHOSTS file must be on each and every subnet's master browser with an entry to the domain master browser to work. It must also be updated manually any time there are changes to the LMHOSTS list. The LMHOSTS file needs to be placed in the `winnt-root\system32\drivers\etc` directory. There are sample TCP/IP files already you can use to reference. It is just a regular text file that can be created by using any text editor. There is no file extension, and Windows NT will look and reference the file in this location whenever it needs to. The two items needed in the LMHOSTS file for it to work across a subnet are as follows:

* IP address and computer name of the domain master browser

* The domain name preceded by `#PRE` and `#DOM:`

For example:

```
129.62.101.5     server1          #PRE #DOM:try
129.62.101.17    server2          #PRE
129.62.101.25    server3          #PRE
```

The `#PRE` statement preloads the specific line it is on into memory as a permanent entry in the name cache, making it easily available without having to first access the domain.

`#DOM:<domain_name>` allows for logon validation over a router, account synchronization, and, in this case, browsing. Every time the computer sends a broadcast to a domain, it also sends it to every computer that has a `#DOM:` in its LMHOSTS file. These types of broadcasts do go across routers, but are not sent to workgroups. There are many difficulties to watch out for, each of which is discussed in the following subsections.

Domain Master Browser

For the domain master browser, you need an LMHOSTS file set up with entries pointing to each of the remote subnet master browsers. You should also have a `#DOM:` statement in each master browser's LMHOSTS file pointing to each of the other subnet master browsers. If any of them gets promoted to the domain master browser, you then do not have to change all your LMHOSTS files.

Duplicate Names

If it finds duplicate LMHOSTS entries for a single domain, the master browser decides which relates to the domain master browser by querying each IP address for each entry it has. None of the master browsers respond; only the domain master browser does that. Therefore it narrows down the list of duplicates; and because only the real one responds, it communicates with the one that responds and proceeds to exchange browse lists.

LMHOSTS File Placement

The placement of the LMHOSTS file is in the `\etc` directory of the client, as mentioned previously. For Windows NT, for example, it is placed in `\systemroot\system32\drivers\etc`. For Windows 95 and Windows for Workgroups, it is placed in `\system_root` (`c:\windows`).

LMHOSTS File Problems

The most common problems you might have with the LMHOSTS file are the following:

♦ The NetBIOS name is misspelled.

♦ The IP address is incorrect.

♦ An entry is not listed for that host.

♦ There are too many entries for a host, whereas only the first entry is used. If there are multiple entries in the LMHOSTS file for the same host computer, for example, only the first one listed will be used.

♦ The LMHOSTS file is in the incorrect location and is not being read.

The LMHOSTS file certainly has its place in IP internetwork browsing, but it is certainly not the ultimate solution. This brings the discussion here to the last name resolution method: WINS.

Using the WINS Solution

WINS (Windows Internet Naming Service) helps fix the problem of NetBIOS broadcast difficulties by dynamically registering the IP address and NetBIOS name, and keeping track of them in a database. Keeping these computer names in its database greatly enhances the network performance. Whenever they need to find a server, clients access the WINS server rather than broadcast on the network. Accessing the WINS server directly allows for a more direct approach when looking for network resources. And, it makes updating much easier because you do not have to manually configure anything. Using a WINS server also provides easier browsing capability because you can freely use NetBIOS names in the place of IP address. The following is an example of using the Ping utility with the NetBIOS name instead of specifying the entire IP address.

```
ping Server2
```

rather than

```
ping 207.0.58.33
```

Domain Browser

If the computer is made a WINS client, the domain master browser periodically queries the WINS server to update its database of all the domains listed in the WINS database, thereby providing a complete list of all the domains and subnets including remote ones. This list has only domain names and their IP address, not the names of the master browsers of each particular subnet as before.

Client Access

When a client needs access to a network resource, it calls up the WINS server directly and asks for a list of domain controllers in the domain. WINS provides a list of servers of up to 25 domain controllers, referred to as an *Internet group*. The client can then quickly access the domain controller it needs without a complete network broadcast.

WHAT IS IMPORTANT TO KNOW

The following bullets summarize the chapter and accentuate the key concepts to memorize for the exam:

- Telnet allows a computer to become a dumb terminal on another hosts—accessing and running files and applications over there. A key note is that Telnet cannot download or upload files, and can only run them.

- If a RAS server is used for Dial-Up Networking, you must leave the default gateway information blank because this is provided by the ISP.

CHAPTER 4

Monitoring and Optimization

UTILITIES USED TO MONITOR TCP/IP TRAFFIC

Optimization changes are primarily made through the Registry Editor (Regedt32.exe or Regedit.exe), although there are two tools primarily used for monitoring TCP/IP traffic:

+ Performance Monitor
+ Network Monitor

A number of other utilities do not perform actual monitoring, but can be used to gather configuration and statistical information. Most of these other utilities are discussed in other sections, but you must know what they offer when compared to Performance Monitor and Network Monitor, and when you would use each one. For that purpose, a short description of each of them is also included here.

Performance Monitor

The Performance Monitor is the Windows NT all-around tool for monitoring a network, using statistical measurements called counters. It has the capability to collect data on both hardware and software components, called objects, and its primary purpose is to establish a baseline from which everything can be judged. It offers the ability to check/monitor/identify the following:

+ The demand for resources
+ Bottlenecks in performance
+ The behavior of individual processes
+ The performance of remote systems
+ Generate alerts to exception conditions
+ Export data for analysis

Every object has a number of counters. Some to be familiar with include those for the Paging File object: %Usage and %Usage Peak, which will tell whether a paging file is reaching its maximum size.

To get numeric statistics, use the Report (columnar) view. To see how counters change over a period of time, use the log feature. To spot abnormalities that occur in data over a period of time, use the Chart view.

To monitor a number of servers and be alerted if a counter exceeds a specified number, create one Performance Monitor alert for each server on your workstation. Enter your username in the Net Name on the Alert Options dialog box (below Send Network Message tab) and you will be alerted when the alert conditions arise. Only one name can be placed in here, and the name can be that of a user or group, but cannot be multiple users or groups. (This is not to be confused with the Alert option in Server Manager.)

If you are monitoring a number of performance counters and that monitoring is slowing down other operations on your workstation, the best remedy to the situation is to increase the monitoring interval.

To tune or optimize Windows NT you will need to be able to look at the performance of the server on many different levels.

NOTE
Two important pieces of knowledge to remember: You *must* install the Network Monitor Agent to be able to see several of the network performance counters, and SNMP service *must* be installed in order to gather TCP/IP statistics.

Network Monitor

Network Monitor is a Windows tool that enables you to see network traffic that is sent or received by a Windows NT computer. Network Monitor is included with Windows NT 4.0, but must be installed to be active.

To install Network Monitor, open Control Panel, Network, and then add the Network Monitor Tools and Agent from the Services tab. The version of Network Monitor that comes with Windows NT 4.0 is a simple version; it captures traffic only for the local machines (incoming and outgoing traffic).

Microsoft's System Management Server, a network management product, comes with a more complete version of Network Monitor that enables you to capture packets on the local machine for the entire local network segment. Both versions enable you to capture the packets flowing into and out of your computer. The full version that comes with SMS also provides extra functionality such as the capability to capture all packets on the local network or on remote networks, edit those packets, and derive statistics about protocols and users on the network.

There are two pieces to the Network Monitor: the Agent, which will capture the data; and the Monitor Tool, which can be used to view the data. You can also filter out traffic that isn't important to the troubleshooting process.

The Network Monitor can be used to diagnose more complex issues with connectivity by enabling you to see the actual packets that are flowing on the network, verifying which steps are being used to resolve names or which port numbers are being used to connect.

Other Utilities

At A Glance: Utilities

Utility	Purpose
ARP	Check IP to MAC address resolution
Event log	View system messages
IPCONFIG	Check IP configuration parameters
NBTSTAT	Check NetBIOS to IP address resolution
NETSTAT	Obtain network statistics
NSLOOKUP	Verify DNS entries
PING	All-purpose connection verification
ROUTE	See entries in the routing table
SNMP	Check network, and in particular TCP/IP, networking statistics
TRACERT	Trace the route a packet takes to reach its destination

You can use a number of tools to help troubleshoot and isolate the source of TCP/IP problems. Each tool gives you a different view of the process used to resolve an IP address to a hardware address, and then route the IP packet to the appropriate destination. As a general rule of thumb, however, the following items apply to the tools listed here:

- If TCP/IP cannot communicate from a Microsoft host to a remote host system, the utilities discussed in this chapter will not work correctly.

- If the systems are on different subnets, and cannot communicate, remember that TCP/IP requires routing to communicate between subnets.

- If the systems could previously communicate, but can no longer communicate, suspect either your router(s) or changes in software configuration.

- Utilities that require usernames and passwords on the remote host need a user account on the remote system. If you have an account on a Windows NT system, the remote host system does not know or care. Trust relationships are not the same as achieving connectivity.

- On Windows NT computers, never forget to consult the Event Viewer. Any messages that are out of the ordinary may provide valuable clues to the cause of the problem.

ARP

After the name has been resolved to an IP address, you computer must resolve the IP address to a MAC address. This is handled by the Address Resolution Protocol (ARP).

ARP, as a utility, can be used to see the entries in the Address Resolution table, which maps network card addresses (MAC addresses) to IP addresses. You can check to see whether the IP addresses you believe should be in the table are there and whether they are mapped to the computers they should be. Usually, you do not know the MAC addresses of the hosts on your network. If you cannot contact a host, or if a connection is made to an unexpected host, however, you can check this table with the ARP command to begin isolating which host is actually assigned an IP address.

The ARP utility enables you to view the addresses that have been resolved, with the following syntax options.

```
C:\>arp /?Displays and modifies the IP-to-Physical address
translation tables used by address resolution protocol (ARP).

ARP -s inet_addr eth_addr [if_addr]
ARP -d inet_addr [if_addr]
ARP -a [inet_addr] [-N if_addr]

   -a             Displays current ARP entries by interrogating the
                  current protocol data.  If inet_addr is specified,
                  the IP and Physical addresses for only the specified
                  computer are displayed.  If more than one network
                  interface uses ARP, entries for each ARP table are
                  displayed.
   -g             Same as -a.
   inet_addr      Specifies an internet address.
   -N if_addr     Displays the ARP entries for the network interface
                  specified by if_addr.
   -d             Deletes the host specified by inet_addr.
   -s             Adds the host and associates the Internet address
                  inet_addr with the Physical address eth_addr.  The
                  Physical address is given as 6 hexadecimal bytes
                  separated by hyphens. The entry is permanent.
   eth_addr       Specifies a physical address.
   if_addr        If present, this specifies the Internet address of
                  the interface whose address translation table should
                  be modified. If not present, the first applicable
                  interface will be used.
```

Event Log

The Event Log in Windows NT is used to track events and errors. The System Event Log in Windows NT is where all critical system messages are stored, and not just those related to TCP/IP.

IPCONFIG

One of the key areas that causes problems with TCP/IP is configuration. Windows NT provides a utility that enables you to view the configuration of a workstation so that you can verify the configuration. The following listing provides a summary of the usage of IPCONFIG.

```
C:\>ipconfig /?Windows NT IP Configurationusage: ipconfig [/? | /all
| /release [adapter] | /renew [adapter]]
/?       Display this help message.       /all    Display full
configuration information.
        /release Release the IP address for the specified adapter.
        /renew   Renew the IP address for the specified adapter.

The default is to display only the IP address, subnet mask and
default gateway for each adapter bound to TCP/IP.

For Release and Renew, if no adapter name is specified, then the IP
address leases for all adapters bound to TCP/IP will be released or
renewed.
```

NBTSTAT

NBTSTAT is a command-line utility that enables you to check the resolution of NetBIOS names to TCP/IP addresses. With NBTSTAT, you can check the status of current NetBIOS sessions. You can also add entries to the NetBIOS name cache from the LMHOSTS file or check your registered NetBIOS name and the NetBIOS scope assigned to your computer, if any.

> **NOTE**
> Whereas NETSTAT deals with all the connections that your system has with other computers, NBTSTAT deals with only the NetBIOS connections.

NBTSTAT also enables you to verify that name resolution is taking place by providing a method to view the name cache. A number of parameters can be used with the utility, as shown in the following list.

```
C:\>nbtstat /?

Displays protocol statistics and current TCP/IP connections using
NBT (NetBIOS over TCP/IP).

NBTSTAT [-a RemoteName] [-A IP address] [-c] [-n]
        [-r] [-R] [-s] [-S] [interval] ]

  -a   (adapter status) Lists the remote machine's name table given
                        its name
  -A   (Adapter status) Lists the remote machine's name table given
                        its IP address.
```

-c	(cache)	Lists the remote name cache including the IP addresses
-n	(names)	Lists local NetBIOS names.
-r	(resolved)	Lists names resolved by broadcast and via WINS
-R	(Reload)	Purges and reloads the remote cache name table
-S	(Sessions)	Lists sessions table with the destination IP addresses
-s	(sessions)	Lists sessions table converting destination IP addresses to hostnames via the hosts file.

RemoteName	Remote host machine name.
IP address	Dotted decimal representation of the IP address.
interval	Redisplays selected statistics, pausing interval seconds between each display. Press Ctrl+C to stop redisplaying statistics.

NETSTAT

NETSTAT is a command-line utility that enables you to check the status of current IP connections. Executing NETSTAT without switches displays protocol statistics and current TCP/IP connections.

After you have determined that your base-level communications are working, you will need to verify the services on your system. This involves looking at the services that are listening for incoming traffic and/or verifying that you are creating a session with a remote station. The NETSTAT command enables you to do this.

A number of parameters can be used with the utility, as shown in the following list.

```
C:\>netstat /?

Displays protocol statistics and current TCP/IP network connections.

NETSTAT [-a] [-e] [-n] [-s] [-p proto] [-r] [interval]
```

-a	Displays all connections and listening ports. (Server-side connections are normally not shown).
-e	Displays Ethernet statistics. This may be combined with the -s option.

-n	Displays addresses and port numbers in numerical form.
-p proto	Shows connections for the protocol specified by proto; proto may be tcp or udp. If used with the -s option to display per-protocol statistics, proto may be tcp, udp, or ip.
-r	Displays the contents of the routing table.
-s	Displays per-protocol statistics. By default, statistics are shown for TCP, UDP and IP; the -p option may be used to specify a subset of the default.
interval	Redisplays selected statistics, pausing interval seconds between each display. Press CTRL+C to stop redisplaying statistics. If omitted, netstat will print the current configuration information once.

NSLOOKUP

NSLOOKUP is a command-line utility that enables you to verify entries on a DNS server. You can use NSLOOKUP in two modes: interactive and noninteractive. In interactive mode, you start a session with the DNS server in which you can make several requests. In noninteractive mode, you specify a command that makes a single query of the DNS server. If you want to make another query, you must type another noninteractive command.

NOTE One of the key issues in using TCP/IP is the capability to resolve a hostname to an IP address—an action usually performed by a DNS server.

A number of parameters can be used with the utility, as shown in the following list.

```
Usage:    nslookup [-opt ...]             # interactive mode using
default server    nslookup [-opt ...] - server    # interactive mode
using 'server'    nslookup [-opt ...] host       # just look up
'host' using default server    nslookup [-opt ...] host server # just
look up 'host' using 'server'
```

Ping

The Ping command is one of the most useful commands in the TCP/IP protocol. It sends a series of packets to another system, which in turn sends back a response. This utility can be extremely useful in troubleshooting problems with remote hosts.

The Ping utility is used as a command line program, and accepts the following parameters:

```
Usage: ping [-t] [-a] [-n count] [-l size] [-f] [-i TTL] [-v TOS]
[-r count] [-s count] [[-j host-list] | [-k host-list]]
[-w timeout] destination-listOptions:     -t           Pings the
specified host until interrupted   -a            Resolves
addresses to hostnames
     -n count      Number of echo requests to send.
     -l size       Sends buffer size
     -f            Sets Don't Fragment flag in packet
     -i TTL        Time to Live
     -v TOS        Type of Service
     -r count      Records route for count hops
     -s count      Time stamp for count hops
     -j host-list  Loose source route along host-list
     -k host-list  Strict source route along host-list
     -w timeout    Time-out in milliseconds to wait for each reply
```

The Ping command indicates whether the host can be reached, and how long it took for the host to send a return packet. On a local area network, the time is indicated as less than 10 milliseconds; across wide area network links, however, this value can be much greater.

ROUTE

ROUTE is a command-line utility that enables you to see the local routing table and add entries to it. Occasionally, it is necessary to check how a system will route packets on the network. Normally, your system will just send all packets to the default gateway; in cases where you are having problems communicating with a group of computers, however, the ROUTE command may provide an answer.

A number of parameters can be used with the utility, as shown in the following list.

```
C:\>routeManipulates network routing tables.ROUTE [-f] [command
[destination] [MASK netmask] [gateway] [METRIC metric]]
   -f          Clears the routing tables of all gateway entries.  If
               this is used in conjunction with one of the commands,
               the tables are cleared prior to running the command.

   -p          When used with the ADD command, makes a route
               persistent across boots of the system. By default,
               routes are not preserved when the system is
               restarted. When used with the PRINT command,
               displays the list of registered persistent routes.
               Ignored for all other commands, which always affect
               the appropriate persistent routes.

   command     Specifies one of four commands
                  PRINT     Prints a route
                  ADD       Adds a route
                  DELETE    Deletes a route
                  CHANGE    Modifies an existing route

   destination Specifies the host.

   MASK        If the MASK keyword is present, the next parameter is
               interpreted as the netmask parameter.

   netmask     If provided, specifies a sub-net mask value to be
               associated with this route entry.  If not specified,
               it defaults to 255.255.255.255.

   gateway     Specifies gateway.

   METRIC      specifies the metric/cost for the destination
```

```
All symbolic names used for destination are looked up in the network
database file NETWORKS. The symbolic names for gateway are looked up
in the hostname database file HOSTS. If the command is print or
delete, wildcards may be used for the destination and gateway, or
the gateway argument may be omitted.
```

SNMP

The SNMP protocol enables TCP/IP to export information to troubleshooting tools such as Performance Monitor or other third-party tools. By itself, SNMP does not report any troubleshooting information. If you are using tools that depend on SNMP, however, you cannot see all the information available from these tools until you install SNMP. To install SNMP, open Control Panel, Network, and then add SNMP from the Services tab.

The SNMP service is an additional component of Windows NT TCP/IP software. It includes the four supported MIBs; each is a dynamic link library and can be loaded and unloaded as needed. It provides SNMP agent services to any TCP/IP host running SNMP management software. It also performs the following:

* Reports special happenings, such as traps, to multiple hosts

* Responds to requests for information from multiple hosts

* Can be set up on any system running Windows NT and TCP/IP

* Sets up special counters in Performance Monitor that can be used to monitor the TCP/IP performance related to SNMP

* Uses hostnames and IP addresses to recognize which hosts it receives, and requests information

NOTE   Security is based on community names as well as hostnames and IP addresses.

The SNMP service can be installed for the following reasons:

* You want to monitor TCP/IP with Performance Monitor.

* You want to monitor a Windows NT-based system with a third-party application.

* You want to set up your computer as an SNMP agent.

TRACERT

TRACERT is a command-line utility that enables you to verify the route to a remote host. Execute TRACERT *hostname*, where *hostname* is the computer name or IP address of the computer whose route you want to trace. TRACERT will return the different IP addresses the packet was routed through to reach the final destination. The results also include the number of hops needed to reach the destination. Execute TRACERT without any options to see a help file that describes all the TRACERT switches.

The TRACERT utility determines the intermediary steps involved in communicating with another IP host. It provides a road map of all the routing an IP packet takes to get from host A to host B.

A number of parameters can be used with the utility, as shown in the following list.

```
Usage: tracert [-d] [-h maximum_hops] [-j host-list] [-w timeout]
target_nameOptions:    -d
Does not resolve addresses to hostnames    -h maximum_hops
Maximum number of hops to search for target
    -j host-list        Loose source route along host-list
    -w timeout          Wait time-out milliseconds for each reply
```

As with the Ping command, TRACERT returns the amount of time required for each routing *hop*.

WHAT IS IMPORTANT TO KNOW

The following bullets summarize the chapter and accentuate the key concepts to memorize for the exam:

- The Registry Editor (Regedt32.exe or Regedit.exe)   Used for optimization changes.

- Event Log   Can track events and errors. The System Event Log in Windows NT is where all critical system messages are stored, and not just those related to TCP/IP.

- Network Monitor   Can analyze a problem by capturing packets coming and going.

- Performance Monitor   Can look for bottlenecks and analyze performance. The Performance Monitor is the Windows NT all-around tool for monitoring a network, using statistical measurements called counters.

▶ Diagnose and resolve IP addressing problems

▶ Use Microsoft TCP/IP utilities to diagnose configuration problems

▶ Identify which Microsoft TCP/IP utility to use to diagnose IP configuration problems

▶ Diagnose and resolve name resolution problems

CHAPTER 5

Troubleshooting

DIAGNOSING AND RESOLVING IP ADDRESSING PROBLEMS

Three main parameters specify how TCP/IP is configured: the IP address, the subnet mask, and the default gateway, which is the address of the router. These parameters are configured through the Protocols tab of the Network Properties dialog box. Although it is possible to receive an IP address from a DHCP server, for the moment this discussion focuses on parameters that are manually configured (DHCP related issues are discussed later in "DHCP Client Configuration Problems").

These TCP/IP parameters must be configured correctly or you cannot connect with TCP/IP. An incorrect configuration can result from typos; if you type the wrong IP address, subnet mask, or default gateway, you may not connect properly or even be able to connect at all. To illustrate, if you dial the wrong number when making a telephone call, you can't reach the party you're calling. If you read the wrong phone number out of the phonebook, you won't ever make a correct call even if you dial the number you think is correct time and time again.

Whether the TCP/IP configuration parameters are wrong due to a typo or due to a mistaken number, the incorrect parameters affect communications. Different types of problems occur when each of these parameters has a configuration error.

IP Address Configuration Problems

An incorrect TCP/IP address might not even cause any problems. If you configure an IP address that is on the correct subnet, but uses the wrong host ID, and is not a duplicate, the client may be able to communicate just fine. If, however, the correct IP address has been entered in a static file or database that resolves hostnames to IP addresses, such as an LMHOSTS file or a DNS database file, there are some communication problems. Typically, therefore, an incorrect IP address does cause some problems.

Incorrect configuration of the TCP/IP parameters can cause different symptoms for each type of parameter. The following sections examine the effects that each TCP/IP parameter can have on IP communications.

IP Address

A TCP/IP address has two or possibly three components that uniquely identify the computer the address is assigned to. At the very least, the IP address specifies the network address and host address of the computer. Also, if you are subnetting (using part of the host address to specify a subnet address), the third part of the address specifies the subnet address of the host.

If the incorrect host (143.168.3.9) sends a message to a local client (133.168.3.20), the TCP/IP configuration of the sending host indicates this is a remote address because it doesn't match the network address of the host initiating the communication. The packet won't ever reach the local client, because the address 133.168.3.20 is interpreted as a remote address.

If a local client (133.168.3.6) sends a message to the incorrect host (143.168.3.9), the message never reaches its intended destination. The message is either routed (if the local client sends the message to the IP address as written) or it stays on the local subnet (if the local client sends it to what should have been the address, 133.168.3.9). If the message is routed, the client for whom it was intended cannot receive the message because it is on the same segment of the network as the local client. If the message is not routed, the message still does not reach the incorrect client because the IP address for the destination host (133.168.3.9) does not match the address as configured on the incorrect client (143.168.3.9).

Figure 5.1 gives an example of an incorrect IP address. In this case, a class A address is used, 33.x.x.x. The subnet mask (255.255.0.0) indicates the second octet is also being used to create subnets. In this case, even though the client has the same network address as the other clients on the same subnet, the client has a different subnet number because the address was typed incorrectly. This time the incorrect address specifies the wrong subnet ID. The client 33.5.8.4 is on subnet 5, but the other clients on the subnet have the address 33.4.x.x. In this case, if the client 33.5.8.4 tries to contact other clients on the same subnet, the message is routed because the subnet ID doesn't match the subnet number of the source host. If the client 33.5.8.4 tries to send a message to a remote host, the message is routed, but the message isn't returned to the client because the router doesn't handle subnet 5, only subnet 4.

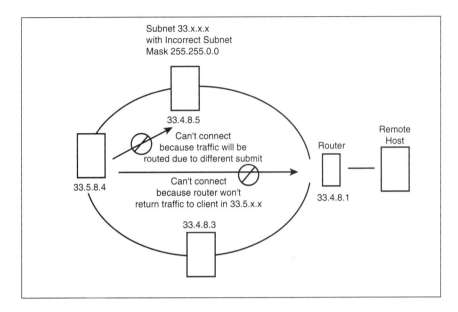

FIGURE 5.1
Incorrect subnet address.

If a local client tries to send a message to 33.5.8.4, the message doesn't reach the client. If the local client uses the address as configured, the message is routed, which isn't the correct solution because the destination host is local. If the local client sends the message to what should have been the IP address, 33.5.8.4 doesn't receive the message because the IP address isn't configured correctly. The last component of an IP addresses that can cause communication problems is the host address.

An incorrect host address may not always cause a problem, however. In Figure 5.2, a local client has the wrong IP address, but only the host address portion of the address is wrong. The network address and subnet match the rest of the clients on the subnet. In this case, if a client sends a message to the client with the incorrect address, the message still reaches the client. If someone tries to contact the client with what should have been the address, however, he doesn't contact the client. In fact, he could contact another host that ended up with the address that was supposed to be given to the original host. If the original host ends up with the same IP address as another host through the configuration error, the first client to boot works, but the second client to

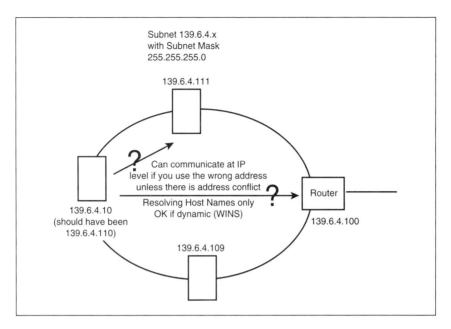

FIGURE 5.2
Incorrect host address.

boot may note the address conflict and not load the TCP/IP stack at all. In this case, the second client to boot cannot make any TCP/IP communications.

Another problem comes in when the correct address was registered in static files, such as an LMHOSTS file or a DNS database. In this case, no one can communicate with this client by name because the name resolution for this host always returns the correct address, which can't be used to contact the host because the address has been typed incorrectly. Basically, the problems you encounter with an incorrect host address are intermittent. If the host was configured to be a WINS client, however, the hostname is registered along with the incorrect address. Another WINS client trying to connect with this computer receives an accurate mapping for the hostname.

Subnet Mask

The subnet mask specifies which portion of the IP address specifies the network address and which portion of the address specifies the host address. Also, the subnet mask can be used to take part of what would have been the host address and use it to further divide the network into subnets. If the subnet mask is not configured correctly, your clients may not be able to communicate at all, or you may see partial communication problems.

Figure 5.3 shows a subnet on a TCP/IP network. The network uses a Class B network address of 138.13.x.x. The third octet is used in this case for subnetting, however, so all the clients in the figure should be on subnet 4, as indicated by the common addresses 138.13.4.x. Unfortunately, the subnet mask entered for one client is 255.255.0.0. When this client tries to communicate with other hosts on the same subnet, it should be able to contact them because the subnet mask indicates they are on the same subnet, which is correct. If the client tries to contact a host on another subnet such as 138.13.3.x, however, the client fails. In this case, the subnet mask still interprets the destination host to be on the same subnet and the message is never routed. Because the destination host is on another subnet, the message never reaches the intended destination. The subnet mask is used to determine whether the host

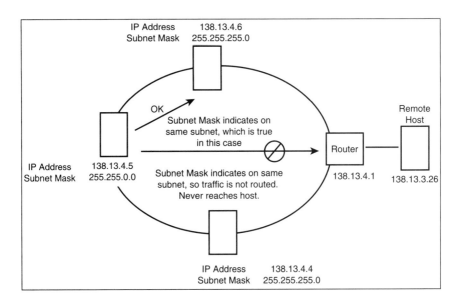

FIGURE 5.3
Incorrect subnet mask—missing third octet.

is local or remote, so the client with the incorrect subnet mask can receive incoming messages. When the client tries to return communications, however, the message isn't routed if the source host is on the same network but on a different subnet. So in actuality, the client really can establish communications with only one side of the conversation. Contact with hosts outside the local network still works because those contacts are routed.

Figure 5.4 shows a subnet mask that masks too many bits. In this case, the subnet mask is 255.255.255.0. The network designers had intended the subnet mask to be 255.255.240.0, however, with 4 bits of the third octet used for the subnet and 4 bits as part of the host address. If the incorrect client tries to send a message to a local host and the third octet is the same, the message is not routed and therefore reaches the local client. If the local client has an address that differs in the last 4 bits of the third octet, however, the message is routed and never reaches its destination. If the incorrect client tries to send a message to another client on another subnet, the message is routed because the third octet is different.

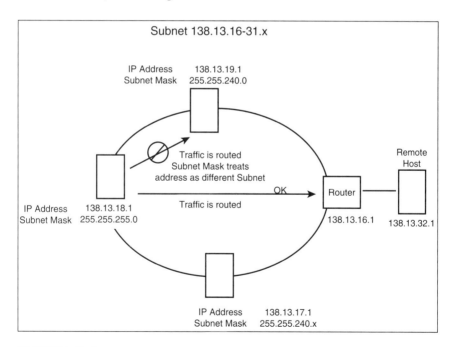

FIGURE 5.4
Incorrect subnet mask—incorrect third octet.

> **NOTE** Problems with the subnet mask also lead to intermittent connections. Sometimes the connection works, sometimes it doesn't. The problems show up when the IP address of the destination host causes a packet to be routed when it shouldn't or to remain local when the packet should be routed.

Default Gateway

The default gateway address is the address of the router, the gateway to the world beyond the local subnet. If the default gateway address is wrong, the client with the wrong default gateway address can contact local hosts but cannot communicate at all beyond the local subnet. It is possible for the incorrect client to receive a message, because the default gateway is used only to send packets to other hosts. As soon as the incorrect client attempts to respond to the incoming message, however, the default gateway address doesn't work and the message doesn't reach the host that sent the original message.

DHCP Client Configuration Problems

All the TCP/IP parameters mentioned previously can cause communication problems if they are not configured correctly. Using a DHCP server can greatly reduce these configuration problems. If the DHCP scope is set up properly, without any typos or other configuration errors, DHCP clients shouldn't have any configuration problems. It is impossible to completely eliminate human error, but using DHCP should reduce the points of potential errors to just the DHCP servers rather than every client on the network.

Even when there are no configuration problems with DHCP addresses, DHCP clients can get a duplicate IP address from a DHCP server. If you have multiple DHCP servers in your environment, you should have scopes on each DHCP server for different subnets. Usually, you have scopes with a larger number of addresses for the local subnet where the DHCP server is located and smaller scopes for other subnets. Creating multiple scopes on one server provides backup for giving clients IP addresses. If the server on the local scope is busy or down, the client can still receive an address from a remote DHCP server. When the router forwards this DHCP request to another subnet, it includes the address of the subnet it came from so that the remote DHCP server knows from which scope of addresses to lease an address to the remote client. Using this type of redundancy, however, can cause problems if you don't configure the scopes on all the DHCP servers correctly.

> **NOTE** The router will forward the request as long as it has BOOTP forwarding capability. DHCP Relay Agent would work if the routers don't have this capability.

The most important part of the configuration is to make sure you don't have duplicate addresses in the different scopes. On one server, for example, you could have a scope in the range 131.107.2.100 to 131.107.2.170. On the remote DHCP server, you could have a scope of 131.107.2.171 to 131.107.2.200. By setting up the scopes without overlap, you should not have any problems with clients receiving duplicate IP addresses. DHCP servers do not communicate with each other, so one server does not know anything about the addresses the other server has leased. Therefore, you must ensure the servers never give out duplicate information by making sure the scopes for one subnet on all the different DHCP servers have unique IP addresses.

> **NOTE** Microsoft uses the guidelines of 75% on one DHCP server and 25% on the remote DHCP server.

Another common problem with having multiple scopes on one server is entering the configuration parameters correctly. If you enter the default gateway as 131.107.3.1 (rather than 131.107.2.1) for the scope 131.107.2.100 to 131.107.2.170, for example, the clients receiving these addresses cannot communicate beyond the local subnet, because they have the wrong router address. With one scope on a DHCP server, you are usually quite sure of what all the configuration parameters should be. With multiple scopes on one server, however, it is easy to get confused about which scope you are editing and what the parameters should be for that scope. To avoid this type of problem, check each scope's parameters very carefully to make sure the parameters match the address of the scope, not the subnet where the DHCP server is located.

Also, if the client doesn't receive an address because the server is down or doesn't respond in a timely manner, the client cannot contact anyone. Without an IP address, the IP stack does not initialize and the client can't communicate at all with TCP/IP.

MICROSOFT CONFIGURATION UTILITIES

If you configure the TCP/IP address and other TCP/IP parameters manually, you can always verify the configuration through the Network Properties dialog box. If the client receives an address from a DHCP server, however, the only information available in the Network Properties dialog box is that the client is receiving its address from DHCP. Because the configuration information for a DHCP client is received dynamically, you must use a utility that can read the current configuration to verify the settings.

The command-line utility IPCONFIG can be used to see how the local host is configured, whether the parameters come from manual configuration or from a DHCP server. Running IPCONFIG from a command prompt, the basic configuration parameters are displayed—the IP address, the subnet mask, and the default gateway. You can see additional information by using IPCONFIG with the /all switch.

IPCONFIG /all executed in a command prompt not only shows the standard parameters, but additional information such as the WINS server address and the DNS server address is also displayed.

NOTE A Windows version of IPCONFIG, called IP Configuration, is included with the Windows NT Resource Kit and is installed under the Internet Utils program group. IP Configuration reports the same information as the IPCONFIG command utility. IP Configuration can also be used to release and renew DHCP addresses, as described in the following section.

When a DHCP client gets an IP that is not configured correctly or if the client doesn't get an IP address at all, IPCONFIG can be used to resolve these problems. If the client gets incorrect IP parameters, that should be apparent from the results of IPCONFIG /all. You should be able to see that some of the parameters don't match the IP address or that some parameters are completely blank. You could have the wrong default gateway, for example, or the client is not configured to be a WINS client.

When a DHCP client fails to receive an address, the results of IPCONFIG /all are different. In this case, the client has an IP address of 0.0.0.0— an invalid address—and the DHCP server is 255.255.255.255—a broadcast address.

To fix this problem, you can release the incorrect address with IPCONFIG /release and then try to obtain a new IP address with IPCONFIG /renew. The IPCONFIG /renew command sends out a new request for a DHCP address. If a DHCP server is available, the server responds with the lease of an IP address.

In many cases, the DHCP client will acquire the same address after releasing and renewing. That the client receives the same address indicates the same DHCP server responded to the renewal request and gave out the address that had just been released back into the pool of available addresses. If you need to renew an address because the parameters of the scope are incorrect, you must fix the parameters before releasing and renewing the address. Otherwise, the client could receive the same address again with the same incorrect parameters.

> **NOTE** The IPCONFIG utility reports address information per NIC, and also RAS connection.

> **NOTE** Occasionally, a DHCP client will not acquire an address regardless of how many times you release and renew the address. One way to try to fix the problem is to manually assign the client a static IP address. After the client is configured with this address, which you can verify by using IPCONFIG, switch back to DHCP.

MICROSOFT IP CONFIGURATION TROUBLESHOOTING UTILITIES

A number of tools come with TCP/IP when the protocol is installed on a Windows NT computer. After you have resolved any problems caused by the Windows NT network configuration, you can then focus on using the TCP/IP tools to solve IP problems. Some tools can be used to verify the configuration parameters. Other tools can be used to test the connectivity capabilities of TCP/IP as configured.

Ping is a command-line tool included with every Microsoft TCP/IP client (any DOS or Windows client with the TCP/IP protocol installed). You can use Ping to send a test packet to the specified address and then, if things are working properly, the packet is returned. Figure 5.5 shows the results of a successful Ping command. Note that four successful responses are returned. Unsuccessful Pings can result in different messages, depending on the type of problem Ping encounters in trying to send and receive the test packet.

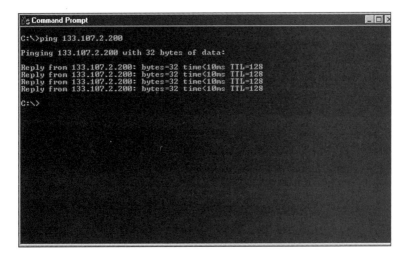

FIGURE 5.5
The results of a successful Ping command.

Although Ping is a simple tool to use (from the command prompt, just type **Ping** with the IP address or hostname you want to Ping), choosing what to Ping is the key to using it for successful troubleshooting. The remainder of this section covers which IP addresses or hosts you should Ping to troubleshoot TCP/IP connectivity problems.

Troubleshooting IP Protocol Installation by Pinging the Loopback Address

The first step in troubleshooting many problems is to verify that TCP/IP installed correctly on the client. You can look at the configuration through the Network Properties dialog box or with IPCONFIG, but to actually test the working status of the protocol stack, you should try to Ping the loopback address. The loopback address is 127.0.0.1. When you Ping this address, a packet is not sent on the network. Ping just sends a packet down through the layers of the IP architecture and then up the layers again. If TCP/IP is installed correctly, you should receive an immediate successful response. If IP is not installed correctly, the response fails.

To correct problems of this type, you should verify the Windows NT network configuration and the protocol installation. You can check the following items:

- Make sure TCP/IP is listed on the installed protocols.
- Make sure the network adapter card is configured correctly.
- Make sure TCP/IP shows up in the bindings for the adapter card and that the bindings are not disabled for TCP/IP.
- Check the System Log for any errors indicating that the network services didn't start.

If you try the preceding steps, including rebooting the system, and have no success, you may have to remove TCP/IP and install it again. Sometimes Windows NT gets hung up somewhere and it thinks things are really installed when they are not. Removing the protocol and then installing it again can often resolve this halfway state.

Troubleshooting Client Address Configuration by Pinging Local Address

Another step in verifying the TCP/IP configuration, after you have verified that TCP/IP is installed correctly, is to Ping the address of the local host. Just Ping the IP address that you think is configured for the client. You should receive an immediate successful reply if the client address is configured as specified in the Ping command. You can also Ping the name of the local host, but problems with name resolution are discussed later in the section titled "Name Resolution Problems." For the moment, you are concerned with raw TCP/IP connectivity—the capability to communicate with another IP host by using its IP address.

Correcting a failure at this level concerns checking the way the client address was configured. Was the address typed in correctly? Did the client receive the IP address from the DHCP server that you expected? Also, does the client have a connection on the network? Pinging the local host address does not cause a packet to be sent on the network; therefore, if you have lost network connectivity, this Ping won't indicate a network failure.

Troubleshooting Router Problems by Pinging the Default Gateway

If you can communicate with hosts on the same subnet but cannot establish communications with hosts beyond the subnet, the problem may be with the router or the way its address is configured. To communicate beyond the subnet, a router must be enabled with an address that matches the subnet address for the clients on the local subnet. The router also has other ports configured with different addresses so that it can send packets out to the network at large. Pinging the default gateway address tests the address you have configured for the router and also tests the router itself.

If the default gateway Ping fails, there are several possible sources for the error:

- **The router has failed or is down.** In this case, you cannot make connections outside the subnet until the router is brought up again. However, you should be able to communicate with hosts on the same subnet.

- **The client has lost a physical connection with the router or with the network.** You can test a network connection at a hardware level and also through the software by trying to establish a session with a server with another protocol (such as NetBEUI, for example). If you only have TCP/IP on your network, you can temporarily install NetBEUI on the client and on another computer on the same subnet. Test connectivity by connecting to a file share on the other computer. Remember, the computer should be on the same subnet because NetBEUI packets don't usually route.

- **The IP address on the router may be configured incorrectly.** The router address must match the client's default gateway address so that packets can move outside the subnet.

- **The client has the wrong router address.** Of course, if you Ping the correct router address and it works, you also want to make sure the default gateway address configured on the client matches the address you successfully Pinged.

- **The wrong subnet mask is configured.** If the subnet mask is wrong, packets destined for a remote subnet may not be routed.

You should also Ping each of the IP addresses used by the different ports on your router. It's possible that the local interface for your subnet is working but other interfaces on the router, which actually connect the router to the other subnets on the network, have some type of problem.

Pinging a Remote Host

As a final test in using Ping, you can Ping the IP address of a remote host, a computer on another subnet, or even the IP address of a Web server or FTP server on the Internet. If you can successfully Ping a remote host, your problem doesn't lie with the IP configuration; you are probably having trouble resolving hostnames.

If Pinging the remote host fails, your problems may be with the router, the subnet mask, or the local IP configuration. If you have followed the earlier steps of Pinging the loopback, local host address, and the default gateway address, you have already eliminated many of the problems that could cause this Ping to fail.

When a remote host Ping fails after you have tried the other Ping options, the failure may be due to other routers beyond the default gateway used for your subnet. If you know the physical layout of your network, you can Ping other router addresses along the path to the remote host to see where the trouble lies. Remember to Ping the addresses on both sides of the router: the address that receives the packet and the address that forwards the packet on. You can also use the Route command, as described in the following section, to find the path used to contact the remote host.

It is also possible that there is not a physical path to the remote host due to a router crash, a disruption in the physical network, or a crash on the remote host.

Many troubleshooters prefer to just try this last step when using Ping to troubleshoot IP configuration and connectivity. If you can successfully Ping a remote host, the other layers of TCP/IP must be working correctly. For a packet to reach a remote host, IP must be installed correctly, the local client address must be configured properly, and the packet must be routed. If a Ping to the remote host works, you can look to other sources (usually name resolution) for your connection problems. If the Ping fails, you can try each preceding step until you find the layer where the problem is located. Then you can resolve the problem at this layer. You can either start by Pinging the loopback address and working up through the architecture, or you can Ping the remote host. Of course, if Pinging the remote host works you can stop. If not, you can work back through the architecture until you find a layer where Ping succeeds. The problem must therefore be at the next layer.

DIAGNOSING AND RESOLVING NAME RESOLUTION PROBLEMS

Name resolution problems are easily identified as such with the Ping utility. If you can Ping a host by using its IP address, but cannot Ping it by its hostname, you have a resolution problem. If you cannot Ping the host at all, the problem lies elsewhere.

Problems that can occur with name resolution and their solutions fit into the following generalities:

1. **The entry is misspelled.** Examine the HOSTS or LMHOSTS file to verify that the hostname is correctly spelled. If you are using the HOSTS file on a system prior to Windows NT 4.0, capitalization is important, as this file is case sensitive; LMHOSTS, on the other hand, is not case sensitive (regardless of the Windows NT version number).

2. **Comment characters prevent the entry from being read.** Verify that a pound sign is not at the beginning of the line, or anywhere on the line prior to the hostname.

3. **There are duplicate entries in the file.** Because the files are read in linear fashion, with any duplication, only the first entry is read and all others ignored. Verify that all hostnames are unique.

4. **A host other than the one you want is contacted.** Verify that the IP address entered in the file(s) is valid and corresponds to the hostname.

5. **The wrong file is used.** Although similar in nature, HOSTS and LMHOSTS are really quite different, and not all that interchangeable. HOSTS is used to map IP addresses to hostnames, and LMHOSTS is used to map NetBIOS names to IP addresses.

In addition to Ping, the all-purpose, TCP/IP troubleshooting tool, useful name resolution utilities include the following:

- nbtstat
- hostname

NBTSTAT

The nbtstat utility (NetBIOS over TCP/IP) displays protocol statistics and current TCP/IP connections. It is useful for troubleshooting NetBIOS name resolution problems, and has a number of parameters and options that can be used with it:

- ◆ -a (adapter status)—Lists the remote machine's name table given its name.

- ◆ -A (Adapter status)—Lists the remote machine's name table given its IP address.

- ◆ -c (cache)—Lists the remote name cache including the IP addresses.

- ◆ -n (names)—Lists local NetBIOS names.

- ◆ -r (resolved)—Lists names resolved by broadcast and via WINS.

- ◆ -R (Reload)—Purges and reloads the remote cache name table.

- ◆ -S (Sessions)—Lists sessions table with the destination IP addresses.

- ◆ -s (sessions)—Lists sessions table converting destination IP addresses to hostnames via the HOSTS file.

Hostname

The hostname.exe utility, located in \systemroot\System32 returns the name of the local host. This is used only to view the name, and cannot be used to change the name. The hostname is changed from the Network Control Panel applet.

If you have configured TCP/IP correctly and the protocol is installed and working, the problem with connectivity is probably due to errors in resolving hostnames. When you test connectivity with TCP/IP addresses, you are testing a lower level of connectivity than users generally use. When users want to connect to a network resource, such as mapping a drive to a server or connecting to a Web site, they usually refer to that server or Web site by its name rather than its TCP/IP address. In fact, users do not usually know the IP address of a particular server. The name used to establish a connection must be resolved down to an IP address so that the networking software can make a connection. After you have tested the IP connectivity, the next logical step is to check the resolution of a name down to its IP address. If a name cannot be resolved to its IP address or if it is resolved to the wrong address, users will not be able to connect to the network resource with that name, even if you can connect to it by using an IP address.

Two types of computer names are used when communicating on the network. A NetBIOS name is assigned to a Microsoft computer, such as a Windows NT Server or a Windows 95 client. A hostname is assigned to a non-Microsoft computer, such as a UNIX server. (Hostnames can also be assigned to a Windows NT Server running Internet Information Server. For example, the name www.microsoft.com refers to a Web server on the Microsoft Web site. This server is running on Windows NT.) In general, when using Microsoft networking, such as connecting to a server for file sharing, print sharing, or applications, you refer to that computer by its NetBIOS name. When executing a TCP/IP-specific command, such as FTP or using a Web browser, you refer to that computer by its hostname.

A NetBIOS name is resolved to a TCP/IP address in several ways. Figure 5.6 shows how NetBIOS names are resolved. The TCP/IP client initiating a session first looks in its local name cache. If the client cannot find the name in a local cache, it queries a WINS server, if configured to be a WINS client. If the WINS server cannot resolve the name, the client tries a broadcast that only reaches the local subnet, because routers, by

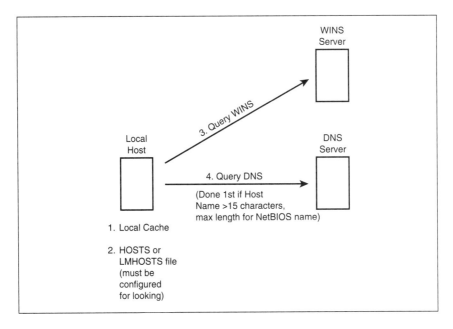

FIGURE 5.6
Resolving NetBIOS names.

default, are not configured to forward broadcasts. If the client cannot find the name through a broadcast, it looks for any LMHOSTS or HOSTS files, if it has been configured to do so. Finally, if the client cannot resolve a name in any other way, it queries a DNS server if it has been configured to be a DNS client. If the client specifies a name longer than 15 characters (the maximum length of a NetBIOS name), the client first queries DNS before trying a HOSTS file or WINS.

Hostnames are resolved in a similar manner. The client, however, checks sources that are used solely to resolve hostnames before trying sources that are used to resolve NetBIOS names. In resolving hostnames, the client first checks the HOSTS file, and then the DNS server, if configured to be a DNS client. These two sources resolve only hostnames. If the client cannot resolve the name, it checks the WINS server, if configured as a WINS client, tries a broadcast, and then looks in the LMHOSTS file. The last three methods to resolve a name are used to resolve NetBIOS names, but it is possible for a hostname to be listed in these sources.

Several tools are available to test name resolution. The following sections discuss these tools.

Testing Name Resolution with Ping

Just as you can use Ping to verify the TCP/IP configuration, you can also use Ping to verify hostname resolution. If you can successfully Ping a hostname, you have verified TCP/IP communication from the Network Interface layer of the TCP/IP architecture to the Transport layer. When you Ping a hostname, a successful reply shows the IP address of the host. This shows that the name has been successfully resolved to an IP address and that you can communicate with that host.

Testing NetBIOS Name Resolution by Establishing a Session

The ultimate test of connectivity is to establish a session with another host. If you can establish a session through mapping a drive or by executing a Net Use command (which is the command-line equivalent of mapping a drive), you have made a NetBIOS connection. If you can FTP, Telnet, or establish a Web session with another host, you have made a Sockets connection. A NetBIOS connection or a Sockets connection are the two main types of connections made by a TCP/IP client.

After the drive has been mapped with Net Use, you can switch to the new drive letter, view files and directories, and do any other things that are specified in the permissions of the share mapped to the drive letter. To get more information about the syntax of the Net Use command, type **net help use** in a command prompt.

A common problem in making NetBIOS connections is that the wrong NetBIOS name is used. Verify that the destination host has the same name that you are using to make the connection. Another potential problem with the name configuration occurs when NetBIOS scope IDs are used. Only NetBIOS hosts with the same scope ID can communicate with each other. The scope ID is configured through the advanced TCP/IP parameters. Incorrect share permissions can prevent you from establishing a NetBIOS session. When you try to connect a drive to a share where you have No Access, you receive an Access Denied message. This message indicates that you can connect to the server, but your rights did not allow you to make a connection to this specific share. This type of failure has nothing to do with TCP/IP connectivity. Remember that if the administrator changes your permissions to give you access, and you want to try again, you must log off and log on again to receive a new access token with the updated permissions.

NOTE   For an access token to be created, you must have an open connection with the server. The preceding example shows that the server has denied access; therefore no access token was ever created.

To resolve NetBIOS connectivity problems, you must know what sources are used to resolve NetBIOS names. The first place a client looks to resolve a NetBIOS name is the local cache. You can view the contents of the NetBIOS cache with the NBTSTAT command. You should verify that no incorrect entry is in the cache that maps the NetBIOS name to an incorrect IP address. If there is, however, you can remove the entry and then try to make another connection.

The next place to attempt NetBIOS name resolution is in a query to a WINS server. The client must be configured to be a WINS client. You can verify the address of the WINS server through the Advanced Properties of TCP/IP or by using IPCONFIG /all. You can view the contents of the WINS database by using WINS Manager on the WINS server. Verify that the hostname is in the database and, if so, make sure it is mapped to the correct IP address.

If the WINS server is configured to do a DNS lookup, you have another way to get NetBIOS resolution. The WINS server queries DNS if the WINS server cannot resolve the name from its own database. You can view the contents of the DNS database files by using DNS Manager on the DNS server or by using the NSLOOKUP utility from any client.

The client next tries a broadcast to resolve NetBIOS names, although you cannot configure what the client finds through the broadcast. The next place the client looks for NetBIOS name resolution is the LMHOSTS file. You can configure the contents of this file. The client must be configured for LMHOSTS lookup in the advanced TCP/IP configuration. Also, the LMHOSTS file must be located in the correct directory path. On a Windows NT computer, the LMHOSTS file must be in the path <winnt root>\system32\drivers\etc.

Next, verify the entries in the LMHOSTS file. The correct hostname and IP address must be entered in this file. If you have multiple entries in the file for a hostname, only the first entry is used. If you added another entry for a host in the file, you must delete the other entry listed earlier in the file so that it will not be used.

Domain names are another source of potential problems with LMHOSTS files. The domain name must be registered with the IP address of the primary domain controller (PDC) and #DOM (a switch that registers the server as a domain controller) on the same line. This entry is necessary to log on to the domain as well as to see the domain in a Browse list.

Another problem with LMHOSTS files doesn't prevent connectivity, but it can greatly delay it. If you have #INCLUDE statements at the top of the LMHOSTS file, the files specified by #INCLUDE are included first before any other entries lower in the LMHOSTS file are searched. You can speed connections to hosts entered in the LMHOSTS file by moving the #INCLUDE entries to the bottom of the LMHOSTS file.

Testing TCP Name Resolution by Establishing a Session

Typical TCP/IP connections from a Microsoft client, such as FTP or Telnet, use Windows Sockets. To test connectivity at this level, try establishing an FTP or Telnet session or try to connect to a Web server. When you successfully connect to a Web server, you see the site's Web page, and you can navigate through the page. When the connection fails, you receive a message on your Internet browser that the connection failed.

To resolve problems with a Windows Sockets connection, you must understand how a client resolves TCP hostnames. The first place a client looks to resolve a hostname is the local hostname. You can see what TCP/IP thinks is the local hostname by executing the `hostname` command. Verify that the local host is what you expect it to be. You can modify the hostname in the DNS tab of the TCP/IP properties.

The next place the client looks is in a HOSTS file. This file must be located in the path `<winnt root>\system32\drivers\etc`. Verify that any entry in the file for the host is correct, with the correct hostname and IP address. If multiple entries for the same hostname are in the file, only the first name is used. The HOSTS file can also have links to HOSTS files on other servers. If links are specified in the local HOSTS file, you should make sure entries in the other HOSTS files are also correct.

The final place a client can use for hostname resolution is a DNS server. The client must be configured to use DNS in the advanced properties of TCP/IP. The DNS server must have a zone file corresponding to the domain name specified in the hostname, or it must be able to query another DNS server that can resolve the name.

WHAT IS IMPORTANT TO KNOW

The following bullets summarize the chapter and accentuate the key concepts to memorize for the exam:

- Troubleshooting problems typically fall into one of two categories: configuration or name resolution.

- Configuration problems typically involve incorrect subnet masks (which can not distinguish between local and remote hosts), but could also be the IP address (duplicates or invalid numbers) or the default gateway (which prevents routing messages outside a subnet—remember that the default gateway must always be located on the same logical network as the host IP address).

- Tools to use in troubleshooting are: ARP (shows the Address Resolution Protocol cache of MAC addresses), IPCONFIG (shows the IP configuration information for the host), NETSTAT (gives all the TCP/IP protocol statistics), NSLOOKUP (shows DNS server entry information), PING (all-purpose troubleshooting utility that can be used with IP addresses or hostnames to verify that you can get to another host), ROUTE (shows the routing table and lets you add entries with ROUTE ADD, or see the table with ROUTE PRINT), TRACERT (like PING, except it traces the route being taken).

- Name resolution problems are easily identified as such with the Ping utility. If you can Ping a host using its IP address, but cannot Ping it by its hostname, you have a resolution problem. If you cannot Ping the host at all, the problem lies elsewhere.

- Problems that can occur with name resolution and their solutions fit into the following generalities:

    1. **The entry is misspelled.** Examine the HOSTS or LMHOSTS file to verify that the hostname is correctly spelled.

    2. **Comment characters prevent the entry from being read.** Verify that a pound sign is not at the beginning of the line, or anywhere on the line prior to the hostname.

    3. **There are duplicate entries in the file.** Because the files are read in linear fashion, with any duplication, only the first entry is read and all others ignored. Verify that all hostnames are unique.

4. A host other than the one you want is contacted. Verify that the IP address entered in the file(s) is valid and corresponds to the hostname.

5. The wrong file is used. Although similar in nature, HOSTS and LMHOSTS are really quite different, and not all that interchangeable. HOSTS is used to map IP addresses to hostnames, and LMHOSTS is used to map NetBIOS names to IP addresses.

♦ In addition to Ping, the all-purpose, TCP/IP troubleshooting tool, useful name resolution utilities include `nbtstat` and `hostname`.

♦ The `nbtstat` utility (NetBIOS over TCP/IP) displays protocol statistics and current TCP/IP connections. It is useful for troubleshooting NetBIOS name resolution problems, and has a number of parameters and options that can be used with it.

♦ The `hostname.exe` utility, located in `\systemroot\System32` returns the name of the local host. This is used only to view the name, and cannot be used to change the name. The hostname is changed from the Network Control Panel applet.

Think of this as your personal study diary. Your documentation of how you beat this exam.

The following section of Objective Review Notes is provided so you can personalize this book to maximum effect. This is your workbook, study sheet, notes section, whatever you want to call it. YOU will ultimately decide exactly what information you'll need, but there's no reason this information should be written down somewhere else. As the author has learned from his teaching experiences, there's absolutely no substitute for taking copious notes and using them *throughout* the study process.

There's a separate section—two to a page—for each subobjective covered in the book. Each subobjective section falls under the main exam objective category, just as you'd expect to find it. It is strongly suggested that you review each subobjective and immediately make note of your knowledge level; then return to the Objective Review Notes section repeatedly and document your progress. Your ultimate goal should be to be able to review this section alone and know if you are ready for the exam.

OBJECTIVE REVIEW NOTES

Suggested use:

1. Read the objective. Refer to the part of the book where it's covered. Then ask yourself the following questions:

   • Do you already know this material? Then check "Got it" and make a note of the date.

   • Do you need some brushing up on the objective area? Check "Review it" and make a note of the date. While you're at it, write down the page numbers you just checked, because you'll need to return to that section.

   • Is this material something you're largely unfamiliar with? Check the "Help!" box and write down the date. Now you can get to work.

2. You get the idea. Keep working through the material in this book and in the other study material you probably have. The better you understand the material, the quicker you can update and upgrade each objective notes section from "Help!" To "Review it" to "Got it".

3. Cross reference the materials YOU are using. Most people who take certification exams use more than one resource at a time. Write down the page numbers of where this material is covered in other books you're using, or which software program and file this material is covered on, or which video tape (and counter number) it's on, or whatever you need that works for you.

Planning

►Objective: Given a scenario, identify valid network configurations.

☐ **Got it**
Date:_____

☐ **Review it**
Date:_____

☐ **Help!**
Date:_____

Notes:

_____

_____

_____

_____

Fast Track cross reference, see pages:

_____

_____

Other resources cross reference, see pages:

_____

_____

_____

►Objective: Given a scenario, select the appropriate services to install when using Microsoft TCP/IP on a Microsoft Windows NT Server computer.

☐ **Got it**
Date:_____

☐ **Review it**
Date:_____

☐ **Help!**
Date:_____

Notes:

_____

_____

_____

_____

Fast Track cross reference, see pages:

_____

_____

Other resources cross reference, see pages:

_____

_____

_____

OBJECTIVE REVIEW NOTES

Installation and Configuration

► Objective: On a Windows NT Server Computer, configure Microsoft TCP/IP to support multiple network adapters.

☐ Got it
  Date:

☐ Review it
  Date:

☐ Help!
  Date:

Notes:

_____
_____
_____
_____

Fast Track cross reference, see pages:

_____
_____

Other resources cross reference, see pages:

_____
_____
_____
_____

► Objective: Configure scopes by using DHCP Manager.

☐ Got it
  Date:

☐ Review it
  Date:

☐ Help!
  Date:

Notes:

_____
_____
_____
_____
_____

Fast Track cross reference, see pages:

_____
_____

Other resources cross reference, see pages:

_____
_____
_____
_____

OBJECTIVE REVIEW NOTES

►Objective: Install and configure a WINS server.

☐ **Got it**　　　☐ **Review it**　　　☐ Help!
　*Date:*_____　　*Date:*_____　　*Date:*_____

Notes:

_____
_____
_____
_____
_____

Fast Track cross reference, see pages:

_____
_____

Other resources cross reference, see pages:

_____
_____
_____
_____

►Objective: Import LMHOSTS files to WINS.

☐ **Got it**　　　☐ **Review it**　　　☐ Help!
　*Date:*_____　　*Date:*_____　　*Date:*_____

Notes:

_____
_____
_____
_____
_____

Fast Track cross reference, see pages:

_____
_____

Other resources cross reference, see pages:

_____
_____
_____
_____

OBJECTIVE REVIEW NOTES

► Objective: Run WINS on a multihomed computer.

☐ Got it   ☐ Review it   ☐ Help!
   Date:_____   Date:_____   Date:_____

Notes:
_____
_____
_____
_____
_____
_____

Fast Track cross reference, see pages:
_____
_____

Other resources cross reference, see pages:
_____
_____
_____
_____

► Objective: Configure WINS replication.

☐ Got it   ☐ Review it   ☐ Help!
   Date:_____   Date:_____   Date:_____

Notes:
_____
_____
_____
_____
_____
_____

Fast Track cross reference, see pages:
_____
_____

Other resources cross reference, see pages:
_____
_____
_____
_____

OBJECTIVE REVIEW NOTES

► Objective: Configure static mappings in the WINS database.

☐ **Got it**   ☐ **Review it**   ☐ Help!
  *Date:*_____   *Date:*_____   *Date:*_____

Notes:

_____

_____

_____

_____

_____

Fast Track cross reference, see pages:

_____

_____

Other resources cross reference, see pages:

_____

_____

_____

_____

► Objective: Configure subnet masks.

☐ **Got it**   ☐ **Review it**   ☐ Help!
  *Date:*_____   *Date:*_____   *Date:*_____

Notes:

_____

_____

_____

_____

_____

_____

Fast Track cross reference, see pages:

_____

_____

Other resources cross reference, see pages:

_____

_____

_____

_____

OBJECTIVE REVIEW NOTES

►Objective: Configure a Windows NT Server computer to function as an IP router.

☐ Got it   ☐ Review it   ☐ Help!
   Date:_____   Date:_____   Date:_____

Notes:
_____
_____
_____
_____
_____
_____

Fast Track cross reference, see pages:
_____
_____

Other resources cross reference, see pages:
_____
_____
_____
_____

►Objective: Install and configure the DHCP Relay Agent.

☐ Got it   ☐ Review it   ☐ Help!
   Date:_____   Date:_____   Date:_____

Notes:
_____
_____
_____
_____
_____
_____

Fast Track cross reference, see pages:
_____
_____

Other resources cross reference, see pages:
_____
_____
_____
_____

► Objective: Install and configure the Microsoft DNS Server service on a Windows NT Server computer.

☐ **Got it**
*Date:*_____

☐ **Review it**
*Date:*_____

☐ **Help!**
*Date:*_____

Notes:

_____
_____
_____
_____
_____
_____

Fast Track cross reference, see pages:

_____
_____

Other resources cross reference, see pages:

_____
_____
_____
_____

► Objective: Integrate DNS with other name servers.

☐ **Got it**
*Date:*_____

☐ **Review it**
*Date:*_____

☐ **Help!**
*Date:*_____

Notes:

_____
_____
_____
_____
_____
_____

Fast Track cross reference, see pages:

_____
_____

Other resources cross reference, see pages:

_____
_____
_____
_____

OBJECTIVE REVIEW NOTES

► Objective: Connect a DNS server to a DNS root server.

☐ Got it	☐ Review it	☐ Help!
Date:	Date:	Date:

Notes:

_____
_____
_____
_____
_____

Fast Track cross reference, see pages:

_____
_____

Other resources cross reference, see pages:

_____
_____
_____
_____

► Objective: Configure DNS server roles.

☐ Got it	☐ Review it	☐ Help!
Date:	Date:	Date:

Notes:

_____
_____
_____
_____
_____
_____

Fast Track cross reference, see pages:

_____
_____

Other resources cross reference, see pages:

_____
_____
_____
_____

OBJECTIVE REVIEW NOTES

► Objective: Configure HOSTS and LMHOSTS files.

☐ **Got it**   ☐ **Review it**   ☐ **Help!**
   *Date:*_____   *Date:*_____   *Date:*_____

Notes:

_____

_____

_____

_____

_____

Fast Track cross reference, see pages:

_____

_____

Other resources cross reference, see pages:

_____

_____

_____

_____

► Objective: Configure a Windows NT Server computer to support
TCP/IP printing.

☐ **Got it**   ☐ **Review it**   ☐ **Help!**
   *Date:*_____   *Date:*_____   *Date:*_____

Notes:

_____

_____

_____

_____

_____

Fast Track cross reference, see pages:

_____

_____

Other resources cross reference, see pages:

_____

_____

_____

_____

OBJECTIVE REVIEW NOTES

►Objective: Configure SNMP.

☐ **Got it**
Date:_____

☐ **Review it**
Date:_____

☐ **Help!**
Date:_____

Notes:

_____
_____
_____
_____
_____
_____

Fast Track cross reference, see pages:

_____
_____

Other resources cross reference, see pages:

_____
_____
_____
_____

Connectivity

►Objective: Given a scenario, identify which utility to use to connect to a TCP/IP-based UNIX host.

☐ **Got it**
Date:_____

☐ **Review it**
Date:_____

☐ **Help!**
Date:_____

Notes:

_____
_____
_____
_____
_____

Fast Track cross reference, see pages:

_____
_____

Other resources cross reference, see pages:

_____
_____
_____

OBJECTIVE REVIEW NOTES

► Objective: Configure a RAS server and dial-up networking for use on a TCP/IP network.

☐ **Got it**   ☐ **Review it**   ☐ **Help!**
   *Date:*_____   *Date:*_____   *Date:*_____

Notes:

_____

_____

_____

_____

_____

Fast Track cross reference, see pages:

_____

_____

Other resources cross reference, see pages:

_____

_____

_____

_____

► Objective: Configure and support browsing in a multiple-domain routed network.

☐ **Got it**   ☐ **Review it**   ☐ **Help!**
   *Date:*_____   *Date:*_____   *Date:*_____

Notes:

_____

_____

_____

_____

_____

_____

Fast Track cross reference, see pages:

_____

_____

Other resources cross reference, see pages:

_____

_____

_____

OBJECTIVE REVIEW NOTES

Monitoring and Optimization

▶ Objective: Given a scenario, identify which tool to use to monitor TCP/IP traffic.

☐ Got it   ☐ Review it   ☐ Help!
  Date:_____   Date:_____   Date:_____

Notes:

_____
_____
_____
_____
_____

Fast Track cross reference, see pages:

_____
_____

Other resources cross reference, see pages:

_____
_____
_____
_____

Troubleshooting

▶ Objective: Diagnose and resolve IP addressing problems.

☐ Got it   ☐ Review it   ☐ Help!
  Date:_____   Date:_____   Date:_____

Notes:

_____
_____
_____
_____
_____

Fast Track cross reference, see pages:

_____
_____

Other resources cross reference, see pages:

_____
_____
_____
_____

OBJECTIVE REVIEW NOTES

► Objective: Use Microsoft TCP/IP utilities to diagnose configuration problems.

☐ **Got it**   ☐ **Review it**   ☐ **Help!**
   *Date:*_____   *Date:*_____   *Date:*_____

Notes:

_____
_____
_____
_____
_____
_____

Fast Track cross reference, see pages:

_____
_____

Other resources cross reference, see pages:

_____
_____
_____
_____

► Objective: Identify which Microsoft TCP/IP utility to use to diagnose IP configuration problems.

☐ **Got it**   ☐ **Review it**   ☐ **Help!**
   *Date:*_____   *Date:*_____   *Date:*_____

Notes:

_____
_____
_____
_____
_____

Fast Track cross reference, see pages:

_____
_____

Other resources cross reference, see pages:

_____
_____
_____
_____

OBJECTIVE REVIEW NOTES

► Objective: Diagnose and resolve name resolution problems.

☐ **Got it**   ☐ **Review it**   ☐ **Help!**
*Date:*_____   *Date:*_____   *Date:*_____

Notes:

_____
_____
_____
_____
_____
_____

Fast Track cross reference, see pages:

_____
_____

Other resources cross reference, see pages:

_____
_____
_____
_____

OBJECTIVE REVIEW NOTES

INSIDE EXAM 70-059

Part II of this book is designed to round out your exam preparation by providing you with chapters that do the following:

- "Fast Facts Review" is a digest of all "What Is Important to Know" sections from all Part I chapters. Use this chapter to review just before you take the exam: It's all here, in an easily-reviewable format.

- "Insider's Spin on Exam 70-059" grounds you in the particulars for preparing mentally for this examination and for Microsoft testing in general.

- "Sample Test Questions" provides a full-length practice exam that tests you on the actual material covered in Part I. If you mastered the material there, you should be able to pass with flying colors here.

- "Hotlist of Exam-Critical Concepts" is your resource for cross-checking your tech terms. Although you're probably up-to-speed on most of this material already, double-check yourself anytime you run across an item you're not 100 percent certain about; it could make a difference at exam time.

- "Did You Know?" is the last-day-of-class bonus chapter: A brief touching-upon of peripheral information designed to be helpful and of interest to anyone using this technology to the point that they wish to be certified in its mastery.

6 Fast Facts Review

7 Insider's Spin on Exam 70-059

8 Sample Test Questions

9 Hotlist of Exam-Critical Concepts

10 Did You Know?

The exam is divided into five objective categories:

- ▶ Planning
- ▶ Installation and Configuration
- ▶ Connectivity
- ▶ Monitoring and Optimization
- ▶ Troubleshooting

CHAPTER **6**

Fast Facts Review

WHAT TO STUDY

A review of the key topics discussed in the preceding five chapters follows. After you are certain that you understand the principles given in those five chapters, study these key points on the day of the exam prior to writing it.

Planning

Support and implementation of the TCP/IP protocol is built in to Windows NT 4.0 (Server and Workstation). To use TCP/IP, **every host (computer) must have a unique IP address.**

Windows NT enhances TCP/IP by including services for DNS and DHCP.

Installation and Configuration

IP addresses are 32-bit binary numbers, most often **written in four octets** of decimal numbers. An example of an address in decimal form is 192.14.200.2, or in binary form:

11000000.00001110.11001000.00000010

To simplify the conversion, always break the number given (whether it is decimal or binary) into the four parts, and then do the conversion. The following illustrates *IP binary to decimal conversion:*

Binary	1	1	1	1	1	1	1	1
Decimal	128	64	32	16	8	4	2	1

Memorizing this table will enable you to easily convert numbers between binary and decimal values. A decimal number of 131 is equivalent to 128+2+1, for example, so the binary representation is 10000011. Likewise, 191 is 128+32+16+8+4+2+1, or 10111111. 255 is 11111111, and 0 is 00000000. Going the opposite way, a binary number of 01010101 is equal to 64+16+4+1, or 85.

Within the octets, the first set of numbers identifies the class of network, and the last set identifies the host. Those in between essentially form the network ID. There are three possible classes:

Address	Class	Number of Possible Hosts	Default Subnet Mask
01-126	A	16,777,214	255.0.0.0
128-191	B	65,534	255.255.0.0
192-223	C	254	255.255.255.0

Notice that **address 127** is not used. This is **reserved for a "loopback" address**. The number of hosts available remains such if the default subnet mask does not change. The subnet mask, however, enables you to decrease the number of hosts and increase the number of sites (subnets) that you can have. The tradeoff is shown in the following *valid subnet addresses:*

Subnet Address	Additional Bits Required	Maximum Number of Subnets	Maximum Number of Hosts, C Network	Maximum Number of Hosts, B Network	Maximum Number of Hosts, A Network
0	0	0	254	65,534	16,777,214
192	2	2	62	16,382	4,194,302
224	3	6	30	8,190	2,097,150
240	4	14	14	4,094	1,048,574
248	5	30	6	2,046	524,286
252	6	62	2	1,022	262,142
254	7	126	Invalid	510	131,070
255	8	254	Invalid	254	65,534

IP addresses can be manually assigned to every machine on your network, or a DHCP server can issue them. DHCP—an extension of the BOOTP protocol (for diskless workstations)—eliminates configuration problems and simplifies IP administration by issuing clients an address from a pool of addresses (called a scope). Not only does it issue them an IP address, but it can also send the subnet mask and default gateway address. The IP address and subnet mask are the two things needed for any TCP/IP client to properly operate; the default gateway is optional, and is the only other piece of information that TCP/IP uses that requires input. A DHCP server can also define DNS and WINS entries for a client.

The issuing of a DHCP address is called leasing, and the address is given for a period of time called a lease period. Approximately halfway through that period, the client will try to renegotiate the lease to keep it longer. If it does not get an acknowledgment, the client will try again at regular intervals. If the lease expires, the client will try to get another one from that or another DHCP server. A DHCP server cannot be a DHCP client (it must have its own static IP address, subnet mask, and default gateway address), and it must have at lease one scope. Multiple DHCP servers should have portions of each other's scopes so that they can serve their clients in the event the other server is down.

Client reservation means that a DHCP client will always get the same IP address from the DHCP server. Addresses within a scope can also be marked off as reserved if they are not to be issued because hosts not employing DHCP (such as a UNIX server, DNS server, or WINS server) statically use them.

The HOSTS file is a static, ASCII-readable file that can be used to map hostnames (common system names) to IP addresses for address resolution. The LMHOSTS file is similar, but used to map NetBIOS names (MS computer names) to IP addresses. The LMHOSTS file (which should at a minimum contain each domain controller on the local domain and the PDC of every remote domain) also enables you to choose to load portions of the file in memory so that the file does not need to be read each time a name resolution takes place. Both HOSTS and LMHOSTS are static files. DNS and WINS servers carry out these procedures on larger scales, respectively.

DNS servers map hostnames given in the format of **FQDNs** (fully qual-ified domain names, such as iquest.net) to IP addresses. There should be two DNS servers in each zone, one primary and one secondary.

WINS servers map NetBIOS names to IP addresses and make the need for LMHOSTS files unnecessary. WINS servers work with Microsoft clients, but cannot integrate with Macintosh clients (for which you would need DNS). Unique entries are those that manually map a com-puter name to an IP address. Four other static entry types are domain name, group, Internet group, and multihomed.

TCP/IP printing can take place between UNIX and Windows NT hosts. The UNIX host can send print jobs to the Windows NT Server, or the Windows NT Server can send print jobs to the UNIX host. The key to both is using the LPR (line printer request) command to submit the job, and having the LPD (line printer daemon) service running on the UNIX host (if you are doing the latter). On the Windows NT side, the TCP/IP Printing service must be installed, and **LPR clients** need to know the IP address of the **LPD print server**.

SNMP allows events to be trapped and sent across a network for network management. To do such, the SNMP service must be installed on the server, and the trap messages must be configured for a destina-tion they are to be sent to. The destination must be running the SNMP Manager.

Connectivity

Telnet allows a computer to become a **dumb terminal** on another host—accessing and running files and applications over there. A key note is that Telnet **cannot download or upload files**, and can only run them.

If a RAS server is used for Dial-Up Networking, you must leave the default gateway information blank because this is provided by the ISP.

Monitoring and Optimization

Optimization changes are primarily made through the Registry Editor (Regedt32.exe or Regedit.exe). Monitoring, on the other hand, can be done with three tools:

- The *Event Log* **can track events and errors**. The System Event Log in Windows NT is where all critical system messages are stored, and not just those related to TCP/IP.

- The *Network Monitor* **analyzes a problem by capturing packets** coming and going. Filters enable you to limit what you are viewing and keep the data from being overwhelming. The most commonly used filters are INCLUDE and EXCLUDE, which capture or avoid capturing, specific data. The Network Monitor included with Windows NT Server can monitor only the specific system on which it is installed, unlike the Network Monitor in SMS, which can monitor other systems on the network.

- The *Performance Monitor* **can look for bottlenecks** and analyze performance. The Performance Monitor is the Windows NT all-around tool for monitoring a network using statistical measurements called counters. It has the capability to collect data on both hardware and software components, called objects, and its primary purpose is to establish a baseline from which everything can be judged. For Performance Monitor to collect TCP/IP information, SNMP must be installed.

Troubleshooting

Troubleshooting **problems typically fall into one of two categories: configuration or name resolution**. Configuration problems typically involve incorrect subnet masks (which cannot distinguish between local and remote hosts), but could also be the IP address (duplicates or invalid numbers) or the default gateway (which prevents routing messages outside a subnet—remember that the default gateway must always be located on the same logical network as the host IP address).

Tools to use in troubleshooting include the following:

- **ARP.** Shows the Address Resolution Protocol cache of MAC addresses. **NetBIOS names are cached as they are resolved, and ARP will display them.**

- **IPCONFIG.** As the name implies, **shows the IP configuration** information for the host. The IPCONFIG /ALL command will show not only TCP/IP configuration, but also DNS, WINS, DHCP, and NetBIOS information.

- **NETSTAT.** Gives all the TCP/IP **protocol statistics**.

- **NSLOOKUP.** Shows **DNS server** entry information.

- **PING.** All-purpose troubleshooting utility that **can be used with IP addresses or hostnames to verify that you can get to another host.** It can also be used to verify that all is working properly in your host. When used with the loopback address, the physical layer is not really tested, only the IP layer.

- **ROUTE.** Mentioned in the "Connectivity" section, it **shows the routing table** and enables you to add entries with ROUTE ADD, or to see the table with ROUTE PRINT.

- **TRACERT.** Like PING, only it **traces the route** being taken.

Name resolution problems are easily identified as such with the PING utility. If you can Ping a host using its IP address, but cannot Ping it by its hostname, you have a resolution problem. If you cannot Ping the host at all, the problem lies elsewhere.

Problems that can occur with name resolution and their solutions fit into the following generalities:

- **The entry is misspelled.** Examine the HOSTS or LMHOSTS file to verify that the hostname is spelled correctly.

- **Comment characters prevent the entry from being read.** Verify that a pound sign is not at the beginning of the line, or anywhere on the line prior to the hostname.

- **There are duplicate entries in the file.** Because the files are read in linear fashion, with any duplication, only the first entry is read and all others ignored. Verify that all hostnames are unique.

- **A host other than the one you want is contacted.** Verify that the IP address entered in the file(s) is valid and corresponds to the hostname.

- **The wrong file is used.** Although similar in nature, HOSTS and LMHOSTS are really quite different, and not all that interchangeable. HOSTS is used to map IP addresses to hostnames, and LMHOSTS is used to map NetBIOS names to IP addresses.

In addition to PING, the all-purpose, TCP/IP troubleshooting tool, useful name resolution utilities include `nbtstat` and `hostname`.

The `nbtstat` utility (NetBIOS over TCP/IP) displays protocol statistics and current TCP/IP connections. It is useful for troubleshooting NetBIOS name resolution problems, and has a number of parameters and options that can be used with it:

- `-a` (adapter status). Lists the remote machine's name table given its name

- `-A` (Adapter status). Lists the remote machine's name table given its IP address

- `-c` (cache). Lists the remote name cache including the IP addresses

- `-n` (names). Lists local NetBIOS names

- `-r` (resolved). Lists names resolved by broadcast and via WINS

- `-R` (Reload). Purges and reloads the remote cache name table

- `-S` (Sessions). Lists sessions table with the destination IP addresses

- `-s` (sessions). Lists sessions table converting destination IP addresses to hostnames via the hosts file

The **hostname.exe** utility, located in `\systemroot\System32` **returns the name of the local host**. This is used only to view the name, and cannot be used to change the name. The hostname is changed from the Network Control Panel applet.

In the Insider's Spin, you get the author's word on exam details specific to 70-059, as well as information you possibly didn't know—but could definitely benefit from—about what's behind Microsoft's exam preparation methodology. This chapter is designed to deepen your understanding of the entire Microsoft exam process. Use it as an extra edge; inside info brought to you by someone who teaches this material for a living.

CHAPTER 7

Insider's Spin on Exam 70-059

At A Glance: Exam Information

Exam Number	70-059
Minutes	90*
Questions	58*
Passing Score	750*
Single Answer Questions:	Yes
Multiple Answer With Correct Number Given	Yes
Multiple Answer Without Correct Number Given	Yes
Ranking Order	Yes
Choices of A–D	Yes
Choices of A–E	Yes
Objective Categories	5

These exam criteria will no longer apply when the exam goes to an adaptive format.

On this exam, there are 58 questions, and a candidate has 90 minutes to answer them with a required passing score of at least 750. Translated into more meaningful numbers, this means you pass with 44 right answers, and fail with anything less.

Two types of multiple-choice questions are on the exam: single answer (always readily identified by a radio button), and multiple answer (with the correct number given). There are no multiple-answer questions without the correct number given. The questions, overall, are extremely verbose and include a large number of exhibits. Choices typically range from A–D; many questions do include an E choice. Of the ones offering five choices, the vast majority are *multiple-ranking* questions.

With a multiple-ranking question, a scenario is given, a solution is offered, a number of required results are listed, and a number of optional desired results are also listed. You then must choose how well the solution met the results desired. These questions are very tricky and difficult. (One word of advice is to mark them the first time through and check them again after the rest of the exam, to make certain you read and answered correctly.)

Although Microsoft no longer releases specific exam information, at one time it was quoted that 85% of all who take a certification exam fail it. Common logic then indicates that only 15 out of every 100 people who think they know a product know it well enough to pass—a remarkably low number.

Quite often, administrators who *do* know a product very well and use it on a daily basis fail certification exams. Is it because they don't know the product as well as they think they do? Sometimes. More often than not, however, it is because of other factors:

1. They know the product from the real-world perspective, and not from Microsoft's perspective.

2. They are basing their answers on the product as it currently exists, and not on when it was first released.

3. They are not accustomed to so many questions in such a short time, or they are not accustomed to the electronic test engine.

4. They don't use all of the testing tools available to them.

The purpose of this chapter is to try to prepare you for the exam and help you overcome the four items in the preceding list. If you have been taking exams on a daily basis, and don't think you need this information, skim the chapter and go on—odds are that you will still uncover some tips that can help you. On the other hand, if you have not taken a lot of electronic exams, or have been having difficulty passing them by as wide a margin as you should, read this chapter carefully.

GET INTO MICROSOFT'S MINDSET

When taking the exams, remember that Microsoft is the party responsible for the authoring of the exam. Microsoft employees do not actually write the exams themselves, but instead "experts" in the field are hired on a contract basis for each exam to write questions. All questions, however, must adhere to certain standards and be approved by Microsoft before they make it into the actual exam. What that translates into is that Microsoft will never have anything in an exam that reflects negatively on them. They will also use the exams as promotional marketing as much as possible.

To successfully answer questions and pass the exams, you must put yourself into the Microsoft mindset and see questions from their standpoint. Take the following question, for example:

1. Which network operating system is the easiest to administer in a small real estate office:

   A. NetWare 3.12

   B. SCO Unix

   C. Windows NT 4.0

   D. LAN server

Although you could look at the question and make a sincere argument for at least three of the answers, there is only one that will be correct on a Microsoft exam. Don't try to read too much between the lines, and don't think that you're going to put a comment at the end of the exam arguing your case why another choice would be better—if you answer anything other than C, you might as well write this one off as a missed question.

UNDERSTAND THE TIMEFRAME OF THE EXAM

When you take an exam, find out when it was written. In almost all cases, an exam goes live within three months of the final release of the product it is based on. Prior to the release of the exam, it goes through a beta process where all of the questions that can be on the exam are written. It is then available for a short time (typically a week), during which scores on each question can be gathered. Questions that exam takers get right every time are weeded out as being too easy, and those that are too hard are weeded out, as well.

When you take something like a major operating system (to remain nameless in this example) and create an exam for it, what you end up with is a timeframe similar to the following:

1. Product goes into early beta.

2. A survey is done (mostly of beta testers) to find out which components of the product they spend most time with and consider to be

the most important. Their findings are used to generate the objectives and the weighting for each.

3. Product goes to final beta.

4. Contract writers are hired to write questions on the product, using the findings from the survey.

5. Product goes live.

6. Exam is beta tested for one to two weeks. After which, results on each question are evaluated, and the final question pool is chosen.

7. Service Pack for the product is released.

8. Exam goes live.

9. Another Service Pack to fix problems from the first Service Pack and add additional functionality is released.

10. Yet another Service Pack comes out.

11. Option Pack—incorporating service packs—is released.

12. You take the exam.

Now suppose the product happens to be Windows NT Server 4, and you receive a question such as this:

1. What is the maximum number of processors Windows NT Server 4.0 can handle?

　A. 2

　B. 4

　C. 8

　D. 16

In the real world, the answer is D. When Windows NT 4.0 first came out, however, the answer was B. Because the original exam questions were written to the final beta, the answer then was B, and is now B. Microsoft has maintained the stance that they will only test on core products, and not add-ons. Service Packs, Option Packs, and the like are considered to be something other than core product.

With this in mind, you must therefore *always* answer every question as if you are addressing the product as it exists when you pull it from the box, and before you do anything else with it—because that is exactly what the exam is written to. You must get into this mindset and understand the timeframe in which the exam was written, or you will fail exams consistently.

GET USED TO ANSWERING QUESTIONS QUICKLY

Every exam has a different number of questions, and most stick with the 90-minute timeframe in which to answer those questions. If you run out of time, every question you have not answered is graded as a wrong answer. Therefore:

1. Always answer every single question, and never leave any unanswered. If you start running out of time, answer all the remaining questions with the same answer (C, D, and so on), and then go back and start reading them. Using the law of averages, if you do run out of time, you should get 25% of the remaining ones correct.

2. Time yourself carefully. A clock runs at the top right of each screen. Mark all questions that require a lot of reading or that have exhibits and come back to them after you have answered all the shorter questions.

3. Practice, practice, practice. Get accustomed to electronic questioning and answering questions in a short period of time. With as many exam simulators as there are available, there is no reason for anyone to not run through one or two before plunking down $100 for the real thing. Some of the simulators are not worth the code they are written in, and others are so close in style to the actual exam that they prepare you very well. If money is an issue, and it should be, look for demos and freebies on Web sites. For a great sample that is accessible over the Web, go to http://www.MeasureUp.com, where you can try some sample exams online.

When you get into a situation where you do run out of time, spend as much time as you want to on the last question. You will never time out with a question in front of you, and will only be timed out when you click Next to go from that question to the next one.

BECOME ACQUAINTED WITH ALL THE THINGS AVAILABLE TO YOU

An enormous amount of common sense is important here, and much of that common sense only comes as you get more used to the testing procedure. The following list summarizes a typical sequence of events:

1. You study for an exam for a considerable period of time.

2. You call Sylvan Prometric (1-800-755-EXAM) and register for the exam.

3. You drive to the testing site, sit in your car, and cram on those last-minute details that won't stick with the others.

4. You walk into the center, sign your name, show two forms of ID, and walk back to a computer.

5. Someone enters your ID in the computer and leaves. You're left with the computer, two pieces of plain paper, and two #2 pencils.

6. You click the button on the screen to begin the exam, and the 90 minutes begins.

When you call Sylvan, be certain to ask how many questions are on the exam so that you know before you go in. Sylvan is allowed to release very little information (for example, they can't tell you the passing score), and this is one of the few pieces of information they can pass along.

The exam begins the minute you click the button to start it. Prior to that time, your 90 minutes haven't started. After you walk into the testing center and sit down, you're free (within reason) to do whatever you want to. Why not dump everything from your brain (including those last-minute facts you just crammed in the parking lot) onto those two sheets of paper before you before starting the exam? The two sheets provide you with four sides—more than enough to scribble everything out you have remembered and refer back to then during the 90 minutes.

After you click start, the first question appears. A number of different types of questions are asked, and Figure 7.1 shows but one. Because Microsoft does not readily make available (for obvious reasons) the

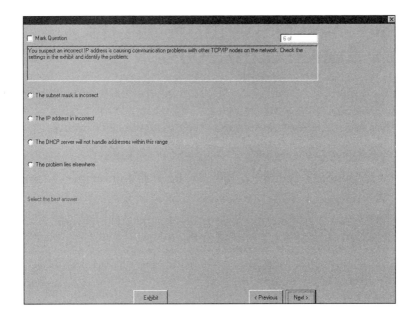

FIGURE 7.1
A sample test question.

ability to take screen shots of the exams, Figure 7.1 and all figures in this chapter are from a third-party emulator closely resembling the real thing.

Look at the question briefly, but more importantly, look at the information on the screen. First, you have the ability to mark this question; doing so will enable you to see (at the end of the exam) any questions you thought were difficult and jump back to them. Never mark a question and go to the next one without choosing some answer. Even if you don't read the question at all, and are saving it for later, mark it and answer C. That way if you run out of time, you have a chance of getting it right.

In the right-hand corner, you see the question number that you are on. In the real exam, you also see the time remaining here. Beneath the question are the possible answers. The radio buttons to the left of each indicate that there can only be one possible answer.

Although not always true, many times when there are four possibilities one will be so far off the mark as to not even be considerable, one will be too much of a give-me to be true, and you are left with two possibilities that you must choose between. For example:

1. In Windows NT Server 4.0, to view the Application log, what tool must you use:

A. Application Viewer

B. Event Viewer

C. Event Observer

D. Performance Monitor

In this case, choice A is the give-me of a non-existent tool which fits the question too perfectly. Choice D is the blow-off answer so far away from what's possible as to not be considered. That leaves choices B and C to choose from.

Even if you knew nothing about Windows NT Server at all, a clue that B and C are legitimate possibilities is the closeness in wording of each. Anytime you see two possibilities worded so closely, assume them to be the ones to focus on.

The buttons at the bottom of the screen enable you to move to the next question, or to a previous question. The latter is important, because if you ever come across a question where the wording of it provides the answer to a question you were asked before, *always* use the previous button to go back and change or check your first answer. Never walk away from a sure thing.

If there is an exhibit associated with the question, the command button for it will be displayed as well. The problem with exhibits is that they layer on top of the question, or can be tiled in such a way that you can't see either. Whenever you have an exhibit, read the question carefully, open the exhibit, memorize what is there (or scribble information about it on your two sheets of paper), close the exhibit, and answer the question.

Figure 7.2 shows an example of a question with more than one correct answer—a fact made obvious by check boxes rather than radio buttons appearing to the left of the choices.

There are two types of these questions: one where you are told how many answers are correct (choose 2, choose 3, and so forth), and the other where you are not. In the example shown, you are told to choose all correct answers, and do not know whether that is 2, 3, or 4. The only

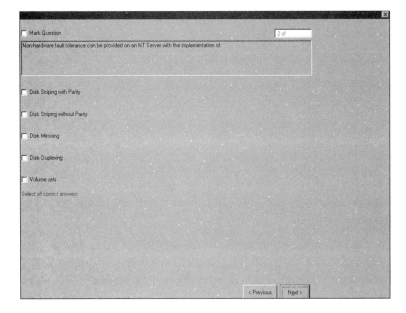

FIGURE 7.2
Another sample test question.

thing you do know is that it is not 1 and not 5—Microsoft will not use
check boxes if radio boxes will work, and will never have an all-of-the-
above–type question.

The vast majority of multiple-answer questions offer four possibilities,
meaning you must choose 2 or 3, but five possibilities (as in the Figure
7.2) are not uncommon. With these questions, read the question as carefully as possible, and begin eliminating choices. The question in Figure
7.2 specifically says non-hardware, for example, and one of the choices
is duplexing. Duplexing requires a hardware enhancement over mirroring, so choice D is not correct. You are now left with four possibilities,
and must rely on your knowledge to choose the right ones.

The biggest problem with multiple answers is that there is no such thing
as partial credit. If you are supposed to choose four items, and choose
only three, the question still counts as being wrong. If you should
choose two, picking one right answer and one wrong answer, you missed
the whole question. Spend much more time with multiple-answer questions than single-answer questions, and always come back, if time allows,
after the exam and reread them carefully.

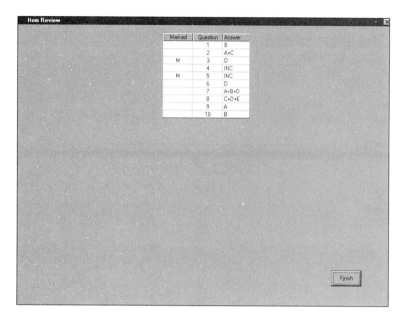

Marked	Question	Answer
	1	B
	2	A+C
M	3	D
	4	INC
M	5	INC
	6	D
	7	A+B+D
	8	C+D+E
	9	A
	10	B

Finish

FIGURE 7.3
The Item Review at the completion of the exam.

After you complete the exam, if there is time remaining, you come to an item review section, similar to that shown in Figure 7.3.

From here you can see the questions that you marked and jump back to them. If you have already chosen an answer on that screen, it remains chosen until you choose something else (the question also remains marked until you unmark it). The command buttons at the bottom of the question will now include an Item Review choice to enable you to jump back to the Item Review screen without going through additional questions.

Use the ability to mark and jump as much as you possibly can. All lengthy questions should be marked and returned to in this manner. Also note all incomplete answers. You can ill afford to not answer any question, so be certain to go back and fill them in before choosing to finish the exam (or running out of time).

After you click Finish, grading is done, and the Examination Score Report appears. The one shown in Figure 7.4 is a bit misleading. Typically, the bar graphs appear along with a message that indicates passing or failing only. The Section Analysis does not appear onscreen; it

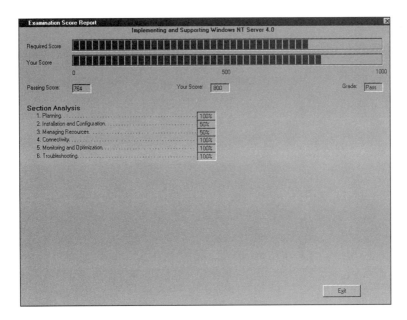

FIGURE 7.4
The Examination Score Report.

appears only on the printed documentation you walk out of the testing center with. The pass/fail score is determined on the beta of the exam, and statistics gathered from the performance of those who partook in it.

If you fail an exam, and every one will occasionally, *never* be lulled into a false sense of confidence by the Section Analysis. If it says you scored 100% in a particular section, you should still study that section before retaking the exam. Too many test-takers study only the sections they did poorly on. That 100% in Monitoring and Optimization could be the result of the first question pool containing only one question and you had a 25% chance of guessing it correctly. What happens next time when there are three questions in the random pool from that objective category, and you don't know the answers? You're handicapping yourself right off the bat.

A good rule of thumb if you do fail an exam is to rush back to your car as quickly as you can and write down all the questions that you can remember. Have your study materials in the vehicle with you and look up the answers then and there. If you wait until later, you will forget many of them.

The new policy from Microsoft allows you to retake an exam that you fail once without any waiting period (other than registering for it, and so on). If you fail it again, however, you must wait 14 days before you can retake it a third time (and 14 days from that point for the fourth try, and so forth). This is to prevent people from actually memorizing the exam. Do your best to never fall into this category. If you fail an exam once, start all over again and study anew before trying it the second time. Make the second attempt within a week of the first, however, so that topics are fresh in your mind.

WHERE THE QUESTIONS COME FROM

Knowing where the questions come from can be as instrumental as anything in knowing how to prepare for the exam—the more you know about it, the better your odds of passing. Earlier, the timeframe used to create the exam was outlined, noting that contract writers are hired for the exam. The contract writers are given a sizeable document detailing how questions must be written. If you really want to pursue the topic with more fervor, contact Microsoft and inquire about a contract writing position. A few tidbits that can be gleaned from multiple-choice authoring, however, include the following:

1. No question should have an *All of the above* answer. When available, this is almost always the case, and thus not a fair representation of a valid multiple-choice question.

2. For the same reason, there should never be a *None of the above* answer.

3. Scenarios should be used when they will increase the value of the question.

4. All subjective words (best, most, and so on) should be left from questions.

5. Although there can be only one correct answer for the question, all other possibilities should appear plausible, and avoid all rationale or explanations.

6. Single answers must be mutually exclusive (no A+C, B+C, and so on).

7. Negative words should be avoided (not, cannot, and so forth).

DIFFERENT FLAVORS OF QUESTIONS

At one time, all questions were either single answer, or multiple answer. There is a push today to go more toward *ranking* questions, and performance-based questions. Older exams still have only the first two question types; newer ones offer the latter.

Ranking questions provide you with a scenario, a list of required objectives, a list of optional objectives, a proposed solution, and then ask you to rank how well the solution meets the objectives. A rudimentary example is as follows:

1. Evan is a teenager who just got his driver's license. He wants to buy a fast car and ask Betty Lou to the movies on Friday.

   Required objectives: Buy a fast car
                           Ask Betty Lou to movies

   Optional objectives: Earn money for movies
                           Earn money for car

   Solution: Take part-time job at the Qwik-E-
                           Mart and buy classic '67 Cougar

   Rank the solution in terms of the objectives:

   A. The solution meets both required and optional objectives.

   B. The solution meets both required objectives and only the first optional objective.

   C. The solution meets both required objectives and only the second optional objective.

   D. The solution does not meet the required objectives.

In this over-simplified example, the answer is D—the solution does not include asking Betty Lou to the movies, so it does not meet the required objectives. With ranking questions, it is often the case that the required objectives are needed in all but the last answer, so read the question backward, if you will, and see whether the required objectives are being met. If they are not, you can answer the question quickly without reading any further and go on to the next question.

Performance-based questions have been incorporated in electronic testing for a long time, just not with Microsoft testing. If I really wanted to test and see how well you knew a product before hiring you, the best way to do so is to turn you loose with the product and tell you to do something. If you can, I will hire you; if you can't, I won't.

Taking that scenario into the testing center becomes difficult. Why? First and foremost, you can't be allowed unrestricted access to the product within the confines of something (a shell) grading your actions. Second, the stability of the operations on most testing centers' antiquated machines is questionable at best. And, the amount of time allotted cannot exceed a reasonable amount or you will become exhausted, and the testing center will not be able to move as many people through each day.

The solution to many of these problems is to keep the number of performance-based questions to a minimum, and have you work with an emulator of some type. The emulator can come onscreen when you click the button and bring up something that looks like what the configuration information in the real product would be, without the time and overhead involved of bringing up the real product.

How do you prepare for performance-based questions? Know your product—plain and simple. Focus on the administrative side of it—how to add new users, sites, servers, directories, and so on. Then you should have no difficulties. If you are very good at guessing multiple-choice answers, and really don't know the product at all, these questions will ferret that out. On the other hand, if you know you're product extremely well, and just aren't good at multiple-choice guessing, then you will find these questions a god-send.

Regardless of your familiarity, or lack thereof, with the product, be very careful with all of the performance-based questions. Although the emulator can load much quicker than the actual product in question, it is still very time-consuming, and the amount of time required to answer each question is far from minute. These questions take *a lot* of time, and you need to budget for them accordingly.

IN THE FUTURE

The study of test delivery and grading is known as *psychometrics*, and a good many people are employed in this profession. Microsoft uses many of them to help with the design and implementation of their exams. It should come as no surprise (if you have any experience with other certifications, such as Novell's) that the next big push will be to adaptive testing.

Under adaptive testing, the amount of time for each exam can be reduced from 90 minutes to somewhere near 30, and the number of questions can drop from 50–70, down to 15 or so. This benefits you greatly, and allows more students to be tested each day at training centers, as well.

The premise behind adaptive testing is fairly simple: The first question you get is totally at random and pulled from a pool. Beyond that first question, every other question presented to you is in some way related to how well you answered the preceding question.

Suppose, for example, that I want to give you a general exam on astronomy. The first question that comes up asks you how many planets there are in our solar system. You answer correctly (nine). I now ask you to name the third planet from the sun, and you also answer it correctly (Earth). I can now assume that you know your planets very well, and the next question will be about quasars. This continues for 15 questions. If you answer them all correctly, I will assume that you really know astronomy and pass you.

If, on the other hand, you answered Mars to the second question, the next question will be about planets again—giving you a chance to redeem yourself. If you miss that one, I will probably ask the most difficult question known to mankind about planets to see whether you can get it right—if you can't, you don't know planets; therefore you don't know astronomy, and you will fail. In some versions of adaptive testing, you bomb out right then, because there is no chance of redemption; on others, you are just given bogus questions for the remainder of the exam to make you feel like you're getting your money's worth, even though you are going to fail anyway.

Again, it differs per style/vendor but with most adaptive tests, if you answer the 15 questions and have not passed, yet are very close to doing so, you can be asked additional questions. The additional questions give you the opportunity to redeem yourself and achieve a passing score.

The key to adaptive testing, besides each question's relationship to the one preceding it, is that every question has a point value associated with it. The first question presented is assumed to be of medium value. If you miss a question on a topic, the next one asked will be more difficult, and of higher point value, to allow the chance for redemption. If you answer the first correctly, the next question will be of lesser value, and lesser difficulty.

There is no Item Review in adaptive testing, and there is no going back to the preceding question(s). After you answer a question, you are done with it, and you can draw a fair conclusion of how you did by whether the next question is on a similar topic.

Performance-based testing is in its infancy stages now at Microsoft, and should be rolled out within the year. Again, the best preparation here is to know your topic, and spend time with each question, making certain that you fully understand what is being asked before answering. With performance-based testing, you are given a task to do in an emulator of the product you are testing on. You must perform the action and your performance is graded to see whether you did it in the time and manner in which an administrator should.

This is an exam preparation book. It's the belief of the author and publisher that it's difficult to get too much practice with sample exam questions. There are other study materials available—books and software—that enable you to practice extensively, and we recommend that you give strong consideration to using these in some form.

What follows in this chapter is a practice test designed to reflect the questions you'd likely be challenged with on an actual Microsoft exam. These questions tie in directly to the material covered in this book. Take note that when this exam goes to an adaptive format, the number of questions, passing score, and minutes necessary to take this exam will vary.

Note: Please see the end matter of this book for more information on New Riders TestPrep books and New Riders Top Score exam preparation software, among other New Riders certification study resources.

CHAPTER 8

Sample Test Questions

QUESTIONS

Please note: When this exam goes to an adaptive format, the number of questions, passing score, and minutes given to take the exam will vary.

This sample test has 58 questions, just like the actual exam, and covers each of the five objective categories.

1. *Kristin Ann's Clothing Co. has seven physical plants, each in a different state. The company plans to open five more within the next year if revenue projections continue to hold true. It has a Class C IP address and is using subnets to differentiate each plant. Assuming that Kristin Ann's wishes to have the capability of putting as many hosts at each site as possible, which subnet mask should they use?*

   A. 255
   B. 254
   C. 252
   D. 248
   E. 240

2. *In reference to question 1, how many hosts would this subnet mask allow for at each site?*

   A. 62
   B. 30
   C. 14
   D. 6
   E. 2

3. *D S Widgets is a startup company with no mentionable network at present. It has tremendous growth potential, however, and wants to plan now for future growth. The company is currently considering which networking protocols to standardize their operations on. Of the following, which should they consider to be unroutable?*

   A. TCP/IP
   B. NetBEUI
   C. IPX/SPX
   D. NWLink IPX/SPX-compatible transport protocol

4. *Custom Cabinet Creations has a network ID of 192 and needs a minimum of six subnets, yet it never anticipates needing more than 20 hosts at any subnet. Which of the following subnets should be recommended for this situation?*
   A. 192
   B. 224
   C. 240
   D. 248
   E. 252

5. *Which of the following services require a daemon that is not provided with Windows NT?*
   A. REXEC
   B. FTP
   C. LPQ
   D. LPR

6. *Bill wants to gather detailed host information for remote management of his network. Which of the following protocols will he need to install?*
   A. ICMP
   B. LPD
   C. ARP
   D. SNMP

7. *Pistols are drawn as two of your administrators begin arguing over what item it is that DHCP reservations are actually assigned to. To ease the tension, you correctly answer the question that the assignments are issued to each:*
   A. Computer
   B. Network adapter card
   C. Domain
   D. Workgroup

8. *Which of the following command-line utilities compacts a DHCP database?*
   A. Compress
   B. Compact
   C. Pack
   D. Jetpack

9. *The default subnet mask assigned to an IP address of 100.100.100.200 is*

   A. 0.0.0.0
   B. 255.0.0.0
   C. 255.255.0.0
   D. 255.255.255.0

10. *Evan's Worldwide Tractors and Trailers has more than 20 plants around the world manufacturing parts. The tractor and trailer market is on the decline, and Evan's does not anticipate opening more plants in the near future. It has a Class B IP address and uses subnets to differentiate each plant. Assuming that Evan's wants to be able to put as many hosts at each site as possible, and not open new plants, what subnet mask should the company use?*

    A. 255
    B. 254
    C. 252
    D. 248
    E. 240

11. *In reference to question 10, how many hosts would this subnet mask allow for at each site?*

    A. 254
    B. 510
    C. 1,022
    D. 2,046
    E. 4,094

12. *Which of the following services is used to map IP addresses to NetBIOS names?*

    A. WINS
    B. DHCP
    C. DNS
    D. TCP

13. *Which of the following are examples of NetBIOS names in UNC format?*

    A. www.microsoft.com
    B. ComputerOne
    C. 192.14.2.15
    D. \\ComputerOne

14. *Which protocol is responsible for providing message addressing and routing?*
    A. TCP
    B. IP
    C. UDP
    D. SNMP

15. *A substitute for TCP that performs the same function only on a connectionless basis is*
    A. PPP
    B. IP
    C. UDP
    D. SNMP

16. *An IP address of 222.1.1.2 would have a default subnet mask of*
    A. 0.0.0.0
    B. 255.0.0.0
    C. 255.255.0.0
    D. 255.255.255.0

17. *Which of the following are not valid IP addresses for a host you are adding to a network?*
    A. 200.200.256.1
    B. 127.0.0.1
    C. 191.0.0.1
    D. 1.2.3.4

18. *What is the role of a WINS proxy?*
    A. A WINS proxy is a secondary WINS server.
    B. A WINS proxy is any WINS server configured to provide name registration, renewal, release, and resolution services to non-WINS clients.
    C. A WINS proxy is any WINS client configured to provide name resolution services to non-WINS clients.
    D. A WINS proxy is a WINS server located on a different subnet from a WINS client.

19. *Your network has client computers that are not WINS clients, and you have added a WINS proxy. Which services are not provided by the WINS proxy?*

A. Name registration

B. Name resolution

C. Name renewal

D. Name release

20. *Your Windows NT network has both a primary and a secondary WINS server and replication has been established with them. Which statement is accurate?*

A. If the primary WINS server is unavailable, the secondary WINS server can provide the same services to WINS clients.

B. If the primary WINS server is unavailable, a WINS proxy agent provides name services.

C. If the primary WINS server is unavailable and the secondary WINS server is also unavailable, a workstation automatically becomes a WINS proxy and provides name services.

D. None of the above

21. *When does name renewal occur?*

A. Name renewal occurs when a WINS client is shut down in an orderly fashion.

B. Name renewal occurs when the name registration's time to live expires.

C. Name renewal occurs automatically before the name registration's time to live expires.

D. Name renewal occurs only when initiated by a WINS proxy.

22. *When does name registration occur?*

A. Name registration occurs whenever a WINS client sends a request to a WINS server to obtain the IP address of a NetBIOS host.

B. Name registration occurs when a non-WINS client starts and sends a broadcast to a WINS proxy.

C. Name registration occurs when a WINS client starts and sends a name registration request to a WINS server.

D. Name registration occurs when a WINS client sends a name registration request to a WINS server and then the WINS server sends a negative acknowledgment because the name is already registered.

23. *In architectural models, how many layers are in the OSI model?*

    A. 7
    B. 5
    C. 4
    D. 3
    E. 2

24. *In architectural models, how many layers are in the TCP/IP model?*

    A. 7
    B. 5
    C. 4
    D. 3
    E. 2

25. *By default, what is the network ID for the address 121.212.112.122?*

    A. 121.0.0.0
    B. 121.212.0.0
    C. 121.212.112.0
    D. 0.0.0.122

26. *By default, what is the network ID for the address 198.81.91.119?*

    A. 198.0.0.0
    B. 198.81.0.0
    C. 198.81.91.0
    D. 0.0.0.119

27. *By default, what is the host ID for the address 179.79.234.234?*

    A. 179.0.0.0
    B. 0.0.234.234
    C. 0.79.234.234
    D. 0.0.0.234

28. *A company is assigned the network ID 150.134.0.0 by InterNIC. The company wants to have 15 subnets and up to 1,000 hosts per subnet. How many bits are needed for the custom subnet mask?*

    A. 4
    B. 5
    C. 6
    D. 7

29. *In question 28, what should the company use for the subnet mask?*
    A. 255.255.0.0
    B. 255.255.5.0
    C. 255.255.31.0
    D. 255.255.248.0

30. *An organization is assigned the network ID 114.0.0.0 by InterNIC. The organization currently has five subnets with about 100,000 hosts per subnet. The vice president wants to divide the subnets into 25 new subnets to make each subnet more manageable, and also plan for future growth. How many bits are used for the custom subnet mask?*
    A. 4
    B. 5
    C. 6
    D. 7

31. *In question 30, what should the organization use for the subnet mask?*
    A. 252.0.0.0
    B. 255.0.0.0
    C. 255.252.0.0
    D. 255.255.252.0

32. *How do you create a shortcut to a phonebook entry?*
    A. From the RAS administrator
    B. From the Dial-Up Networking icon
    C. From the Internet Service Manager
    D. Using drag and drop

33. *What do you have to change to use a different DNS for a phonebook entry?*
    A. The Dial-Up Networking properties
    B. The TCP/IP properties
    C. The settings in the RAS Administrator
    D. Dial-Up Networking always uses the default.

34. *If your dial-in server requires you to log on and this procedure cannot be scripted, what can you do?*

   A. Use Windows NT logon.
   B. Bring up a terminal window.
   C. Use Client Services for NetWare.
   D. You will not be able to dial in.

35. *What does autodial do for you?*

   A. Enables you to dial users from User Manager
   B. Enables you to use Windows Messaging to connect to your ISP
   C. Reconnects network resources when accessed
   D. Automatically dials at a given time

36. *What events can cause the Dial-Up Networking Monitor to make a sound?*

   A. On connection
   B. On errors
   C. When the program starts
   D. When the program terminates

37. *Where can you grant a user dial-in permissions?*

   A. From the command prompt
   B. From User Manager
   C. From the RAS administrator
   D. From Server Manager

38. *A DHCP server has been configured to use the wrong DNS server. How can you correct the problem?*

   A. Change the scope options on DHCP, and then renew the lease on the client.
   B. Use IPCONFIG /update:DNS to make the change.
   C. Enter the address of the DNS server in the advanced properties of TCP/IP.
   D. Add an entry for the DHCP client on the other DNS server.

39. *A TCP/IP client had a drive mapped to a Windows NT Server. You have just changed the IP address of the server and rebooted. Now the client can't connect to the new server, even though the server is configured to be a WINS client. What is the most likely cause of this problem?*

   A. The WINS server hasn't copied the new registration to all its clients.

   B. The client has the old IP address cached.

   C. The LMHOSTS file on the Windows NT Server needs to be updated.

   D. The DNS server needs to be updated.

40. *On a Windows NT computer, where does TCP/IP display its error messages?*

   A. In the TCP/IP log file

   B. In the SNMP log file

   C. In the System Log

   D. In the TCP.ERR file

41. *How can you test the installation of an FTP server?*

   A. Ping the FTP loopback address

   B. Ping another FTP server

   C. FTP another server

   D. FTP the loopback address

42. *In a network that has a mixture of Windows NT and remote host systems, you want to administer remote host systems from a Windows NT computer by running remote system jobs. Which of the following utilities enables you to execute a job on a remote system without requiring a logon password?*

   A. TFTP

   B. REXEC

   C. RSH

   D. Telnet

43. *Your network provides a Web server to the Internet through a typical firewall. Which of the following protocols would usually not be available to a client on the other side of your firewall trying to connect to a server inside it?*
    A. HTTP
    B. FTP
    C. TFTP
    D. Telnet

44. *HTML documents are transferred using the HTTP protocol. Which of the following statements accurately describes the HTTP protocol?*
    A. HTTP uses the non-connection–oriented communication features of TCP/IP for data transfer.
    B. HTTP requires a username and password for all HTML documents.
    C. The HTTP protocol uses the connection-oriented communication features of TCP/IP for data transfer.
    D. HTTP can be used only for text files.

45. *Which parameters are required when using the* LPR *command on a Windows NT computer to send a print job to a remote host?*
    A. The remote hostname
    B. Username and password for the remote system
    C. The remote printer name
    D. The name of the file to be printed
    E. The remote system's SMB server name

46. *By creating an LPR printer on a Windows NT computer and sharing the newly created printer, which of the following statements describes the added functions?*
    A. Remote host systems can print to the LPR printer, and Windows NT client computers can print to the LPR printer, but only by using the LPR command.
    B. Remote host systems can print to the LPR printer, and Windows NT computers can print to the LPR printer using Windows NT printing, but other Windows NT computers cannot print to the LPR printer.

C. Remote host systems can print to the LPR printer, Windows NT computers can print to the LPR printer using Windows NT printing, and other Windows NT computers can print to the LPR printer.

D. Remote host systems cannot print to the LPR printer, Windows NT computers can print to the LPR printer using Windows NT printing, and other Windows NT computers can print to the LPR printer.

47. *What is the purpose of the domain suffix search order?*

A. When you look for a hostname, entries here can be used to complete the FQDN.

B. When you look for a NetBIOS name, entries here can be used as the NetBIOS scope ID.

C. Allows your computer to be in more than one domain at a time.

D. Tells your systems which Windows NT domains to search when looking for a logon server.

48. *Which of the following best describes the order in which you should configure the DNS server?*

A. Install the server, create the zone, enter all the records, create the reverse lookup zone, and add the WINS records

B. Install the server, create the reverse lookup zone, add the zone information, add the WINS lookup records, and add the other hosts

C. Create the DNS server database files using a text editor, install the server, and verify the information

D. Install the DNS server and then transfer the zone from the WINS server

49. *What information is contained in an MX record? (Choose all that apply)*

A. A preference entry

B. The mail server name

C. The WWW server name

D. There is no such record.

50. *What is the purpose of the cache file?*

   A. Stores the names of hosts that your server has resolved
   B. Enables you to enter commonly used hosts that will be loaded to the cache
   C. Stores the addresses of root-level servers
   D. Temporarily builds the DNS server information as the server starts

51. *If a domain announcement is sent out to a domain and the domain does not respond, how long is it before the remote domain is removed from the browse list?*

   A. Four announcement periods
   B. Three announcement periods
   C. Two announcement periods
   D. One announcement period

52. *You have a network with three subnets: subnet A, subnet B, and subnet C. What happens if the domain master browser on subnet A goes down?*

   A. Browsing is restricted to each subnet.
   B. Subnet B can see C, but not A.
   C. Subnet C can see B, but not A.
   D. All subnets continue browsing normally.

53. *How can you configure a WINS server to automatically replicate its database with any other WINS servers?*

   A. Specify all servers as push partners for replication.
   B. Turn on the Migrate On/Off switch in WINS Manager.
   C. Set the UseSelfFndPnrs parameter in the Registry to 0.
   D. Turn off the Replicate Only with Partners switch in WINS Manager.

54. *How does a client decide which WINS server to use? (Select the best answer)*

   A. The first WINS server that responds to a broadcast
   B. The WINS server that WINS an election
   C. The initial WINS server configured in TCP/IP
   D. The primary WINS server specified in the DHCP scope options

55. *What happens to a name registration when the host crashes?*

   A. The WINS server marks the record as released after it queries the client at half of TTL.

   B. The name is marked as released after three renewal periods are missed.

   C. The name is scavenged after the registration expires.

   D. The name is released after the TTL is over.

56. *On which platform can you install a WINS server? (Select all that apply)*

   A. On a Windows NT 3.51 member server

   B. On a Windows NT 4.0 Workstation running the WINS proxy agent

   C. On a Windows NT 4.0 backup domain controller

   D. On a Windows NT 4.0 primary domain controller

57. *How many WINS servers should be installed?*

   A. One primary for each subnet and one secondary for every two subnets

   B. One primary for every 2,000 clients and one secondary for each additional 2,000 clients

   C. One primary and one secondary for every 10,000 clients

   D. One primary and one secondary for each domain

58. *How do you configure automatic address resolution for DHCP clients?*

   A. Specify the Create WINS database option in the DHCP scope

   B. Install a WINS server with an address specified by the DHCP scope

   C. Schedule the active leases to be copied from DHCP Manager to an LMHOSTS file

   D. Locate a DHCP relay agent on the same subnet as the WINS server

ANSWERS AND EXPLANATIONS

1. **E**   A subnet mask of 240 is needed to make up to 14 subnets available on a Class C network.

2. **C**   A subnet mask of 240 on a Class C network allows for up to 14 hosts at each subnet.

3. **B**   NetBEUI is considered an unroutable protocol.

4. **B**   A subnet mask of 224 will make six subnets available with up to 30 hosts at each site.

5. **A**   The REXEC daemon support is not provided with standard Windows NT 4.0.

6. **D**   SNMP—Simple Network Management Protocol—obtains detailed host information for remote management.

7. **B**   DHCP reservations are made to network adapter cards.

8. **D**   The Jetpack utility compacts a DHCP database.

9. **B**   The default subnet mask for a Class A network is 255.0.0.0.

10. **D**   A subnet mask of 248 will allow for up to 30 subnets.

11. **D**   A subnet mask of 248 on a Class B network will allow for up to 2,046 hosts at each subnet.

12. **A**   WINS maps IP addresses to NetBIOS names.

13. **B - D**   ComputerOne is a NetBIOS name, as is \\ComputerOne. www.microsoft.com is an example of a fully qualified domain name (FQD); 192.14.2.15 is an example of an IP address.

14. **B**   IP is the protocol that provides message addressing and routing.

15. **C**   UDP is connectionless, whereas TCP is connection oriented.

16. **D**   The default subnet mask for Class C networks is 255.255.255.0.

17. **A - B**   200.200.256.1 exceeds the maximum value in the third octet: 127.0.0.1 is the loopback address.

18. **C**   A WINS proxy is any WINS client configured to provide name resolution services to non-WINS clients.

19. **A - B - C - D**   Services not provided by the WINS proxy to non-WINS clients include name registration, resolution, renewal, and release.

20. **A**   If the primary WINS server is unavailable, the secondary WINS server can provide the same services to WINS clients.

21. **C**   Name renewal occurs automatically before the name registration's time to live expires.

22. **C**   Name registration occurs when a WINS client starts and sends a name registration request to a WINS server.

23. **A**   The OSI model has seven layers.

24. **C**   The TCP/IP model has four layers.

25. **A**   The default network ID for address 121.212.112.122 is 121.0.0.0.

26. **C**   The default network ID for address 198.81.91.119, by default, is 198.81.91.0.

27. **B**   The default host ID for address 179.79.234.234 is 0.0.234.234.

28. **B**   Fifteen subnets are required, which converts to binary 1111. Four bits don't have enough subnets because 0000 and 1111 can't be used. Therefore 5 bits are needed, which allows for 30 subnets. C and D also allow for enough subnets, but more is not always better. Because this is a Class B network, using 6 bits barely allows for 1,000 hosts per subnet (1,022), leaving very little room for growth. Using 7 bits allows for only 510 hosts per subnet.

29. **D**   This subnet mask uses the 5 higher-order bits in the third octet to specify the subnet, as calculated in question 28. A is the default subnet mask, which allows for only one network ID. C is

binary 11111. Remember when converting the required number of bits to a decimal number, you must fill in the lower-order bits with zeroes. The correct binary subnet mask is 11111000, which is decimal 248.

30. **C**   Although B is certainly a correct answer because it allows for 30 subnets, there is very little room for growth in the number of subnets. Because you have a Class A network ID, 524,286 host IDs are possible within each of the 30 subnets. A better approach is to sacrifice one of the host address bits to allow for 62 subnets. This solution still allows for 262,142 hosts on each subnet, 160% more than the original needs.

31. **C**   The subnet mask 255.252.0.0 is correct for a Class A network that allows 62 subnets. A puts the 252 one octet too soon. D puts the octet too late, making it a Class B subnet mask. B is the default subnet mask for a Class A network.

32. **B**   You can create a shortcut to a phonebook entry from the Dial-Up Networking icon.

33. **A**   To use a different DNS for a phonebook entry, you must change the Dial-Up Networking properties.

34. **B**   If your dial-in server requires you to log on and this procedure cannot be scripted, you can bring up a terminal window.

35. **C**   Autodial reconnects network resources when accessed.

36. **A - B**   Events that can cause the Dial-Up Networking Monitor to make a sound include on connection and on errors.

37. **B - C**   You can grant a user dial-in permissions from User Manager or from the RAS administrator.

38. **A**   You can correct the problem by changing the scope options on DHCP and then renewing the lease on the client.

39. **B**   The most likely cause of the problem is that the client has the old IP address cached.

40. **C**   On a Windows NT computer, TCP/IP displays its error messages in the System Log.

41. **D**   You can FTP the loopback address to test the installation of an FTP server.

42. **C**   RSH enables you to execute a job on a remote system without requiring a logon password.

43. **D**   Telnet would usually *not* be available to a client on the other side of a firewall.

44. **C**   The HTTP protocol uses the connection-oriented communication features of TCP/IP for data transfer.

45. **A - C - D**   The LPR command on a Windows NT computer needs the remote hostname, the remote printer name, and the name of the file to be printed.

46. **C**   Remote host systems can print to the LPR printer, Windows NT computers can print to the LPR printer using Windows NT printing, and other Windows NT computers can print to the LPR printer.

47. **A**   The domain suffix search order is used when you look for a hostname. Entries here can be used to complete the FQDN.

48. **B**   Configure the DNS server as follows: install the server, create the reverse lookup zone, add the zone information, add the WINS lookup records, and add the other hosts.

49. **A - B**   An MX record contains a preference entry and the mail server name.

50. **C**   The purpose of the cache file is to store the addresses of root-level servers.

51. **B**   If a domain announcement is sent out to a domain and the domain does not respond, three announcement periods and 45 minutes pass before the remote domain is removed from the Browse list.

52. **A**   Browsing is restricted to each subnet.

53. **D**   A WINS server can automatically replicate with any other WINS server. However, WINS is configured by default to repli-

cate only with specified partners. You must turn off this parameter to enable the automatic replication.

54. **D**   A WINS client communicates only with WINS servers for which the client is configured. You can configure these WINS servers in one of two ways. You can manually specify a WINS server with the primary WINS server address in TCP/IP. Or you can specify the primary WINS server address through the scope options of DHCP for clients that receive their TCP/IP addresses from DHCP.

55. **D**   After a client registers its NetBIOS name with a WINS server, it is the client's responsibility to renew that registration. The WINS server does not initiate any registration renewals with clients. The registration is released if not renewed by the time the TTL expires. However, the entry is not scavenged until the extinction interval and the extinction timeout have expired.

56. **A - C - D**   You can install a WINS server on any Windows NT Server platform.

57. **C**   You should have one primary and one secondary WINS server for every 10,000 WINS clients. Although the secondary server is not required, it can serve as a backup if the primary WINS server goes down.

58. **B**   Resolving addresses for DHCP clients needs to be automated because DHCP clients can end up with a different TCP/IP address every time they reboot. Installing a WINS server, which is configured as part of the DHCP Scope options, is the only practical way to resolve NetBIOS names in this environment.

If you feel you need to practice more exam-like questions, take a look at New Riders' MCSE TestPrep series of certification preparation books, featuring hundreds of review questions and concise explanations of why answer choices are correct or incorrect. These books are specifically designed for exam candidates who want to drill themselves extensively on exam questions.

The breadth and depth of your technical vocabulary is a significant measure of your knowledge as applied to the exam you're about to be tested on. The hotlist of exam-critical concepts is something you should access every time you run across a term or a word you're not sure about. Double-check your knowledge by reviewing this section from time to time. Do you have a slightly different definition for a term? Why? The answer can deepen your understanding of the technology.

Do you need to add your own definitions or new terms? It's more than likely, since no two exam candidates will find the same list of terms equally useful. That's why there's room to add your own terms and concepts at the end of this section.

CHAPTER 9

Hotlist of Exam-Critical Concepts

Term	*Definition*
Account	A user ID and disk area (typically the home directory) restricted for the use of a particular person. Usually password protected.
ACK	Acknowledgment—A response from a receiving computer to a sending computer to indicate successful reception of information. TCP requires that packets be acknowledged before it considers the transmission safe.
Active open	An action taken by a client to initiate a TCP connection with a server.
Address classes	Grouping of IP addresses with each class, defining the maximum number of networks and hosts available. The first octet of the address determines the class.
Address mask	A 32-bit binary number used to select bits from an IP address for subnet masking.
Agent	The software routine in a Simple Network Management Protocol (SNMP)–managed device that responds to get and set requests and sends trap messages.
Alias	A short name that represents a more complicated one. Often used for mail addresses or host domain names.
Analog	A form of electronic communication using a continuous electromagnetic wave, such as television or radio. Any continuous wave form, as opposed to digital on/off transmissions.
Anchor	A hypertext link in the form of text or a graphic that, when clicked, takes you to the linked file.
Annotation	A Mosaic feature that enables you to add a comment to a viewed document.
Anonymous FTP	Enables you to download (and sometimes upload) files without requiring a password.

Term	*Definition*
ANSI	American National Standards Institute—The membership organization responsible for defining U.S. standards in the information technology industry.
API	Application Programming Interface—A language and message format that enables a programmer to use functions in another program or in the hardware.
Archie	A search engine that finds filenames on anonymous FTP services.
Archive	A repository of files available for access at an Internet site. Also, a collection of files, often a backup of a disk or files saved to tape to allow them to be transferred.
Argument	A parameter passed to a subroutine or function.
ARP	Address Resolution Protocol—A protocol in the TCP/IP suite used to resolve an IP address to a physical hardware address.
ARPA	Advanced Research Projects Agency—A government agency that originally funded the research on the ARPAnet (became DARPA in the mid-1970s).
ARPAnet	The first network of computers funded by the U.S. Department of Defense Advanced Projects Agency. An experimental communications network funded by the government that eventually developed into the Internet.
Article	Message submitted to a Usenet newsgroup. Unlike an email message that goes to a specific person or group of persons, a newsgroup message goes to directories (on many machines) that can be read by any number of people.
ASCII	American Standard Code for Information Interchange—A standard character set of data that is limited to letters, numbers, and punctuation.

Term	*Definition*
ATM	Asynchronous Transfer Mode—Broadband technology that increases transfer speeds.
Attribute	A form of a command-line switch as applied to tags in the HTML language. HTML commands or tags can be more specific when attributes are used. Not all HTML tags use attributes.
au	Extension for audio files.
Backbone	Generally very high-speed, T3 telephone lines that connect remote ends of networks and networks to one another; only service providers are connected to the Internet in this way. Can also be the main network segment that connects the network.
Bang	A slang term for an exclamation point. Also known as a bang path.
Bang address	A type of email address that separates hostnames in the address with exclamation points. Used for mail sent to the UUCP (UNIX-to-UNIX copy) network, where specifying the exact path of the mail (including all hosts that pass on the message) is necessary. The address is in the form of machine!machine!userID, in which the number of machines listed depends on the connections needed to reach the machine that stores the account user ID.
Baseband	A network technology that requires all nodes attached to the network to participate in every transmission. Ethernet, for example, is a baseband technology.
Best-effort delivery	A characteristic of a network technology that does not ensure link-level reliability. IP and UDP protocols work together to provide best-effort delivery service to applications.
BGP	Border Gateway Protocol—A routing protocol used to exchange network availability information with other subsystems.

Term	*Definition*
Binary	A file or other data that may contain nonprintable characters, including graphics files, programs, and sound files.
BinHex	A program that encodes binary files as ASCII so that they can be sent through email.
Bitnet	Because It's Time Network—A non-TCP/IP network for small universities without Internet access.
Block	A group of statements enclosed in braces.
Bookmarks	Term used by some World Wide Web browsers for marking URLs you access frequently.
Boolean logic	Logic dealing with true/false values. (The operators AND, OR, and NOT are Boolean operators.)
BOOTP	Bootstrap Protocol—A protocol used to configure systems with an IP address, subnet mask, and a default gateway across internetworks.
Bounce	An email message you receive that tells you that an email message you sent wasn't delivered. Usually contains an error code and the contents of the message that wasn't delivered.
bps	bits per second—A measurement that expresses the speed at which data is transferred between computers.
Bridge	A device that operates at the Data Link layer of the OSI model and connects one physical section of a network to another, often providing isolation.
Broadband	A network technology that multiplexes multiple network carriers into a single cable.
Broadcast	A packet destined for all hosts on the network.
Brouter	A computer device that works as both a bridge and a router. Some network traffic may be bridged, while other traffic is routed.

Term	*Definition*
Browser	A utility that enables you to look through collections of things. A file browser, for example, enables you to look through a file system. Applications that enable you to access the World Wide Web are called browsers.
Buffer	A storage area used to hold input or output data.
CAN	Campus area network—A physical communications network that operates across a campus or similar geographic area.
CERN	The European Laboratory for Particle Physics, where the World Wide Web was first conceived of and implemented.
Checksumming	A service performed by UDP that checks to see whether packets were changed during transmission.
Child	A subprocess called to assist a parent with execution of a task.
CIDR	Classless interdomain routing—A method of allocating and specifying Internet addresses by replacing network numbers with variable-length prefixes.
Client	User of a service. Also often refers to a piece of software that gets information from a server. Additionally, *client* refers to an application that makes a request of a service on a (sometimes) remote computer; the request can be, for example, a function call.
CMIP	Common Management Information Protocol—An OSI network management protocol.
Compress	A program that compacts a file so that it fits into a smaller space. Also can refer to the technique of reducing the amount of space a file takes up.
Concatenate	To join two strings.
Connection	A logical path between two protocol modules that provides a reliable delivery service.

Term	*Definition*
Connectionless service	A delivery service that treats each packet as a separate entity. Often results in lost packets or packets delivered out of sequence.
Context	Many functions return either array values or scalar values depending on the context—that is, whether returning an array or a scalar value is appropriate for the place where the call was made.
CRC	Cyclic Redundancy Check—A computation about a frame of which the result is a small integer. The value is appended to the end of the frame and recalculated when the frame is received. If the results differ from the appended value, the frame has presumably been corrupted and is therefore discarded. CRC is used to detect errors in transmission.
CSMA	Carrier Sense Multiple Access—A simple media access control protocol that enables multiple stations to contend for access to the medium. If no traffic is detected on the medium, the station may send a transmission.
CSMA/CD	Carrier Sense Multiple Access with Collision Detection—A characteristic of network hardware that uses CSMA with a process that detects when two stations transmit simultaneously. If that happens, both back off and retry the transmission after a random time period has elapsed.
Cyberspace	Refers to the entire collection of sites accessible electronically. If your computer is attached to the Internet or another large network, it exists in cyberspace.
Daemon	A program that runs automatically on a computer to perform a service for the operating system or for clients on the network.
DARPA	Defense Advanced Research Projects Agency, originally ARPA—The government agency that funded the research that developed the ARPAnet.

Term	*Definition*
Database	A structured way of storing data in any way, often described in terms of a number of tables; each table is made up of a series of records, and each record contains a number of fields.
Datagram	A packet of data and delivery information.
Debugging	The process of tracking down errors in a program, often aided by examining or outputting extra information designed to help this process.
Dedicated line	See Leased line.
DES	Data Encryption Standard—A private key encryption algorithm developed by the U.S. government to provide security for data transmitted over a network.
DHCP	Dynamic Host Configuration Protocol—A protocol that provides dynamic address allocation and automatic TCP/IP configuration.
Dial-up connection	A connection to the Internet through a modem and telephone line that allows email and running processes to occur on a remote computer.
Digest	A form of mailing list where a number of messages are concatenated (linked) and sent out as a single message.
Digital	Type of communications used by computers, consisting of individual on and off pulses. Compare to analog.
Direct connection	A connection to the Internet through a dedicated line, such as ISDN.
Directed broadcast address	An IP address that specifies all hosts on the network.
Directory of servers	A service that describes what is available on servers throughout the world.
DNS	See Domain name system (DNS).

Term	*Definition*
DNS Name Server	The server(s) that contain information about a portion of the DNS database.
Doc-ID	In a wide area information server (WAIS), an ID that identifies a specific document in a database.
DOD	Department of Defense—A U.S. government agency that originally sponsored the ARPAnet research.
Domain	Highest subdivision of the Internet, for the most part by country (except in the United States, where it's by type of organization, such as educational, commercial, and government). Usually the last part of a hostname; for example, the domain part of ibm.com is .com, which represents the domain of commercial sites in the United States.
Domain name system (DNS)	The system that translates between Internet IP address and Internet hostnames.
Dot address	See Host address.
Download	Move a file from a remote computer to a local computer.
Effective GID	The group identifier of the current process, which may have been changed from the original GID by various means.
Effective UID	The user identifier of the current process, which may have been changed from the original UID by various means.
Email	An electronic message delivered from one computer user to another. Short for electronic mail.
Email address	An address used to send email to a user on the Internet, consisting of the username and hostname (and any other necessary information, such as a gateway machine). An Internet email address is usually in the form username@domainname.

Term	*Definition*
Encryption	The process of scrambling a message so that it can be read only by someone who knows how to unscramble it.
Ethernet	A type of local area network hardware. Many TCP/IP networks are Ethernet-based.
Eudora	The most widely used email system.
Expire	Remove an article from a Usenet newsgroup after a specified interval.
Fair queuing	A technique that controls traffic in gateways by restricting every host to an equal share of gateway bandwidth.
FAQ	Frequently asked question(s)—Often a question and answer approach to common problems. Most Usenet newsgroups have a FAQ to introduce new readers to popular topics in the newsgroup.
FCS	Frame check sequence—A computation about the bits in a frame; the result is appended to the end of the frame and recalculated within the frame as it is received. If the results differ from the appended value, the frame has presumably been corrupted and is therefore discarded. It is used to detect errors in transmission.
FDDI	Fiber Distributed Data Interface—The formal name for fiber wiring, which enables high-speed data transfers.
FDM	Frequency division multiplexing—A technique of passing signals across a single medium by assigning each signal a unique carrier frequency.
Feed	Send Usenet newsgroups from your site to another site that wants to read them. Also known as a newsfeed.
FIFO	First-in first-out—A queue in which the first item placed in the queue is the first item processed when the queue is processed.

Term	*Definition*
File	Basic unit of storage of computer data in a file structure; files can normally be binary or text only (ASCII).
Finger	A program that provides information about users on an Internet host; may include a user's personal information, such as project affiliation and schedule.
Firewall	A device placed on a network to prevent unauthorized traffic from entering the network. Can also, but less commonly, be used to restrict outbound flow.
Flame	Communicate in an abusive or absurd manner. Often occurs in newsgroup posts and email messages.
Flow control	A mechanism that controls the rate at which hosts may transmit at any time. It is used to avoid congestion on the network, which may exhaust memory buffers.
Flushing	When data is output to a text file, it is usually buffered to make processing more efficient. Flushing forces any items in the buffer to be actually written to the file.
Forms	Online data-entry sheets supported by some World Wide Web browsers.
FQDN	Fully qualified domain name—A combination of the hostname and the domain name.
Fragment	A piece that results when a datagram is partitioned into smaller pieces. It is used to facilitate datagrams too large for the network technology in use.
Frame	A set of packets as transmitted across a medium. Differing frame types have unique characteristics.
Frame relay	A type of digital data communications protocol.
Freeware	Software that the author makes available at no cost to anyone who wants it (although the author retains rights to the software).

Term	*Definition*
FTP	File Transfer Protocol—A popular Internet communications protocol that enables you to transfer files between hosts on the Internet.
Gateway	A device that interfaces two networks that use different protocols.
GIF	Graphics Interchange Format—An image format.
Gigabit	Very high-speed (1 billion bits per second) data communications.
Gigabyte	A unit of data storage approximately equal to 1 billion bytes of data.
Global variables	Variables that can be referred to anywhere within a package.
Gopher	An application that enables you to access publicly available information on Internet hosts that provide Gopher service.
Gopherbook	An application that uses an interface resembling a book to access Gopher servers.
Gopherspace	Connected Gopher services.
GOSIP	Government Open Systems Interconnection Profile—A U.S. government document that defines a specification of a set of OSI protocols that agencies may use.
Greenwich Mean Time	An international time standard reference, also known as Universal time.
GUI	Graphical User Interface—A computer interface based on graphic symbols rather than text. Windowing environments and Macintosh environments are GUIs.
Hacking	Originally referred to playing around with computer systems; now often used to indicate destructive computer activity.

Term	*Definition*
Hardware address	The physical address of a host used by networks.
Hash lookup	Find the value associated with a specified key in an associative array.
Hash table	A method used for implementing associative arrays, which allows the keys to be converted to numbers for internal storage purposes.
HDLC	High Level Data Link Control—A standard Data Link level protocol.
Header	Data inserted at the beginning of a packet that contains control information.
Home page	The document that serves as the entry way for all the information contained in a company's WWW service. Your World Wide Web browser loads this page when it starts up.
Hop-check	A utility that enables you to find out how many routers are between your host and another Internet host.
Host	A server connected to the Internet.
Host address	A unique number assigned to identify a host on the Internet (also called an IP address or a dot address). This address is usually represented as four numbers between 1 and 254 and separated by periods (for example, 192.58.107.230).
Host ID	The portion of an IP address that identifies the host in a particular network. It is used with network IDs to form a complete IP address.
Hostname	A unique name for a host that corresponds to the host address.
Hosts	Individual computers connected to the Internet.
HOSTS file	A text file that contains mappings of IP addresses to hostnames.

Term	*Definition*
Hotlist	A list of your favorite World Wide Web sites that can be accessed quickly by your WWW browser.
html	The extension for HTML files.
HTML	Hypertext Markup Language—The formatting language/protocol used to define various text styles in a hypertext document, including emphasis and bulleted lists.
HTTP	Hypertext Transfer Protocol—The communications protocol used by WWW services to retrieve documents quickly.
Hyperlinks	See Links.
Hypertext	An online document that has words or graphics containing links to other documents. Usually, selecting the link area onscreen (with a mouse or keyboard command) activates these links.
IAB	Internet Architecture Board—An independent group responsible for policies and standards for TCP/IP and the Internet.
ICMP	Internet Control Message Protocol—A maintenance protocol that handles error messages to be sent when datagrams are discarded or when systems experience congestion.
IEEE	Institute of Electrical and Electronics Engineers—The professional society for electrical and computer engineers.
IETF	Internet Engineering Task Force—A group of volunteers who help develop Internet standards.
IGMP	Internet Group Management Protocol—A protocol used to carry group membership information in a multicast system.

Term	*Definition*
IGP	Interior Gateway Protocol—A generic term that applies to any routing protocol used within an autonomous system.
Index files	Files created by waisindex that make up the WAIS source database.
Internet	The term used to describe all the worldwide interconnected TCP/IP networks.
InterNIC	The NSFnet manager sites on the Internet that provide information about the Internet.
IP	Internet Protocol—The communications protocol used by computers connected to the Internet.
IP address	See Host address.
Ipng	Internet Protocol, next generation.
IPv4	Internet Protocol, version 4.
IPv6	Internet Protocol, version 6.
ISDN	Integrated Services Digital Network—A dedicated telephone-line connection that transmits digital data at rates of 64kbps and 128kbps. In reality, because of the overhead, the data transfers are approximately 56/112.
ISO	International Standards Organization—An organization that sets worldwide standards in many different areas.
ISP	Internet Service Provider—A provider of Internet services, including connectivity, for individuals and companies.
Java	A programming language developed by Sun Microsystems that is platform-independent.
JPEG	Joint Photographic Expert Group—A compression standard.

Term	*Definition*
LAN	Local area network—A network of computers that is usually limited to a small physical area, such as a building.
LATA	Local access and transport area.
Leased connection	A connection to the Internet through a local phone company that allows your company to set up—for example—FTP, WWW, and Gopher services on the Internet at a permanent address.
Leased line	A dedicated phone line used for network communications.
LIFO	Last-in first-out—A queue in which the last item placed in the queue is the first item processed when the queue is addressed.
Links	The areas (words or graphics) in an HTML document that cause another document to be loaded when the user clicks them.
List	A series of values separated by commas; lists are often enclosed in parentheses to avoid ambiguity and these parentheses are often necessary.
List context	Same as Array. Context.
Listproc	Software that automates the management of electronic mailing lists.
LISTSERV	Software that automates the management of electronic mailing lists.
LLC	Logical Link Control—A protocol that provides a common interface point to the media access control (MAC) layers.
Local host	The computer you are currently using.
Local variables	Local variables can be accessed only in the current block and in subroutines called from that block.

Term	*Definition*
Logical operators	Boolean operators: that is, those dealing with true/false values.
Logon	The process of entering your user ID and password at a prompt to gain access to a service.
MAC	Media Access Control—A protocol that governs the access method a station has to the network.
Mail bridge	A gateway that screens mail between two networks to make certain they meet administrative constraints.
Mailers	Applications that enable you to read and send email messages.
Mailing list	A service that forwards an email message sent to it to everyone on a list, enabling a group of people to discuss a particular topic.
Majordomo	Software that automates the management of electronic mailing lists.
MAN	Metropolitan area network—A physical communications network that operates across a metropolitan area.
Match	A string that fits a specified pattern.
Metacharacters	Characters that have a special meaning and so may need to be escaped to turn off that meaning.
MIB	Management Information Base—A database made up of a set of objects that represent various types of information about devices. It is used by SNMP to manage devices.
MIME	Multipurpose Internet Mail Extension—A protocol that describes the format of Internet messages. Also, an extension to Internet mail that supports the inclusion of nontextual data such as video and audio in email.
Modem	An electronic device that allows digital computer data to be transmitted via analog phone lines.

Term	*Definition*
Moderator	A person who examines all submissions to a newsgroup or mailing list and allows only those that meet certain criteria to be posted. Usually, the moderator makes sure that the topic is pertinent to the group and that the submissions aren't flames.
Mosaic	A graphical interface for the World Wide Web that employs hypertext, images, video clips, and sound.
Motd	Message of the day—A message posted on some computer systems to let people know about problems or new developments.
MSS	Maximum segment size—The largest amount of data that can be transmitted at one time; negotiated by sender and receiver.
MTU	Maximum transmission unit—The largest datagram that can be sent across a given physical network.
Multihomed host	A TCP/IP host that is attached to two or more networks, requiring multiple IP addresses.
Name resolution	The process of mapping a computer name to an IP address. WINS and LMHOSTS are two ways of resolving names.
Netiquette	Network etiquette conventions used in written communications; usually referring to Usenet newsgroup postings, but also applicable to email.
Netnews	A collective way of referring to the Usenet newsgroups.
Netscape	A popular commercial World Wide Web browser manufacturer.
Network	A number of computers physically connected to enable communication with one another.
Network ID	The portion of an IP address that identifies the network. It is used with host IDs to form a complete address.

Term	*Definition*
Newsgroups	The electronic discussion groups of Usenet.
Newsreaders	Applications that enable you to read (and usually post) articles in Usenet newsgroups.
NFS	Network file system—A file system developed by Sun Microsystems that is now widely used on many different networks.
NIC	Network information center—A service that provides administrative information about a network.
NIC	Network interface card—An add-on card to allow a machine to access a LAN (most commonly an Ethernet card).
NIS	Network information service—A naming service from SunSoft that provides a directory service for network information.
NNTP	Network News Transport Protocol—The communications protocol that is used to send Usenet news on the Internet.
Nodes	Individual computers connected to a network.
NSFnet	Network funded by the National Science Foundation, now the backbone of the Internet.
Null character	A character with the value 0.
Null list	An empty list represented as empty parentheses.
OSF	Open Software Foundation—A nonprofit organization formed by hardware manufacturers who attempt to reduce standard technologies for open systems.
OSI	Open Systems Interconnection—A set of ISO standards that define the framework for implementing protocols in seven layers.

Term	*Definition*
OSPF	Open shortest path first—Routing protocol that dynamically sends updates to the routing table rather than the whole table.
Packet	The unit of data transmission on the Internet. A packet consists of the data being transferred with additional overhead information, such as the transmitting and receiving addresses.
Packet switching	The communications technology that the Internet is based on, where data being sent between computers is transmitted in packets.
Parallel	Means of communication in which digital data is sent multiple bits at a time, with each simultaneous bit being sent over a separate line.
Parameter	An Argument.
Pattern	An expression defining a set of strings that match the pattern and a set that do not.
Peer-to-peer	Internet or network services that can be offered and accessed by anyone, without requiring a special server.
Perl	Practical Extraction and Report Language, a language well-suited to text-file processing as well as other tasks.
PGP	Pretty Good Privacy—An application that enables you to send and receive encrypted email.
PID	Process identifier—A number indicating the number assigned by the operating system to that process.
Ping	Packet Internet Groper—A utility that sends out a packet to an Internet host and waits for a response (used to check whether a host is up).
Pipe	The concept in an operating system where the output of one program is fed into the input of another.
POP	Point of presence—Indicates availability of a local access number to a public data network.

Term	*Definition*
Port (hardware)	A physical channel on a computer that enables you to communicate with other devices (printers, modems, disk drives, and so on).
Port (network)	An address to which incoming data packets are sent. Special ports can be assigned to send the data directly to a server (FTP, Gopher, WWW, Telnet, or email) or to another specific program.
Port ID	The method used by TCP and UDP to specify which application is sending or receiving data.
Post	To send a message to a Usenet newsgroup.
Postmaster	An address to which you can send questions about a site (asking whether a user has an account there or whether it sells a particular product, for example).
PPP	Point-to-Point Protocol—A driver that enables you to use a network communications protocol over a phone line; used with TCP/IP to enable you to have a dial-in Internet host.
PPTP	Point-to-Point Tunneling Protocol—A revision to PPP used mostly for virtual private networks.
Precedence	The order in which operators are evaluated is based on their precedence.
Process	In multitasking operating systems such as UNIX, many programs may be run at once, and each one as it is running is called a process.
Protocol	The standard that defines how computers on a network communicate with one another.
Proxy	A connection through a modem and telephone line to the Internet, which enables clients to access this service through a host.
Public domain software	Software made available by the author to anyone who wants it. (In this case, the author gives up all rights to the software.)

Term	*Definition*
RARP	Reverse Address Resolution Protocol—A protocol that enables a computer to find its IP address by broadcasting a request. It is usually used by diskless workstations at startup to find their logical IP address.
Recursion	When a subroutine makes a call to itself.
Regular expressions	A way of specifying a pattern so that some strings match the pattern and some strings do not. Parts of the matching pattern can be marked for use in operations such as substitution.
Relevance feedback	In WAIS, a score between 0 and 1,000 that represents how closely a document satisfies search criteria.
Remote	Pertaining to a host on the network other than the computer you now are using.
Remote host	A host on the network other than the computer you currently are using.
Repeater	Device that enables you to extend the length of your network by amplifying and repeating the information it receives.
Resolver	Client software that enables access to the DNS database.
RFC	Request for Comments—A document submitted to the Internet governing board to propose Internet standards or to document information about the Internet.
RIP	Routing Information Protocol—A router-to-router protocol used to exchange information between routers. RIP supports dynamic routing.
rlogin	A UNIX command that enables you to log on to a remote computer.
RMON	Remote Network Monitor—A device that collects information about network communications.

Term	*Definition*
Route	The path that network traffic takes between its source and its destination.
Router	Equipment that receives an Internet packet and sends it to the next machine in the destination path.
RPC	Remote Procedure Call—An interface that allows an application to call a routine that executes on another machine in a remote location.
Script	An interpreted set of instructions in a text file.
Segment	A protocol data unit consisting of part of a stream of bytes being sent between two machines. It also includes information about the current position in the stream and a checksum value.
Serial	Means of communication in which digital data is sent one bit at a time over a single physical line.
Server	A provider of a service; a computer that runs services. It also often refers to a piece of hardware or software that provides access to information requested from it.
Service	An application that processes requests by client applications (for example, storing data or executing an algorithm).
SGML	Standard Generalized Markup Language—A language that describes the structure of a document.
Shareware	Software that is made available by the author to anyone who wants it, with a request to send the author a nominal fee if the software is used on a regular basis.
Signal	A means of passing information between the operating system and a running process; the process can trap the signal and respond accordingly.
Signature	A personal sign-off used in email and newsgroup posts, often contained in a file and automatically appended to the mail or post. Often contains organization affiliation and pertinent personal information.

Term	*Definition*
Site	A group of computers under a single administrative control.
SLIP	Serial Line Internet Protocol—A way of running TCP/IP via the phone lines to enable you to have a dial-up Internet host.
SmartList	Software that automates the management of electronic mailing lists.
SMTP	Simple Mail Transport Protocol—The accepted communications protocol standard for exchange of email between Internet hosts.
SNA	System Network Architecture—A protocol suite developed and used by IBM.
SNMP	Simple Network Management Protocol—A communications protocol used to control and monitor devices on a network.
Socket	A means of network communications via special entities.
Source	In WAIS, describes a database and how to reach it.
Source route	A route identifying the path a datagram must follow that is determined by the source device.
String	A sequence of characters.
Subnet	Any lower network that is part of the logical network; identified by the network ID.
Subnet mask	A 32-bit value that distinguishes the network ID from the host ID in an IP address.
Subscribe	Become a member of a mailing list or newsgroup; also refers to obtaining Internet provider services.
Surfing	Jumping from host to host on the Internet to get an idea of what can be found. Also refers to briefly examining a number of different Usenet newsgroups.

Term	*Definition*
Syntax	A statement that contains programming code.
T1	A dedicated telephone line that transfers data at the rate of 1.544MB/sec.
T3	A dedicated telephone line that transfers data at the rate of 45MB/sec.
Tag	A slang reference for annotations used by HTML, such as <H2>, </H2>.
TCP	Transmission Control Protocol—The connection-oriented network protocol used by hosts on the Internet.
TCP/IP	Transmission Control Protocol/Internet Protocol—A communications protocol suite that allows computers of any make to communicate when running TCP/IP software.
Telnet	A program that allows remote logon to another computer.
Terminal emulation	Running an application that enables you to use your computer to interface with a command-line account on a remote computer as if you were connected to the computer with a terminal.
TFTP	Trivial File Transfer Protocol—A basic, standard protocol used to upload or download files with minimal overhead. TFTP depends on UDP and is often used to initialize diskless workstations, as it has no directory and password capabilities.
Thread	All messages in a newsgroup or mailing list pertaining to a particular topic.
TIFF	Tag Image File Format—A graphics format.
TLI	Transport layer interface—An AT&T-developed interface that enables applications to interface to both TCP/IP and OSI protocols.

Term	*Definition*
Token ring	A network protocol for LAN, based on a token-passing communications scheme.
Traceroute	A utility that enables you to find out how many routers are between your host and another Internet host. See also Hop-check.
Traffic	The information flowing through a network.
Transceiver	A device that connects a host interface to a network. It is used to apply signals to the cable and sense collisions.
Trap	A block of data that indicates some request failed to authenticate. An SNMP agent will issue a trap when a specified event has occurred. For example, the SNMP service sends a trap when it receives a request for information with an incorrect community name.
TTL	Time to Live—A measurement of time, usually defined by a number of hops, that a datagram can exist on a network before it is discarded. It prevents endlessly looping packets.
UDP	User Datagram Protocol—A simple protocol that enables an application program on one machine to send a datagram to an application program on another machine. Delivery is not guaranteed; there is also no guarantee that the datagrams will be delivered in proper order.
Universal time	An international time standard reference, also known as Greenwich Mean Time.
Upload	Move a file from your local computer to a remote computer.
URL	Universal resource locator—A means of specifying the location of information on the Internet for WWW clients. Also known as uniform resource locator.
Usenet	An online news and bulletin board system accommodating more than 7,000 interest groups.

Term	*Definition*
Username	The ID used to log on to a computer.
UFudecode	A program that enables you to construct binary data from text that was uuencoded.
Uuencode	A program that enables you to send binary data through email by converting text to binary.
Veronica	A tool that helps you find files on Gopher servers.
Viewer applications	Software that gives you access to the images, video, and sounds stored on Internet servers.
Viewers	Applications used to display nontext files, such as graphics, sound, and animation.
Virus	A computer program that covertly enters a system by means of a legitimate program, usually doing damage to the system; compare to worm.
VMS	Virtual memory system—An operating system used on hosts made by Digital Equipment Corporation.
VRML	Virtual Reality Modeling Language—An experimental language that enables you to display 3D objects in Web documents.
WAIS	Wide area information server—A tool that helps you search for documents using keywords or selections of text as search criteria.
WAIS client	An application that formats user-defined search criteria to be used by waisserver; the goal is to find matches between search criteria and data files (of all types)
WAIS sources	Databases created by waisindex that include, for example, a table of all unique words contained in a document.
waisindex	A mechanism that extracts data from raw data files (of most types) to put into databases, called WAIS sources, which allow waisserver to match search criteria to data files quickly.

Term	*Definition*
waisserver	A mechanism that compares search criteria, supplied by a WAIS client, to WAIS sources.
WAN	Wide area network—A network of computers that are geographically dispersed.
Web	Short for World Wide Web (WWW).
Web chat	An application that enables you to carry on live conversations over the World Wide Web.
Web Crawler	A Web search tool.
WHOIS	A service that enables you to look up information about Internet hosts and users.
World Wide Web	WWW or Web—A hypertext-based system that allows browsing of available Internet resources.
Worm	A computer program that invades other computers over a network, usually nondestructively; compare to virus.
X.25	A CCITT standard for connecting computers to a network that provides a reliable stream transmission service, which can support remote logons.
X.400	A CCITT standard for message transfer and interpersonal messaging, like electronic mail.
X-modem	A communication protocol that enables you to transfer files over a serial line. See also Y-modem and Z-modem.
XBM	X bitmapped—A graphics format.
XDR	External Data Representation—A data format standard developed by Sun Microsystems that defines data types used as parameters and encodes these parameters for transmission.

Term	Definition
Y-modem	A communication protocol that enables you to transfer files over a serial line. See also X-modem and Z-modem.
Z-modem	A communication protocol that enables you to transfer files over a serial line.

Additional Terms and Concepts

Not every interesting item the instructor has to share with the class is necessarily related directly to the exam. That's the case with 'Did You Know?' Think of the information in here as the intriguing sidebar, or the interesting diversion, you might wish the instructor would share with you during an aside.

CHAPTER 10

Did You Know?

The following interesting items are *not* relevant to the exam:

1. Switching is a vast improvement on routing, and allows multiple paths to be used to deliver the data. This decreases the amount of time necessary for delivery, and provides redundancy in paths. There are three types of switching technologies currently employed:

- ◆ Circuit switching
- ◆ Message switching
- ◆ Packet switching

The following sections look at each of these.

CIRCUIT SWITCHING

Circuit switching establishes a path that remains fixed for the duration of the connection, and is similar to telephone switching equipment. In the telephone world, switching equipment establishes a route between your telephone in the Midwest and a telephone in New York, and maintains that connection for the duration of your call. The next time you call, the same path may or may not be used.

The advantages of circuit switching include the use of dedicated paths and a well-defined bandwidth. The disadvantages include the establishment of each connection (which can be time consuming) and the inability of other traffic to share the dedicated media path. The latter can lead to inefficiently utilized bandwidth. Due to the need to have excess (or rather a surplus of) bandwidth, the technology tends to be expensive when compared to other options.

MESSAGE SWITCHING

Message switching treats each message as an independent entity, and is not concerned with what came before or will come after. Each message carries its own address information and details of its destination. The information is used at each switch to transfer the message to the next switch in the route. Message switches are programmed with information concerning other switches in the network that can be used to forward messages to their destinations. They can also be programmed with information about which of the routes is the most efficient, and can send different messages through the network to the same destination via different routes (and routers).

In message switching, the complete message is sent from one switch to the next and the whole message is stored there before being forwarded on. Because the switches hold what is coming in and wait until it is all there before sending anything out, they are often called store-and-forward networks, and common uses for such technology are with email, calendaring, and groupware applications.

The advantage of message switching is that it can use relatively low-cost devices, data channels are shared among communicating devices, priorities can be assigned to manage traffic, and bandwidth is used rather efficiently. The disadvantage is that it is completely unacceptable for real-time applications.

PACKET SWITCHING

When most administrators think of adding switches to their network, they inherently mean packet switches. Here, messages are divided into smaller packets—each containing source and destination address information, and capable of being routed through the internetwork independently. Packet size is restricted to the point where the entire packet can remain in memory of the switching devices and there is no need to temporarily store the data anywhere. For this reason, packet switching routes the data through the network much more rapidly and efficiently than is possible with message switching.

A number of different types of packet switches exist, with the most common being datagram and virtual circuit. With datagram packet switching, each switch node decides which network segment should be used for the next step in the packet's route. This enables switches to bypass busy segments and take other steps to speed packets through the internetwork—making it ideally suited for LANs.

Virtual circuit packet switching establishes a formal connection between two devices and negotiates communication parameters such as the maximum message size, communication window, network path, and so on—thus creating a virtual circuit that remains in effect until the devices stop communicating. When a virtual circuit is there on a temporary basis, you will hear the buzzword switched virtual circuit (SVC). When the virtual circuit is there for an undetermined amount of time, the buzzword used is permanent virtual circuit (PVC).

The most popular implementation of packet switching is ATM (asynchronous transfer mode), which uses fixed-length 53-byte packets (that ATM advocates call cells) and sends them across the internetwork. By standardizing on a size of 53-bytes, the process of negotiating packet size with each connection is eliminated, thus allowing for an increase in transfer speed.

Regardless of the technology employed, packet switching advantages include the capability to optimize the use of bandwidth and enable many devices to route packets through the same network channels. At any time, a switch may be routing packets to several different destination devices, adjusting the routes as required to get the best efficiency possible. The only disadvantage is the initial cost of the equipment, which can be sizeable.

INDEX

SYMBOLS

10BASE-2 coaxial cable
  connections, 23
10BASE-T unshielded twisted
  pair cable connections, 23

A

AAAA DNS record, 121
accounts, 302
ACK (acknowledgment), 14,
  33-34, 302
Active Leases dialog box, 71
active open actions, 14, 302
adaptive testing, 278-279
Add Reserved Clients dialog
  box, 71
address classes, 14, 302
address masks, 14, 302
address reservations, 70
address resolution, 14
Address Resolution Protocol
  (ARP), 40-41, 197, 259, 303
addresses
  bang, 304
  directed broadcast, 308
  dot, 309, 313
  email, 309
  hardware, 17, 313
  host, 17, 313

IP (Internet Protocol)
  components, 209
  configuring, 216-217
  DHCP detection, 51
  DHCP scopes, 67-76
  testing, 218-220
  troubleshooting, 208-211,
    213-214, 220-222
  local, pinging, 220
  loop back, pinging, 219-220
  physical, 23-25
addressing IP (Internet
  Protocol), 36
Advanced Configuration dialog
  box, 83
Advanced Research Projects
  Agency (ARPA), 15, 303
AFSDB DNS record, 121
agents, 302
  Network Monitor, 196
  SNMP, 48, 136-137, 143-144
alerts, Performance Monitor, 195
aliases, 302
American National Standards
  Institute (ANSI), 14, 303
American Standard Code for
  Information Interchange,
  15, 303
analog communication, 14, 302
anchor, 302
annotation, 302
announcement periods, Windows
  NT browsing services, 185

anonymous FTP, 302
ANSI (American National
 Standards Institute), 14, 303
answering questions quickly,
 exam preparation, 268
answering strategies for exam
 questions, 270-273
answers to sample exam, 295-299
API (Application Programming
 Interface), 14, 42-43, 303
Application layer
 Internet Protocol Suite, 29
 network APIs, 42-43
 OSI model, 20
Application Programming
 Interface (API), 14, 42-43, 303
Archie, 303
archives, 303
arguments, 303
ARP (Address Resolution
 Protocol), 14, 28, 40-41, 303
ARPA (Advanced Research
 Projects Agency), 15, 303
arpa domain, 64
ARPAnet, 15, 303
articles, 303, 310
ASCII (American Standard Code
 for Information Interchange),
 15, 303
ascii command (FTP), 155
Asynchronous Transfer Mode
 (ATM), 15, 304
attributes, 304
au extension, 304
authentication, RAS clients, 176
automatic restoration of corrupt
 DHCP databases, 75

B

backbones, 15, 304
backup browsers, 180
Backup on Termination setting,
 configuring WINS Manager, 83

backups for databases
 DHCP, 74
 WINS, 61
bandwidth, circuit switching, 332
bangs, 304
Base I/O Port Address port
 option, 161
basebands, 15, 304
Baud Rate port setting, 160
best-effort delivery, 304
BGP (Border Gateway
 Protocol), 304
binary, 305
binary command (FTP), 155
binary numbers and decimal
 conversions, 254-255
BIND files, installing DNS
 servers, 116
BinHex, 305
Bitnet, 305
bits per second (bps), 15, 305
blocks, 305
bookmarks, 305
Boolean logic, 305
BOOTP (Bootstrap Protocol), 15,
 256, 305
Border Gateway Protocol
 (BGP), 304
bounced email messages, 305
bps (bits per second), 15, 305
bridges, 15
 brouters, 305
 mail, 317
broadband technology, 15, 305
broadcast packets, 15, 305
broadcasts, 36
brouters, 15, 305
browse lists, 176, 183-184
browsers, 306
 IP Internetwork browsing
  directed traffic, 188
  IP routers, 187-188
  LMHOSTS file, 188-190
 network, 176
  clients, 178
  direct approach access, 179

host computers, 178-179
Network Neighborhood, 177
shared resources, 178
roles, 180-182
servicing client requests, 186
Windows NT services
  announcement periods, 185
  collecting browse lists, 183-184
  distributing browse lists, 184
  domain master browser
    failure, 186
  subnets, 185
WINS (Windows Internet
  Naming Service), 190-191
buffers, 15, 306
building
multihomed routers, 111-113
static route tables, 106

C

**caching and configuring DNS
server roles, 123**
**call-back security and RAS
clients, 176**
**campus area networks
(CAN), 306**
**Carrier Sense Multiple Access
with Collision Detection
(CSMA/CD), 307**
cd command (FTP), 155
CERN, 306
**Chart view, Performance
Monitor, 195**
checksumming, 15, 306
child subprocesses, 306
**CIDR (classless interdomain
routing), 306**
circuit switching, 332
classes
address, 14, 302
IP addressing, 36
network IDs, 255
**classless interdomain routing
(CIDR), 306**

Clear to Send (CTS), 160
client-server architecture, 26
clients, 178, 306
browsing services, 186
DHCP, 256
  implementation
    requirements, 53
  troubleshooting, 214-215
  Windows for Workgroups as, 72
  Windows NT/95 as, 71-72
Dial-Up Networking, 169-172
  dial-in permissions, 167
  ISDN, 166
  modems, 159-166
  PPP problems, 168
  PPP versus SLIP, 158
  X.25 protocol, 167
enabling DNS, 114-116
non-WINS, configuring for, 77
printing from to Windows NT
  servers, 133
printing to from Windows NT
  servers, 131-132
RAS, 176
TCP/IP, pinging local
  addresses, 220
WAIS, 327
WINS, 77
  access, 191
  configuring, 60
close command (FTP), 155
**CMIP (Common Management
Information Protocol), 306**
CNAME DNS record, 121
collecting browse lists, 183-184
com domain, 64
COM ports, 159, 161
command-line utilities
IPCONFIG, 216-217
Ping, 218-221
comment characters
hostname resolution
  problems, 223
name resolution problems, 260

Common Management
  Information Protocol
  (CMIP), 306
compacting databases
  DHCP, 73-74
  WINS, 61
Compress Data option,
  modem connections, 164
Compress program, 306
concatenating strings, 306
conditionless service, 15
configuring
  default gateways, 214
  DHCP clients, 214-215
  DHCP Relay Agent, 113
  DHCP server service, 58
  DNS
    BIND files, 116
    DNS Administration tool, 117
    DNS Manager preferences, 118
    enabling on clients, 114-116
    NSLOOKUP, 118-119
    reinstalling Microsoft DNS
      Server, 116
    startup files, updating, 118
    subdomains, creating, 117
  DNS server roles
    for caching only, 123
    for IP forwarders, 123-124
    primary DNS servers, 124
    secondary DNS servers,
      126-127
    SOA (Start of Authority)
      records, 125-126
  HOSTS files, 127-129
  IP addresses, 216-217
  LMHOSTS files, 129-131
  RAS servers, 173-174
  replication, WINS Manager,
    82-83
  SNMP, 133-134, 142
    agents, 136-137, 143-144
    communities, 141
    extension agents, 140

management system, 135-136
    MIB (Management
      Information Base), 137-139
    Microsoft SNMP Service, 140
    security, 141, 143
    SNMP utility, 144-145
static mappings, WINS
  databases, 84
subnet masks, 85, 89-91, 211
    default masks, 92-93
    intermittent connections, 214
    networks, subdividing, 94-99
    subnetting, 86-88
    third octet, 212-213
TCP/IP
    DHCP client problems,
      214-215
    IP address problems, 208-209,
      211-214
    IP address utilities, 216
  Windows NT as an IP router
    default gateways, 103
    dynamic routers, 99, 108-111
    multihomed routers, building,
      111-113
    route tables, 103-106
    static route tables,
      building, 106
    static routers, 99-102
    TRACERT utility, 107
  WINS
    for non-WINS clients, 77
    servers, 76
connection properties and
  modems
  Cancel the call if not connected
    within, 163
  Compress Data option, 164
  Disconnect a call if idle for
    more than, 163
  Extra Settings option, 165
  Modulation Type option, 164
  Record a Log File option, 165
  Required to Connect option, 164

Use Cellular Protocol
option, 164
Use Error Control option, 164
Use Flow Control option, 164
Wait for tone before dialing, 163
connectionless service, 307
connections, 306
circuit switching, 332
dial-up, 308
direct, 308
DNS root servers, 123
intermittent, subnet masks, 214
leased, 316
message switching, 332
network, 23
orientation communication,
31-32
packet switching, 333-334
connectivity, 26, 150
data transfer utilities
FTP, 154-156
HTTP, 157
RCP, 153-154
TFTP, 156-157
Dial-Up Networking, 257
RAS (Remote Access Service)
authentication, 176
call-back security, 176
dial-in permissions, 167
Dial-Up Networking, 169-172
*Dial-Up Networking
Monitor, 175*
ISDN, 166
modems, 159-166
PPP problems, 168
PPP versus SLIP, 158
servers, configuring, 173-174
servers, installing, 172
servers, monitoring from, 175
X.25 protocol, 167
remote execution utilities
passwords, 150
REXEC, 151
RSH, 151-152
Telnet, 152-153, 257

context, 307, 316
Control Panel, port settings, 160
controlling browser roles,
181-182
copying corrupt DHCP databases,
manual restoration, 76
corrupt DHCP databases, 75-76
counters, Performance
Monitor, 194
CRC (Cyclic Redundancy Check),
15, 307
cross-platform architectures, 26
CSMA (Carrier Sense Multiple
Access), 16, 307
CSMA/CD (Carrier Sense
Multiple Access with Collision
Detection), 16, 307
CTS (Clear to Send), 160
cyberspace, 307
Cyclic Redundancy Check (CRC),
15, 307

D

daemons, 307
DARPA (Defense Advanced
Research Projects Agency),
16, 307
Data Bits port setting, 160
Data Encryption Standard
(DES), 308
Data Link layer, OSI model, 21
data transfer utilities
FTP, 154-156
HTTP, 157
RCP, 153-154
TFTP, 156-157
Database Backup Path setting,
configuring WINS Manager, 84
databases, 308
DHCP
backing up, 74
compacting, 73-74
restoring corrupt, 75-76

MIB, 137
  DHCP MIB, 138
  Internet MIB II, 138
  LAN Manager MIB II, 138
  WINS MIB, 139
  WINS, 61, 84
datagram packet switching, 333-334
datagrams, 16, 31, 36-37, 308
debug command (FTP), 156
debugging, 308
decimal numbers and binary conversions, 254-255
dedicated lines, 308
dedicated path, circuit switching, 332
default gateways, 103
  pinging, troubleshooting router problems, 220-221
  troubleshooting, 214
default subnet masks, 92-93
Defense Advanced Research Projects Agency (DARPA), 16, 307
defining subnet masks, 96-98
Department of Defense (DOD), 309
DES (Data Encryption Standard), 308
DHCP (Dynamic Host Configuration Protocol), 16, 47-49, 174, 254
  addresses, 256
  BOOTP protocol, 256
  clients, 214-215, 256
  databases
    backing up, 74
    compacting, 73-74
    restoring corrupt, 75-76
  DHCP Relay Agent, installing/configuring, 113
  implementing TCP/IP
    clients requirements, 53
    DHCPACK phase, 56
    lease renewal, 56-57

  multiple servers, 54
  network requirements, 52-53
  limitations, 51
  MIB, 138
  Relay Agent, 47
  scopes, 67-68, 73-76
    address reservations, 70
    clients, 71-72
    global options, 69-70, 72
    scope options, 69, 72
  server service
    configuring, 58
    installing, 57
  servers, 50
DHCPACK phase, DHCP implementation requirements, 56
DHCPDISCOVER packet, 50
Dial using calling card dialing property, 166
dial-in permissions, 167-168
Dial-In Permissions dialog box, 167
dial-up connections, 308
Dial-Up Networking, 158, 169-172, 257
  dial-in permissions, 167
  ISDN, 166
  modems, 159-166
  PPP problems, 168
  X.25 protocol, 167
Dial-Up Networking Monitor, 175
dialing properties and modems, 165-166
Dialing Properties dialog box, 165
dialog boxes
  Active Leases, 71
  Add Reserved Clients, 71
  Advanced Configuration, 83
  Dial-In Permissions, 167
  Dialing Properties, 165
  Microsoft TCP/IP Configuration, 69

Modem Properties, 163
Network Configuration, 113
Network Properties, 208, 216
Network Settings, 57, 66, 114,
   172-173
New Phonebook Entry, 169
New Zone, 126
Ports, 160
Select Network Protocol, 66
Static Mappings, 78
TCP/IP Configuration, 72, 114
TCP/IP Settings, 115
digests, 308
digital communications, 16, 308
direct approach network
   access, 179
direct connections, 308
directed broadcast addresses,
   16, 308
directed traffic, 188
directory of servers, 308
disk duplexing, 23
disk mirroring, 23
disk striping, 22
distributing browse lists,
   Windows NT services, 184
DLC protocol, 21
DNS (domain name system), 16,
   48, 62, 254, 308
   domains, 64
   history of, 63
   hostnames, 64-65
   installing/configuring
      BIND files, 116
      DNS Administration tool, 117
      DNS Manager preferences, 118
      enabling DNS on clients,
         114-116
      NSLOOKUP, 118-119
      startup files, updating, 118
      subdomains, creating, 117
   integrating with other
      servers, 119
      hosts, adding, 120
      records, adding, 121-122

reverse lookup, 65-66
servers, 123-127, 257
zones, 65
DNS Administration tool, 117
DNS Manager, preferences, 118
DNS Name Server, 309
Doc-ID, 309
DOD (Department of
   Defense), 309
domain browsers, WINS, 191
domain master browsers, 180
   failures, Windows NT browsing
      services, 186
   LMHOSTS file, 189
Domain Name static mapping, 84
domain name system. *See* DNS
domains, 16, 189, 309
dot addresses, 309, 313
downloading, 309
dumb terminals, 257
duplexing, disk, 23
duplicate domain names,
   LMHOSTS file, 189
duplicate entries, name resolution
   problems, 260
Dynamic Host Configuration
   Protocol. *See* DHCP
dynamic routers, 99, 108-111

E

edu domain, 64
effective GID, 309
effective UID, 309
election processes, choosing
   master browsers, 181
email, 309
enabling DNS clients, 114-116
encryption, 310
Entire Network, 177
errors, debugging, 308
Ethernet, 16, 310
Eudora, 310
Event Log, 198

Event Log tool, 258
Examination Score Report, 274
exams
  adaptive testing, 278-279
  failing, reasons for, 265
  passing scores, 264
  performance-based testing, 279
  preparing for
    answering quickly, 268
    answering strategies, 270-273
    exam procedures, 269-274
    Microsoft mindset, 265-266
    performance-based
      questions, 277
    question sources, 275
    ranking questions, 276
    timeframes, 266-267
  psychometrics, 277
  question types, 264
  retaking, 275
  sample questions, 282-295
    answers and explanations,
      295-301
expired articles, Usenet, 310
extension agents, SNMP, 140-141
External Data Representative
  (XDR), 328
external modems, 159
Extinction Interval parameter,
  WINS Manager, 82
Extinction Timeout parameter,
  WINS Manager, 82
Extra Settings option, modem
  connections, 165

F

failing exams, reasons for
  answering slowly, 268
  exam procedures, 269-274
  Microsoft mindset, 265-266
  timeframes, 266-267
fair queuing, 310
FAQs (Frequently Asked
  Questions), 310
fault tolerance, 22

FCS (frame check sequence), 310
FDDI (Fiber Distributed Data
  Interface), 16, 310
FDDI connections, 23
FDM (Frequency Division
  Multiplexing), 16, 310
feeds, Usenet newsgroups, 310
Fiber Distributed Data Interface
  (FDDI), 16, 310
FIFO (first-in first-out), 310
File Transfer Protocol. *See* FTP
files, 311
  DNS zones, 65
  index, 315
  static, storing IP addresses, 211
  WINS, 60-61
filling browser roles, 180-182
finger program, 311
firewalls, 16, 311
first-in first-out (FIFO), 310
flaming, 311
flow control, 311
Flow Control port setting, 160
flushing, 311
forms, 311
FQDN (fully qualified domain
  name), 16, 64-65, 257, 311
fragmentation, IP (Internet
  Protocol), 37
fragments, 311
frame check sequence (FCS), 310
frame relay, 17, 311
frames, 17, 311
freeware, 311
Frequency Division Multiplexing
  (FDM), 16, 310
Frequently Asked Questions
  (FAQs), 310
FTP (File Transfer Protocol), 17,
  26, 29, 312
  anonymous, 302
  data transfer utilities, 154
    options, 155-156
    UNIX syntax, 156
fully qualified domain name
  (FQDN), 16, 64-65, 257, 311

G

Gateway Address column, route tables, 103
gateways, 17, 103, 214, 220-221, 312
get command (FTP), 156
GID, effective, 309
GIF (Graphics Interchange Format), 312
gigabits, 312
gigabytes, 312
global options, DHCP scopes, 69-70, 72
global variables, 312
Gopher, 312
Gopherbook, 312
Gopherspace, 312
GOSIP (Government Open Systems Interconnection), 312
gov domain, 64
Graphical User Interface (GUI), 312
Graphics Interchange Format (GIF), 312
Greenwich Mean Time, 312
GUI (Graphical User Interface), 312

H

hacking, 312
hardware addresses, 17, 313
hash lookup, 313
hash tables, 313
HDLC (High Level Data Link Control), 313
headers, 21, 313
HINFO DNS record, 121
home pages, 313
hop-checks, 313
host addresses, 313
host computers, 178-179
host IDs, 17, 313
    choosing, 99
    subdivision requirements, 95-96

hostname.exe utility, name resolution problems, 224, 226, 261
hostnames, 17, 313
    DNS, 64-65, 257
    pinging problems, 222
    resolution problems
        hostname.exe, 224, 226
        nbtstat utility, 223-224
        NetBIOS sessions, 226-228
        Ping, 226
        Windows Sockets sessions, 229
    Telnet, 152
hosts, 313
    adding, integrating DNS servers, 120
    addresses, 17, 209
    connections, name resolution, 260
    incorrect, troubleshooting IP addresses, 209-210
    local, 316
    maximum, subnetting, 93
    multihomed, 318
    printing between, 257
    remote, 221-222, 322
HOSTS files, 127-129, 256, 313
hotlists, 314
HTML (HyperText Markup Language), 17, 157, 314
html file extension, 314
HTTP (Hypertext Transfer Protocol), 17, 157, 314
hyperlinks, 314
hypertext, 314
HyperText Markup Language (HTML), 17, 157, 314
Hypertext Transfer Protocol (HTTP), 17, 157, 314

I

IAB (Internet Architecture Board), 314
IANA (Internet Assigned Numbers Authority), 30

ICMP (Internet Control Message
Protocol), 17, 28, 38-39, 314
IDs, network classes, 255
IEEE (Institute of Electrical and
Electronics Engineers),
21-22, 314
IETF (Internet Engineering
Task Force), 314
IGMP (Internet Group
Management Protocol), 17, 28,
40, 314
IGP (Interior Gateway
Protocol), 315
IIS (Internet Information
Server), 47
index files, 315
installing
DHCP Relay Agent, 113
DHCP server service, 57
DNS
BIND files, 116
DNS Administration tool, 117
DNS Manager preferences, 118
enabling on clients, 114-116
NSLOOKUP, 118-119
reinstalling Microsoft DNS
Server, 116
startup files, updating, 118
subdomains, creating, 117
modems
Compress Data option, 164
Extra Settings option, 165
Modulation Type option, 164
Port property, 162
Record a Log File option, 165
Required to Connect
option, 164
Speaker Volume property, 162
Use Cellular Protocol
option, 164
Use Error Control option, 164
Use Flow Control option, 164
Network Monitor, 195
RAS servers, 172

SNMP, 141-142
TCP/IP, 66, 219-220
WINS servers, 76
Institute of Electrical and
Electronics Engineers (IEEE),
21-22, 314
Integrated Services Digital
Network (ISDN), 17, 166, 315
integrating DNS, 119
hosts, adding, 120
records, adding, 121-122
interactive mode,
NSLOOKUP, 201
Interface column, route
tables, 104
interfaces between TCP/IP
layers, 29
Interior Gateway Protocol
(IGP), 315
intermittent connections, subnet
masks and, 214
internal modems, 159
Internet Architecture Board
(IAB), 314
Internet Assigned Numbers
Authority (IANA), 30
Internet Control Message
Protocol (ICMP), 17, 28,
38-39, 314
Internet Engineering Task Force
(IETF), 314
Internet Group Managment
Protocol (IGMP), 17, 28,
40, 314
Internet Group static
mapping, 84
Internet Information Server
(IIS), 47
Internet layer
ARP (Address Resolution
Protocol), 40-41
ICMP (Internet Control Message
Protocol), 38-39
IGMP (Internet Group
Management Protocol), 40

Internet Protocol Suite, 28
IP (Internet Protocol), 36-38
Internet MIB II, 138
Internet Protocol Suite (TCP/IP layers), 27
  Application layer, 29
  ARP (Address Resolution Protocol), 40-41
  ICMP (Internet Control Message Protocol), 38-39
  IGMP (Internet Group Management Protocol), 40
  interfaces between, 29
  Internet layer, 28
  IP (Internet Protocol), 36-38
  network APIs, 42-43
  Network Interface layer, 28
  TCP (Transmission Control Protocol)
    acknowledgments, 33-34
    connection-orientation communication, 31-32
    ports and sockets, 30
    sliding windows, 33
  Transport layer, 28
  UDP (User Datagram Protocol), 34-35
Internet Protocol, next generation (Ipng), 315
Internet Protocol. *See* **IP**
Internet Protocol, version 4 (IPv4), 315
Internet Protocol, version 6 (IPv6), 315
Internet Service Providers (ISPs), 315
Internetworks, browsing in, 187-190
InterNIC, 64, 315
IP (Internet Protocol), 36-38, 315
  forwarders, configuring DNS server roles, 123-124
  Internetworks, browsing in, 187-190

routers, 187-188
  default gateways, 103
  dynamic routers, 99, 108-111
  multihomed routers, building, 111-113
  route tables, 103-104
  static route tables, building, 106
  static routers, 99-102
  TRACERT utility, 107
  viewing route tables, 104-106
IP addresses
  components, 209
  configuring, 216-217
  DHCP detection, 51
  DHCP scopes, 67-68
    address reservations, 70
    backing up databases, 74
    binary numbers and decimal conversions, 254-255
    clients, 71-72
    compacting databases, 73-74
    global options, 69-70, 72
    restoring corrupt databases, 75-76
    scope options, 69, 72
  remote hosts, pinging, 221-222
  router problems, pinging default gateways, 220-221
  testing Ping utility, 218-220
  troubleshooting, 208
    default gateways, 214
    incorrect hosts, 209-210
    lost packets, 209-210
    static file address storage, 211
    subnet masks, 211, 213-214
IPCONFIG utility, 24, 198, 216-217, 259
Ipng (Internet Protocol, next generation), 315
IPv4 (Internet Protocol, version 4), 315
IPv6 (Internet Protocol, version 6), 315
IRQs, 159, 161

ISDN (Integrated Services Digital
  Network), 17, 166, 315
ISDN DNS record, 121
IsDomainMaster Registry,
  controlling browser roles, 181
ISP (Internet Service
  Providers), 315

J-K

J50.CHK, 61
J50.LOG, 61
Java, 315
Joint Photographic Expert Group
  (JPEG), 315

keys (Registry), RestoreFlag,
  75-76

L

LAN (local area network),
  17, 316
LAN Manager MIB II, 138
last-in first-out (LIFO), 316
LAT protocol, 21
LATA (local access and
  transport area), 316
layers
    Application, 29, 42-43
    interfaces between, 29
    Internet, 28
        *ARP (Address Resolution
        Protocol), 40-41*
        *ICMP (Internet Control
        Message Protocol), 38-39*
        *IGMP (Internet Group
        Management Protocol), 40*
        IP (Internet Protocol), 36-38
    Internet Protocol Suite, 27
    Network Interface, 28
    OSI model, 20-21
    Transport, 28
        *TCP (Transmission Control
        Protocol), 30-34*
        *UDP (User Datagram
        Protocol), 34-35*

lcd command (FTP), 155
lease renewal, DHCP, 56-57
leased connections, 316
leased lines, 316
leasing DHCP addresses, 256
LIFO (last-in first-out), 316
Line Printer Daemon (LPD),
  47, 257
line printer request, 132, 257
links, 316
listproc, 316
lists, 316-317
LISTSERV, 316
LLC (Logical Link Control),
  17, 316
LMHOSTS files, 188, 256
    configuring, 129-131
    domain master browsers, 189
    duplicate names, 189
    importing to WINS, 78
    placement, 190
    troubleshooting, 190
local access and transport area
  (LATA), 316
local addresses, pinging, 220
local area networks (LANs), 316
local hosts, 316
local variables, 316
Log Detailed Events setting,
  configuring WINS Manager, 83
Logical Link Control (LLC), 316
logical operators, 317
logons, 317
loop back addresses,
  219-220, 255
lost packets, troubleshooting IP
  addresses, 209-210
LPD (Line Printer Daemon),
  47, 257
LPR command-line utility,
  printing to remote clients,
  132, 257
ls command (FTP), 155

M

MAC (Media Access Control),
   17, 317
mail bridges, 317
mailers, 317
mailing lists, 317
majordomo software, 317
MAN (metropolitan area
   networks), 18, 317
Management Information Base
   (MIB), 137-139, 317
management system, SMNP,
   135-136
manually copying to restore
   corrupt DHCP databases, 76
masks
   address, 14, 302
   subnet, 19
master browsers
   domain, 180
      failures, 186
      LMHOSTS file, 189
   election process, 181
   performance costs, 182
matches, string, 317
maximum networks and hosts,
   subnetting, 93
maximum segment size
   (MSS), 318
maximum tranmission unit
   (MTU), 318
MB DNS record, 121
Media Access Control (MAC),
   17, 317
message of the day (motd), 318
message switching, 332
meta characters, 317
Metric column, route tables, 104
metropolitan area network
   (MAN), 317
MG DNS record, 122
MIB (Management Information
   Base), 137-139, 317

Microsoft
   DNS Server, reinstalling, 116
   mindset and exam preparation,
      265-266
   SNMP service, 140
   TCP/IP Configuration dialog
      box, 69
Migrate On/Off setting,
   configuring WINS Manager, 83
mil domain, 64
MIME (Multipurpose Internet
   Mail Extension), 18, 317
MINFO DNS record, 122
mirroring, disk, 23
mnemonics, OSI model, 21
models, OSI, 20-21
Modem Properties dialog
   box, 163
modems, 317
   dialing properties
      Dial using calling card, 166
      I am dialing from, 165
      I am in, 165
      The area code is, 165
      *The phone system at this
         location uses, 166*
      *This location has call
         waiting, 166*
      *To access an outside line,
         first dial, 165*
   external, 159
   installing
      *Cancel the call if not connected
         within property, 163*
      Compress Data option, 164
      *Disconnect a call if idle for
         more than property, 163*
      Extra Settings option, 165
      Maximum Speed property, 163
      Modulation Type option, 164
      *Only connect at this speed
         property, 163*
      Port property, 162
      Record a Log File option, 165

*Required to Connect
option, 164*
Speaker Volume property, 162
*Use Cellular Protocol
option, 164*
Use Error Control option, 164
Use Flow Control option, 164
*Wait for tone before dialing
property, 163*
internal, 159
ports, 159
Base I/O Port Address, 161
Baud Rate setting, 160
COM Port Number, 161
Data Bits setting, 160
Flow Control setting, 160
IRQs, 161
Parity setting, 160
Stop Bits setting, 160
moderators, 318
Modulation Type option,
modem connections, 164
monitoring
Event Log tool, 258
Network Monitor, 195-196
Network Monitor tool, 258
Performance Monitor, 194-195
Performance Monitor tool, 258
from RAS servers, 175
utilities, 196
ARP, 197
Event Log, 198
IPCONFIG, 198
NBTSTAT, 199
NETSTAT, 200
NSLOOKUP, 201
Ping, 202
ROUTE, 202
SNMP protocol, 203-204
TRACERT, 204-205
Mosaic, 318
motd (message of the day), 318
MP (Multilink Protocol), 159
MR DNS record, 122
MSS (maximum
segment size), 318

MTU (maximum
transmission unit), 318
multihomed computers,
running WINS on, 78-79
multihomed host, 318
multihomed routers, building,
111-113
Multihomed static mapping, 84
Multilink Protocol (MP), 159
multiple servers,
DHCP implementation
requirements, 54
multiple-ranking exam
questions, 264
Multipurpose Internet Mail
Extension (MIME), 317
MX DNS record, 122
My Computer icon, 169

N

name resolution, 18, 222,
259-260, 318
hostname.exe, 224, 226
nbtstat, 223-224
NetBIOS sessions, 226-228
Ping, 226
Windows Sockets sessions, 229
names (domain), duplicates, 189
NBTSTAT, 199
nbtstat utility, 223-224, 261
net domain, 64
Net View command, network
browsing, 177
NetBEUI protocol, 21
NetBIOS, 43, 226-228
Netiquette, 318
Netmask column, route
tables, 103
Netnews, 318
Netscape, 318
NETSTAT, 200, 259
Netstat utility, 104
Network Address Column,
route tables, 103

network addresses (IP),
  troubleshooting, 209
network APIs, 42-43
Network Configuration dialog
  box, 113
network file system (NFS), 319
network IDs, 95, 98, 318
network information center
  (NIC), 319
network information service
  (NIS), 319
network interface card
  (NIC), 319
Network Interface layer, Internet
  Protocol Suite, 28
Network layer, OSI model, 21
Network Monitor, 195-196
Network Monitor tool, 258
Network Neighborhood, 177
Network News Transport
  Protocol (NNTP), 319
Network Properties dialog box,
  208, 216
Network Settings dialog box, 57,
  66, 114, 172-173
networks, 318
  browsers, 176
    clients, 178
    direct approach access, 179
    host computers, 178-179
    Network Neighborhood, 177
    roles, 180-183
    shared resources, 178
  connections, 23
  DHCP implementation
    requirements, 52-53
  IDs, classes, 255
  maximum subnetting, 93
  monitoring
    Network Monitor, 195-196
    Performance Monitor, 194-195
  subdividing, 94
    defining subnet masks, 96-98
    host ID requirements, 95-96

  host IDs, choosing, 99
  network ID requirements, 95
  network IDs, choosing, 98
New Phonebook Entry dialog
  box, 169
New Zone dialog box, 126
newsgroups, 310, 319
newsreaders, 319
NFS (network file system),
  18, 319
NIC (network information
  center), 319
NIC (network interface
  card), 319
NIS (network information
  system), 319
NNTP (Network News
  Transport Protocol), 319
No Call Back option, dial-in
  permissions, 168
nodes, 18, 319
non-browsers, 180
noninteractive mode,
  NSLOOKUP, 201
non-routable protocols, 21
Normal Group static mapping, 84
NS DNS record, 122
NSFnet, 319
NSLOOKUP, 118-119, 201, 259
null characters, 319
null lists, 319
num domain, 64

O

objects, Performance Monitor,
  194
open command (FTP), 155
Open Shortest Path First (OSPF),
  99, 320
Open Software Foundation
  (OSF), 319
Open Systems Interconnection
  (OSI), 18, 319

operators, logical, 317
optimization, Registry Editor, 194, 258
org domain, 64
OSF (Open Software Foundation), 319
OSI (Open Systems Interconnection), 18, 319
OSI model, 20-21
OSPF (Open Shortest Path First), 99, 320

P

Packet Internet Groper (Ping), 320
packet switching, 333
packets, 18, 320
   datagrams, 16, 31, 36-37, 308
   DHCPDISCOVER, 50
   lost, troubleshooting IP addresses, 209-210
   switching, 18, 333
   testing IP addresses, Ping utility, 218-219
parallel communication, 320
parameters, 320
   configurating IP addresses, 208-209, 211-214, 216
   DHCP clients, entering correctly, 214-215
   nbtstat utility, 224, 261
   WINS Manager, 82-83
parity, disk striping, 22
Parity port setting, 160
passing scores on exams, 264
passwords, remote execution utilities, 150
patterns, 320
PDCs (primary domain controllers), 180
peer-to-peer networking, 320
performance costs, master browsers, 182
performance-based exam questions, 277

performance-based testing, 279
Performance Monitor, 194-195
Performance Monitor tool, 258
Perl, 320
permanent virtual circuit (PVC), 334
Personal Internet Gopher (Ping), 40
PGP (Pretty Good Privacy), 320
physical addresses, 23-25
Physical layer, OSI model, 21
PID (process identifiers), 320
Ping (Packet Internet Groper), 40, 202, 259, 320
Ping utility, 18, 218
   name resolution problems, 222, 226
   testing protocol installations, 219-220
   troubleshooting
      client addresses, 220
      IP addresses, 221-222
      router problems, 220-221
Pipe, 320
placement, LMHOSTS files, 190
planning, 254
point of presence (POP), 18, 320
Point-to-Point protocol (PPP), 18, 158-159, 168, 321
Point-to-Point Tunneling Protocol (PPTP), 159, 321
POP (point of presence), 18, 320
port IDs, 321
ports
   COM, 159
   hardware, 321
   modem, 159
      Base I/O Port Address, 161
      Baud Rate setting, 160
      COM Port Number, 161
      Data Bits setting, 160
      Flow Control setting, 160
      IRQs, 161
      Parity setting, 160
      Stop Bits setting, 160

network, 321
TCP (Transmission Control
  Protocol), 30
Telnet, 152
Ports dialog box, 160
posting messages, 321
Postmaster, 321
potential browsers, 180
PPP (Point-to-Point Protocol),
  18, 158-159, 168, 321
PPTP (Point-to-Point Tunneling
  Protocol), 159, 321
precedence, 181, 321
preferences, DNS Manager, 118
Presentation layer, OSI model, 20
Preset To option, dial-in
  permissions, 168
primary DNS servers,
  configuring server roles, 124
primary domain controllers
  (PDCs), 180
printing, 131-133
procedures and exam preparation,
  269-274
process, 321
properties
  dialing, 165-166
  modem
    Cancel the call if not connected
      within, 163
    Compress Data option, 164
    Disconnect a call if idle for
      more than, 163
    Extra Settings option, 165
    Maximum Speed, 163
    Modulation Type option, 164
    Only connect at this speed, 163
    Port, 162
    Record a Log File option, 165
    Required to Connect
      option, 164
    Speaker Volume, 162
    Use Cellular Protocol
      option, 164
    Use Error Control option, 164

Use Flow Control option, 164
Wait for tone before
  dialing, 163
protocols, 18, 321
  Address Resolution Protocol, 14,
    28, 40-41, 197, 259, 303
  Internet Control Message
    Protocol, 17, 28, 38-39, 314
  Internet Group Management
    Protocol, 17, 28, 40, 314
  non-routable, 21
  PPP, 158-159
  Simple Mail Transport Protocol,
    19, 29, 324
  SLIP, 19, 158, 324
  Trivial File Transfer Protocol, 19,
    156-157, 325
  User Datagram Protocol, 19, 28,
    34-35, 326
  X.25, 20, 167, 328
  See also DCHP; SNMP; TCP/IP
proxy, 321
proxy agents, WINS, 59
PSTN, 159
psychometrics, 277-279
PTR DNS record, 122
public domain software, 321
push partners, WINS
  replication, 80
put command (FTP), 156

Q-R

questions
  exam question types, 264
  exams
    answering strategies, 270-273
    performance-based, 277
    ranking, 276
    sources, 275
  sample exam, 282-301

RAID, 22
ranking exam questions, 276
RARP (Reverse Address
  Resolution Protocol), 18, 322

RAS (Remote Access Service)
  clients, 176
  Dial-Up Networking, 169-172
    dial-in permissions, 167
    ISDN, 166
    modems, 159-166
    PPP problems, 168
    PPP vs. SLIP, 158
    X.25 protocol, 167
  servers
    configuring, 173-174
    dial-in permissions, 167
    Dial-Up Networking, 169-172
    Dial-Up Networking Monitor, 175
    installing, 172
    ISDN, 166
    modems, 159-166
    monitoring from, 175
    PPP problems, 168
    PPP vs. SLIP, 158
    X.25 protocol, 167
RCP command, data transfer utilities, 153-154
reassembly, IP (Internet Protocol), 37
Record a Log File option, modem connections, 165
records, adding when integrating DNS servers, 121-122
recursion, 322
Regedit.exe, 258
Regedit32.exe, 258
Registry Editor, 194, 258
Registry keys, RestoreFlag, 75-76
regular expressions, 322
reinstalling Microsoft DNS Server, 116
Relay Agent, DHCP, 47
relevance feedback, 322
remote clients and printing, 131-133
remote execution utilities
  passwords, 150
  REXEC, 151

RSH, 151-152
Telnet, 152-153
remote hosts, 221-222, 322
Remote Procedure Calls (RPCs), 323
Renewal Interval parameter, WINS Manager, 82
repeaters, 18, 322
Replicate only with Partners setting, configuring WINS Manager, 83
replication
  WINS, 79-81
  WINS Manager, 82-83
Report view, Performance Monitor, 195
Request for Comments (RFC), 322
Request to Send (RTS), 160
Required to Connect option, modem connections, 164
resolver, 322
RestoreFlag key (Registry), restoring corrupt DHCP databases, 75-76
restoring
  corrupt databases, DHCP, 75-76
  databases, WINS, 61
retaking exams, 275
Reverse Address Resolution Protocol (RARP), 322
reverse lookup, DNS, 65-66
REXEC remote connection utility, 151
RFC (Request for Comments), 322
RIP (Routing Information Protocol), 18, 99, 108, 322
rlogin, 322
RMON, 322
roles
  browser, 180-182
  DNS server, configuring, 123-127

root servers (DNS), connections, 123
ROUTE, 202, 259
route tables
    Gateway Address column, 103
    Interface column, 104
    Metric column, 104
    Netmask column, 103
    Network Address column, 103
    static, building, 106
    viewing, 104-106
routeability, IP (Internet Protocol), 37
routers, 19, 323
    brouters, 305
    dynamic, 99, 108-111
    IP, 103-107, 187-188
    multihomed, building, 111-113
    static, 99-102
    troubleshooting, pinging default gateways, 220-221
routes, 323
Routing Information Protocol (RIP), 99, 322
RP DNS record, 122
RPCs (Remote Procedure Calls), 323
RSH remote connection utility, 151-152
RT DNS record, 122
RTS (Request to Send), 160

S

sample questions, 282-301
scalability, 26
scope options, DHCP scopes, 69, 72
scopes, DHCP, 73-76
    address reservations, 70
    clients, 71-72
    global options, 69-70, 72
    scope options, 69, 72
scores and passing exams, 264
scripts, 323

secondary DNS servers, configuring server roles, 126-127
security
    call-back, RAS clients, 176
    firewalls, 311
    SNMP, 141, 143
segments, 19, 323
Select Network Protocol dialog box, 66
serial communication, 323
Serial Line Internet Protocol (SLIP), 19, 158, 324
servers, 19, 323
    DHCP, 50
        configuring, 58
        installing, 57
        scopes, 67-76
    DNS
        Administration tool, 117
        hostnames, 257
        Name Server, 309
        reinstalling Microsoft DNS Server, 116
        roles, configuring, 123-127
    multiple DHCP implementation requirements, 54
    RAS
        configuring, 173-174
        dial-in permissions, 167
        Dial-Up Networking, 169-172
        Dial-Up Networking Monitor, 175
        installing, 172
        ISDN, 166
        modems, 159-166
        monitoring from, 175
        PPP problems, 168
        PPP versus SLIP, 158
        X.25 protocol, 167
    Windows NT, TCP/IP support, 131-133
    WINS, 76, 257
    WINS/NBNS, 60

services, 19
  browsing, client requests, 186
  DHCP, 48-49
    clients requirements, 53
    DHCPACK phase, 56
    lease renewal, 56-57
    limitations, 51
    multiple servers, 54
    network requirements, 52-53
    scopes, 67-76
    server service, 57-58
    servers, 50
  DNS, 62
    domains, 64
    history of, 63
    hostnames, 64-65
    reverse lookup, 65-66
    zones, 65
  Windows NT browsing
    announcement periods, 185
    collecting browse lists, 183-184
    distributing browse lists, 184
    domain master browser
      failure, 186
    subnets, 185
  WINS, 58
    backing up databases, 61
    clients, 77
    clients, configuring, 60
    compacting databases, 61
    configuring for non-WINS
      clients, 77
    files, 60-61
    LMHOSTS files, importing, 78
    multihomed computers,
      running on, 78-79
    proxy agents, 59
    replication, configuring, 79-81
    restoring databases, 61
    servers, 76
    WINS Manager, 81-83
Session layer, OSI model, 20
sessions
  NetBIOS, 226-228
  Windows Sockets, 229

Set by Caller option, dial-in
  permissions, 168
SGML (Standard Generalized
  Markup Language), 323
shared resources, 178
shareware, 323
signals, 323
signatures, 323
Simple Mail Transport Protocol
  (SMTP), 324
Simple Network Management
  Protocol. *See* SNMP
sites, 324
sliding windows, TCP
  (Transmission Control
  Protocol), 33
SLIP (Serial Line Internet
  Protocol), 19, 158, 324
SmartList, 324
SMTP (Simple Mail Transport
  Protocol), 19, 29, 324
SNA (System Network
  Architecture), 19, 324
SNMP (Simple Network
  Management Protocol), 19, 26,
  29, 203-204, 324
  Agent, 48, 143-144, 302
  configuring, 133-134
    agents, 136-137
    communities, 141
    extension agents, 140
    management systems, 135-136
    MIB (Management
      Information Base), 137-139
    Microsoft SNMP Service, 140
    security, 141, 143
  installing, 141-142
  utility, 144-145
SOA (Start of Authority) records
  configuring server roles, 125-126
  DNS record, 122
sockets, 19, 30, 324
software, public domain, 321
source routes, 324

sources of exam questions, 275
Standard Generalized Markup
  Language (SGML), 323
standards (IEEE 802), 21-22
Start of Authority (SOA), 122,
  125-126
Starting Version Count setting,
  configuring WINS Manager, 83
startup files (DNS),
  updating, 118
static files, storing IP
  addresses, 211
static mappings and configuring
  (WINS databases), 84
Static Mappings dialog box, 78
static routers, 99-102
Stop Bits port setting, 160
streams, 32-33
strings, 324
  concatenating, 306
  matches, 317
striping disk, 22
subdividing networks, 94
  host ID requirements, 95-96
  host IDs, choosing, 99
  network ID requirements, 95
  network IDs, choosing, 98
  subnet masks, defining, 96-98
subdomains, creating, 117
subnet addresses, 209, 255
subnet masks, 19, 255, 324
  configuring, 85, 89-91
    default masks, 92-93
    networks, subdividing, 94-99
    subnetting, 86-88
  defining, 96-98
  troubleshooting, 211-214
subnets, 54, 324
  browsing over, Windows NT
    services, 185
  DHCP network requirements, 52
subscribes, 324
surfing, 324
switched virtual circuit
  (SVC), 334

switching, 18, 320, 332-333
Sylvan Prometric exam
  registration, 269
syntax, 325
System Network Architecture
  (SNA), 324

T

T1 lines, 325
T3 lines, 325
tables, route
  Gateway Address column, 103
  Interface column, 104
  Metric column, 104
  Netmask column, 103
  Network Address column, 103
  static, building, 106
  viewing, 104-106
Tag Image File Format
  (TIFF), 325
tags, 325
taking exams
  performance-based
    questions, 277
  procedures, 269-274
  question sources, 275
  ranking questions, 276
  retaking, 275
TCP (Transmission Control
  Protocol), 28, 325
  acknowledgments, 33-34
  connection-orientation
    communication, 31-32
  ports and sockets, 30
  sliding windows, 32-33
TCP/IP (Transmission Control
  Protocol/Internet Protocol), 25
  ARP (Address Resolution
    Protocol), 40-41
  client-server architecture, 26
  connectivity utilities, 26
  ICMP (Internet Control
    Message Protocol), 38-39

IGMP (Internet Group
Management Protocol), 40
industry-standard support, 26
installing, 66
Internet access, 27
IP (Internet Protocol), 36-38
layers, 28-29
network APIs, 42-43
printing and Windows NT
server support, 131-133
TCP (Transmission Control
Protocol), 28, 30-34, 325
UDP (User Datagram Protocol),
34-35
TCP/IP Configuration dialog
box, 72, 114
TCP/IP Settings dialog box, 115
Telnet remote connection utility,
26, 152-153, 257
10BASE-2 coaxial cable
connections, 23
10BASE-T unshielded twisted
pair cable connections, 23
terminal emulation, 325
terminal types, 152
testing
IP addresses, Ping utility,
218-222
name resolution
NetBIOS sessions, 226-228
Ping, 226
Windows Sockets sessions, 229
tests. See exams
TFTP (Trivial File Transfer
Protocol), 19, 156-157, 325
threads, 325
three-way handshake, connection-
orientation communication, 32
TIFF (Tag Image File
Format), 325
Time to Live (TTL), 37, 326
timeframes and exam preparation,
266-267
TLI (transport layer
interface), 325

token ring connections, 23, 326
traceroutes, 326
TRACERT utility, static routing
environments, 107,
204-205, 259
traffic, 188, 326
transceivers, 19, 326
Transmission Control Protocol.
See TCP
Transmission Control
Protocol/Internet
Protocol. See TCP/IP
Transport layer
Internet Protocol Suite, 28
TCP (Transmission Control
Protocol)
acknowledgments, 33-34
connection-orientation
communication, 31-32
ports and sockets, 30
sliding windows, 33
UDP (User Datagram
Protocol), 34-35
transport layer interface
(TLI), 325
Transport layer, OSI model, 20
traps, 326
Trivial File Transfer Protocol
(TFTP), 19, 156-157, 325
troubleshooting, 258
DHCP clients, 214-215
Event Log, 198
hostname utility, 261
IP addresses, 208
default gateways, 214
incorrect hosts, 209-210
IPCONFIG utility, 216-217
lost packets, 209-210
Ping utility, 218-222
static file address storage, 211
subnet masks, 211, 213-214
IPCONFIG, 198, 216, 259
LMHOSTS files, 190

name resolution problems,
222, 259
host connections, 260
hostname.exe, 224, 226
nbtstat, 223-224, 261
NetBIOS sessions, 226-228
Windows Sockets sessions, 229
NBTSTAT, 199
NETSTAT, 200, 259
NSLOOKUP, 201, 259
Ping, 202, 226, 259
ROUTE, 202, 259
SNMP, 203-204
TRACERT, 204-205, 259
TTL (Time to Live) specification,
37, 326
TXT DNS record, 122

U

UDP (User Datagram Protocol),
19, 28, 34-35, 326
UFudecode, 327
UID, effective, 309
universal resource locators
(URLs), 19, 326
universal time, 326
UNIX, FTP syntax, 156
updating DNS startup files, 118
uploading, 326
URLs (universal resource
locators), 19, 326
Use Cellular Protocol option,
modem connections, 164
Use Error Control option,
modem connections, 164
Use Flow Control option,
modem connections, 164
Usenet, 310, 326
User Datagram Protocol (UDP),
19, 28, 34-35, 326
User Manager for Domains, 167
User Properties sheet, 167
usernames, 327

utilities
command-line
IPCONFIG, 216-217
Ping, 218-222
data transfer
FTP, 154-156
HTTP, 157
RCP, 153-154
TFTP, 156-157
IPCONFIG, 24
LPR, printing to remote
clients, 132
monitoring, 196
ARP, 197
Event Log, 198
IPCONFIG, 198
NBTSTAT, 199
NETSTAT, 200
NSLOOKUP, 201
Ping, 202
ROUTE, 202
SNMP protocol, 203-204
TRACERT, 204-205
name resolution, 222
hostname.exe, 224, 226
nbtstat utility, 223-224
Ping, 226
Netstat, 104
remote execution
passwords, 150
REXEC, 151
RSH, 151-152
Telnet, 152-153
SNMP, 144-145
TRACERT, static routing
environments, 107
Uuencode, 327

V

valid subnet addresses, 255
variables
global, 312
local, 316

Verify Interval parameter, WINS
Manager, 82
Veronica, 327
viewer applications, 327
viewers, 327
viewing route tables, 104-106
views, Performance Monitor, 195
virtual circuit packet
switching, 334
virtual memory systems
(VMS), 327
Virtual Reality Modeling
Language (VRML), 327
viruses, 327
VMS (virtual memory
systems), 327
VRML (Virtual Reality
Modeling Language), 327

W

WAIS
clients, 327
Doc-ID, 309
waisindex, 327
waisserver, 328
WANs (wide area networks),
20, 328
Web chats, 328
Web Crawler, 328
WHOIS service, 328
wide area networks (WANs),
20, 328
windows, sliding, 32-33
Windows 95
DHCP clients, 71-72
filling browser roles, 181
Windows for Workgroups, DHCP
clients, 72
Windows Internet Naming
Service. *See* WINS
Windows NT
browser precedence, 181
browsing services
announcement periods, 185
collecting browse lists, 183-184

distributing browse lists, 184
domain master browser
failure, 186
subnets, 185
DHCP, 48-49
clients, 71-72
clients requirements, 53
DHCPACK phase, 56
lease renewal, 56-57
limitations, 51
multiple servers, 54
network requirements, 52-53
scopes, 67-76
server service, 57-58
servers, 50
DHCP Relay Agent,
installing/configuring, 113
DNS, 62
domains, 64
history of, 63
hostnames, 64-65
installing/configuring,
114-119
integrating with other servers,
119-122
reverse lookup, 65-66
root server connections, 123
server roles, configuring,
123-127
zones, 65
HOSTS files, configuring,
127-129
IP router configurations
default gateways, 103
dynamic routers, 99, 108-111
multihomed routers, building,
111-113
route tables, 103-104
static route tables, building,
106-107
static routers, 99-102
viewing route tables, 104-106
LMHOSTS files, configuring,
129-131
Network Monitor, 195-196

Performance Monitor, 194-195
TCP/IP printing support,
131-133
WINS, 58
clients, 77
clients, configuring, 60
configuring for non-WINS
clients, 77
files, 60
LMHOSTS files, importing, 78
multihomed computers,
running on, 78-79
proxy agents, 59
replication, configuring, 79-81
servers, 76
static mappings,
configuring, 84
WINS Manager, 81-83
Windows NT 4.0, planning, 254
Windows NT Member Servers,
filling browser roles, 181
Windows NT Workstation, filling
browser roles, 181
Windows Sockets API, 26,
42, 229
WINS (Windows Internet
Naming Service), 47, 58, 190
client access, 191
clients, 77
configuring
clients, 60
for non-WINS clients, 77
databases, 61, 84
domain browsers, 191

files
J50.CHK, 61
J50.LOG, 61
WINS.MDB, 60
WINSTMP.MDB, 60
LMHOSTS files, importing, 78
MIB, 139
multihomed computers, running
on, 78-79
proxy agents, 59
replication, 79-81
servers, 76, 257
WINS Manager, 81-83
WINS.MDB, 60
WINS/NBNS servers, 60
WINS/NBT node, 60
WINSTMP.MDB, 60
WKS DNS record, 122
World Wide Web (WWW), 328
Worm, 328

X-Y-Z

X bitmapped (XBM), 328
X-modem protocol, 328
X.25, 20, 167, 328
X.25 DNS record, 122
X.400, 20, 328
XBM (X bitmapped), 328
XDR (External Data
Representative), 328

Y-modem protocol, 329

Z-modem protocol, 329
zones, DNS, 65

MCSE Fast Track: Networking Essentials

1-56205-939-4,
$19.99, 9/98

 **MCSE Fast Track: TCP/IP**

1-56205-937-8,
$19.99, 9/98

 **MCSE Fast Track: Windows 98**

0-7357-0016-8,
$19.99, Q4/98

 MCSE Fast Track: Internet Information Server 4

1-56205-936-X,
$19.99, 9/98

 MCSE Fast Track: Windows NT Server 4

1-56205-935-1,
$19.99, 9/98

 MCSD Fast Track: Solution Architectures

0-7357-0029-X,
$19.99, Q1/99

 **MCSE Fast Track: Windows NT Server 4 Enterprise**

1-56205-940-8,
$19.99, 9/98

 MCSD Fast Track: Visual Basic 6, Exam 70-175

0-7357-0018-4,
$19.99, Q4/98

 MCSE Fast Track: Windows NT Workstation 4

1-56205-938-6,
$19.99, 9/98

 MCSD Fast Track: Visual Basic 6, Exam 70-176

0-7357-0019-2,
$19.99, Q4/98

TRAINING GUIDES

*Complete, Innovative,
Accurate, Thorough*

Our next generation Training Guides
have been developed to help you study
and retain the essential knowledge that
you need to pass the MCSE exams. We
know your study time is valuable, and
we have made every effort to make the
most of it by presenting clear, accurate,
and thorough information.

In creating this series, our goal was to
raise the bar on how MCSE content is
written, developed and presented. From
the two-color design that gives you
easy access to content to the new software simulator that allows you to perform tasks in a simulated operating
system environment, we are confident
that you will be well-prepared for exam
success.

Our New Riders Top Score Software
Suite is a custom-developed set of full-
functioning software applications that
work in conjunction with the Training
Guide by providing you with the following:

Exam Simulator tests your hands-on
knowledge with over 150 fact-based
and situational-based questions
Electronic Study Cards really test your
knowledge with explanations that are
linked to an electronic version of the
Training Guide
Electronic Flash Cards help you retain
the facts in a time-tested method
An Electronic Version of the Book
provides quick searches and compact,
mobile study
Customizable Software adapts to the
way you want to learn

**MCSE Training
Guide: Networking
Essentials, Second
Edition**

1-56205-919-X, $49.99, 9/98

**MCSE Training
Guide: Windows NT
Server 4, Second
Edition**

1-56205-916-5, $49.99, 9/98

**MCSE Training
Guide: Windows NT
Server 4 Enterprise,
Second Edition**

1-56205-917-3, $49.99, 9/98

**MCSE Training
Guide: Windows NT
Workstation 4,
Second Edition**

1-56205-918-1, $49.99, 9/98

**MCSE Training
Guide: Windows 98**

1-56205-890-8, $49.99, Q4/98

**MCSE Training
Guide: TCP/IP,
Second Edition**

1-56205-920-3, $49.99, 10/98

MCSE Training Guide: SQL Server 7 Administration

0-7357-0003-6, $49.99, Q1/99

MCSE Training Guide: SQL Server 7 Design and Implementation

0-7357-0004-4, $49.99, Q1/99

MCSD Training Guide: Solution Architectures

0-7357-0026-5, $49.99, Q1/99

MCSD Training Guide: Visual Basic 6, Exam 70-175

0-7357-0002-8, $49.99, Q1/99

MCSD Training Guide: Visual Basic 6, Exam 70-176

0-7357-0031-1, $49.99, Q1/99

TRAINING GUIDES
First Editions

Your Quality Elective Solution

MCSE Training Guide: Systems Management Server 1.2, 1-56205-748-0

MCSE Training Guide: SQL Server 6.5 Administration, 1-56205-726-X

MCSE Training Guide: SQL Server 6.5 Design and Implementation, 1-56205-830-4

MCSE Training Guide: Windows 95, 70-064 Exam, 1-56205-880-0

MCSE Training Guide: Exchange Server 5, 1-56205-824-X

MCSE Training Guide: Internet Explorer 4, 1-56205-889-4

MCSE Training Guide: Microsoft Exchange Server 5.5, 1-56205-899-1

MCSE Training Guide: IIS 4, 1-56205-823-1

MCSD Training Guide: Visual Basic 5, 1-56205-850-9

MCSD Training Guide: Microsoft Access, 1-56205-771-5

TESTPREP SERIES

Practice and cram with the new, revised Second Edition TestPreps

Questions. Questions. And more questions. That's what you'll find in our New Riders TestPreps. They're great practice books when you reach the final stage of studying for the exam. We recommend them as supplements to our Training Guides.

What makes these study tools unique is that the questions are the primary focus of each book. All the text in these books support and explain the answers to the questions.

Scenario-based questions challenge your experience.

Multiple-choice questions prep you for the exam.

Fact-based questions test your product knowledge.

Exam strategies assist you in test preparation.

Complete yet concise explanations of answers make for better retention.

Two practice exams prepare you for the real thing.

Fast Facts offer you everything you need to review in the testing center parking lot.

MCSE TestPrep: Networking Essentials, Second Edition

0-7357-0010-9, $19.99, 11/98

MCSE TestPrep: Windows 95, Second Edition

0-7357-0011-7, $19.99, 11/98

MCSE TestPrep: Windows NT Server 4, Second Edition

0-7357-0012-5, $19.99, 12/98

MCSE TestPrep: Windows NT Server 4 Enterprise, Second Edition

0-7357-0009-5, $19.99, 1/98

MCSE TestPrep: Windows NT Workstation 4, Second Edition

0-7357-0008-7, $19.99, 11/98

MCSE TestPrep: TCP/IP, Second Edition

0-7357-0025-7, $19.99, 12/98

MCSE TestPrep:
Windows 98

1-56205-922-X, $19.99, Q4/98

TESTPREP SERIES
FIRST EDITIONS

MCSE TestPrep: SQL Server 6.5
Administration, 0-7897-1597-X

MCSE TestPrep: SQL Server 6.5 Design
and Implementation, 1-56205-915-7

MCSE TestPrep: Windows 95 70-64
Exam, 0-7897-1609-7

MCSE TestPrep: Internet Explorer 4,
0-7897-1654-2

MCSE TestPrep: Exchange Server 5.5,
0-7897-1611-9

MCSE TestPrep: IIS 4.0, 0-7897-1610-0

How to Contact Us

IF YOU NEED THE LATEST UPDATES ON A TITLE THAT YOU'VE PURCHASED:

1) Visit our Web site at www.newriders.com.

2) Click on the DOWNLOADS link, and enter your book's ISBN number, which is located on the back cover in the bottom right-hand corner.

3) In the DOWNLOADS section, you'll find available updates that are linked to the book page.

IF YOU ARE HAVING TECHNICAL PROBLEMS WITH THE BOOK OR THE CD THAT IS INCLUDED:

1) Check the book's information page on our Web site according to the instructions listed above, or

2) Email us at support@mcp.com, or

3) Fax us at (317) 817-7488 attn: Tech Support.

IF YOU HAVE COMMENTS ABOUT ANY OF OUR CERTIFICATION PRODUCTS THAT ARE NON-SUPPORT RELATED:

1) Email us at certification@mcp.com, or

2) Write to us at New Riders, 201 W. 103rd St., Indianapolis, IN 46290-1097, or

3) Fax us at (317) 581-4663.

IF YOU WISH TO PREVIEW AN OF OUR CERTIFICATION BOOK FOR CLASSROOM USE:

Email us at pr@mcp.com. Your message sh include your name, title, training company o school, department, address, phone numbe office days/hours, text in use, and enrollme Send these details along with your request desk/examination copies and/or additional information.

IF YOU ARE OUTSIDE THE UNITED STATES AND NEED TO FIND A DISTRIBUTOR IN YOUR AREA:

Please contact our international department at international@mcp.com.

WE WANT TO KNOW WHAT YOU THINK

To better serve you, we would like your opinion on the content and quality of this book. Please complete this card and mail it to us or fax it to 317-581-4663.

Name _____

Address _____

City _____ State_____ Zip _____

Phone _____ Email Address _____

Occupation _____

Which certification exams have you already passed? _____
_____
_____
_____

Which certification exams do you plan to take? __
_____
_____
_____

What influenced your purchase of this book?
❏ Recommendation ❏ Cover Design
❏ Table of Contents ❏ Index
❏ Magazine Review ❏ Advertisement
❏ Publisher's reputation ❏ Author Name

How would you rate the contents of this book?
❏ Excellent ❏ Very Good
❏ Good ❏ Fair
❏ Below Average ❏ Poor

What other types of certification products will you buy/have you bought to help you prepare for the exam?
❏ Quick reference books ❏ Testing software
❏ Study guides ❏ Other

What do you like most about this book? Check all that apply.
❏ Content ❏ Writing Style
❏ Accuracy ❏ Examples
❏ Listings ❏ Design
❏ Index ❏ Page Count
❏ Price ❏ Illustrations

What do you like least about this book? Check all that apply.
❏ Content ❏ Writing Style
❏ Accuracy ❏ Examples
❏ Listings ❏ Design
❏ Index ❏ Page Count
❏ Price ❏ Illustrations

What would be a useful follow-up book to this one for you?_____
Where did you purchase this book?_____
Can you name a similar book that you like better than this one, or one that is as good? Why?_____
_____
_____

How many New Riders books do you own? _____
What are your favorite certification or general computer book titles? _____
_____

What other titles would you like to see us develop? _____
_____

Any comments for us? _____
_____

Fold here and Scotch tape to mail

New Riders
201 W. 103rd St.
Indianapolis, IN 46290